WEBER'S ULTIMATE GRILLING™

Jamie Purviance

Photography by Ray Kachatorian

Houghton Mifflin Harcourt
Boston • New York • 2019

CONTENTS

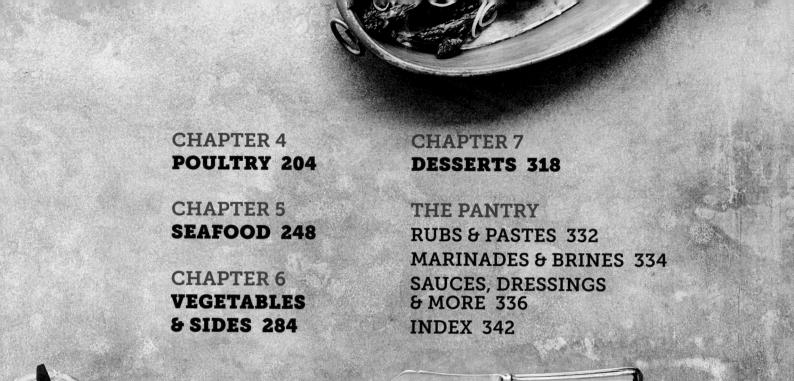

INTRODUCTION

I'll admit it. In my youth, I approached grilling the same way an unskilled, super-psyched teenager picks up a shiny electric guitar for the first time. Forget lessons! I'll just fire up the grill, throw some meat on it, and know intuitively how to manage whatever happens next.

In my case, what usually happened involved an eruption of flames, followed by plumes of dark smoke. As I sheepishly served black meteorites of unrecognizable meat, friends either winced or laughed. Back then no one wanted to eat my food. Not friends. Not pets. Not even me.

Eventually, my desire to eat better led me to The Culinary Institute of America for two years of rigorous training in cooking techniques. That raised my grilling game dramatically. Shortly after, I started working with Weber—a phenomenal opportunity to access grilling know-how from experts at the world's grandest grill company. Within a year, I went from being a guy with halfway decent grilling chops to a cookbook author with a full-blown obsession and a wealth of knowledge about all styles of outdoor cooking.

I mention this to emphasize that none of us is born with grilling skills embedded in our DNA. We all learn along the way. My way was intensive and extreme. Your way will not require professional cooking school or a job with Weber. Your way could be as easy as using this book. What you are holding now is a comprehensive record of nearly everything I've learned about grilling—in professional cooking school, in restaurants, at Weber, and in the backyards of skilled grillers all over the world.

This book may look like just a collection of recipes—and, in a way, it is that. But look a little deeper, as it is actually much more. It's a highly visual exploration of the techniques that will put better food on your plate. I included these particular recipes because I believe they are not only well worth making, but are also prime examples of skills that you can apply to other recipes as well. My mission with this book is to teach you so much about cooking over fire that each time you step up to your grill, whether you are making one of my recipes or one of your own, you will be capable of greatness.

To get started, check out The Four T's (pages 9 to 49). This front section is meant to organize your thinking. When you grill, there are lots of variables potentially at play: fire and embers, sparks and smoke, searing and charring, rubs and marinades, sun and wind, tough and tender ingredients, friends and family, beer and wine flowing, abundant choices of sauces and side dishes, split-second decisions about when to turn and when to take foods off the grill. This section will set your priorities straight. On any given day, with any given recipe, if you focus on "the four T's," you will be a better griller.

Next, I hope you will try at least a few of the ten BBQ Genius recipes in this book, as you will learn the most from them. I've developed a BBQ Genius recipe for each of the most popular (and often most misunderstood) foods: chicken wings, pizza, cheeseburgers, rib-eye steaks, pork chops, baby back ribs, chicken breasts, salmon fillets, shrimp, and asparagus. Each recipe is introduced by essential tips and techniques, as well as a "Grill Science" column that will deepen your understanding of what is happening to your ingredients on and off the grill. Then comes the recipe itself, presented with detailed step-by-step photography so you can look and cook your way through it. Following each BBQ Genius recipe are "Flavor Bomb" variations—easy, weeknight-friendly recipes based on the techniques in the BBQ Genius recipe.

You will be surprised at how quickly your confidence and grilling skills improve when you start cooking with greater attention to techniques. Raising your grilling game is not just a matter of knowing what you are doing but also how and why you are doing it. That's when you approach "ultimate grilling." With more and more recipes and techniques in your repertoire, there will come a time when you are sitting around a table with friends, enjoying tremendously what you have made, and you suddenly say to yourself, "Wow, this food I made came out great." To me, that's ultimate grilling. Let's go there. I'll show you the way.

Temperature

Time

Techniques

Tools

THE FOUR T'S

Grilling, at its best and most elemental, is about simplicity: fire, food, and the ease of the outdoors. What calls cooks back to the grill time and again are the stress-free vibes and peerless flavors that open-air cooking creates. To experience that simplicity, you must first master four critical elements of the art: temperature, time, techniques, and tools.

Let's say you want to grill some steaks. Your first step toward success is to get your grill up to the right temperature and to maintain it there. This is the key to a proper sear and crust. Next, you must keep an eye on the timing so your steak cooks to your desired doneness according to their cut and thickness. Good results rely on solid techniques, too. With steaks, that technique could be "sear and slide" (see page 125), a "reverse sear" (see page 116), or even "coal cooking" (see page 130), in which you set raw steaks directly on burning embers (much easier to master than

it sounds). The final element in the quest for great steaks is your use of tools. Tongs are the obvious choice for turning the steaks. Less obvious but also important is an instant-read thermometer to help you know when your steaks are perfectly cooked.

In the pages that follow, you'll see that if you set up your grill for the right temperature, cook the food for the correct length of time, employ trusted techniques, and use the proper tools, you'll turn out fantastic food and achieve high marks for what might be called the fifth T: taste.

TEMPERATURE

Temperature is paramount in grilling. If it's too low, stuff goes wrong:
food sticks to the grates, barely browns, or overcooks. If it's too high, you
are headed toward different disappointments: food burns, becomes bitter, and
ends up about as tender as a ball of tangled rubber bands. Setting your
grill to the right temperature is easy. Here is how to do it.

DIRECT GRILLING
ON A GAS GRILL

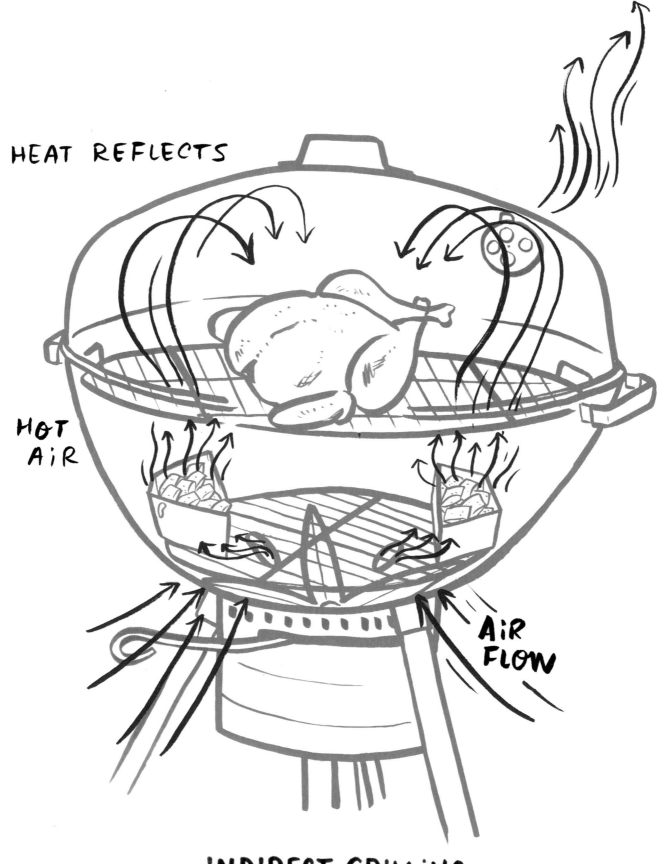

HEAT REFLECTS

HOT
AIR

AIR
FLOW

INDIRECT GRILLING
ON A CHARCOAL GRILL

GAS GRILLS

Lighting a Gas Grill

The convenience and flexibility of a gas grill offers a lot to appreciate. It is easy to light, easy to adjust, and easy to sustain at ideal temperatures for a long time. In most cases, lighting one is as simple as lifting the lid, turning on the gas, and igniting the burners.

1. First, open the lid and make sure all knobs are in the off position. Open the valve on the propane tank all the way (or turn on the natural gas at the source), then wait a minute for the gas to travel through the gas line.

2. With the lid still open, light each burner individually, turning each one to high and making sure it has ignited before turning on the next.

3. Close the lid and preheat the grill to above 500°F; this will take 10 to 15 minutes. Preheating the grill will make the cooking grate easier to clean and ensure a better sear.

Maintaining Temperature

If you can turn a dial, you can operate a gas grill. Turning the knobs left or right will prompt the grill to respond with varying amounts of oxygen and fuel.

Always light the burners on the grill with the lid open. Preheat the grill with the lid closed and all the burners at their maximum setting. When the temperature climbs above 500°F, open the lid, brush the cooking grates clean, and turn the knobs to make any heat adjustments. For example, you may want to turn off one or more burners to create a zone of indirect heat (see opposite).

Now the grill is hot, but how hot do you want it to stay? Very low? Medium? Medium-high? These differences are critical. To achieve and maintain the correct temperature, you need to know the standard ranges as measured by the thermometer inside the lid.

HERE ARE THE TEMPERATURES TO AIM FOR:

VERY LOW HEAT	**(225° TO 250°F)**
LOW HEAT	**(250° TO 350°F)**
MEDIUM-LOW HEAT	**(300° TO 350°F)**
MEDIUM HEAT	**(350° TO 450°F)**
MEDIUM-HIGH HEAT	**(400° TO 450°F)**
HIGH HEAT	**(450° TO 550°F)**

Heat Configurations on a Gas Grill

Two main heat configurations are recommended throughout this book: direct and indirect. Direct heat is used for foods that cook quickly, like steaks and burgers, while indirect heat is used for larger foods or foods that cook more slowly, such as whole chickens or roasts. Setting these up on a gas grill is easy. It's just a matter of which burners you leave on and which burners you turn off.

DIRECT HEAT

For gas grilling over direct heat, leave all the burners on and adjust them for the desired level of heat. Remember to brush the cooking grates clean before adding any food.

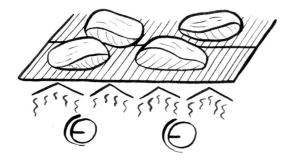

INDIRECT HEAT

For gas grilling over indirect heat, leave some of the burners on and turn one or two of them off. Adjust the burners on each side of the food to the temperature noted in the recipe and turn off the burner(s) directly below where the food will be placed. It's preferable to turn the center burner(s) off so heat comes from both the right and left sides of the grill.

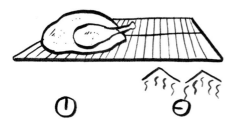

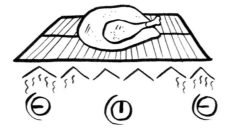

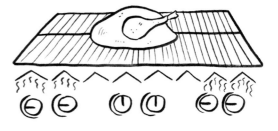

1. If using a two-burner gas grill, light one side of the grill and do the grilling on the opposite side.

2. If using a three-burner gas grill, light the outside burners (right and left) and cook over the unlit center burner.

3. If using a four- to six-burner gas grill, light the outside burners (right and left) and cook over the unlit burners in the center. If your ingredients are small, like whole russet potatoes, you may need to use only one or two unlit burners in the center. If your food is quite large, like a whole turkey, you might need two to four unlit burners in the center.

CHARCOAL GRILLS

Lighting a Charcoal Grill

1. Using a chimney starter, which is an upright metal cylinder with a handle on the outside and a wire rack on the inside (see also page 46), is the easiest way to light a charcoal grill.

2. To light the chimney starter, remove the lid and cooking grate from the grill and open the bottom vents. Place one or two paraffin (wax) lighter cubes on the charcoal grate, then place the chimney over the cube(s). Fill the chimney with charcoal briquettes.

3. Alternatively, fill the space under the wire rack of the chimney with a few sheets of wadded-up newspaper. Fill the space above the rack with charcoal briquettes.

4. Light the cube(s) or newspaper underneath the chimney. If lighting newspaper, you can light it through the holes at the bottom of the chimney. Once the cube(s) or paper have ignited the charcoal, some impressive thermodynamics will begin channeling the heat evenly throughout the charcoal. The briquettes will be ready in 15 to 20 minutes.

5. When the briquettes are lightly covered with white ash, put on a pair of heavy, insulated gloves and grab the two handles on the chimney starter. The swinging handle is there to help you lift the chimney starter and safely aim the coals just where you want them.

Heat Configurations on a Charcoal Grill

Configuring direct and indirect heat on a charcoal grill is more involved than on a gas grill, but once you master them, you are set for a lifetime of grilling success.

DIRECT HEAT

As the term implies, direct heat is the heat directly under your food. If your food is cooking smack dab over hot charcoal, you are cooking with direct heat. As a general rule, the strong radiant energy of direct heat is preferred for foods that cook quickly—burgers, steaks, pork tenderloin, boneless chicken pieces, fish fillets—that is, in less than 20 minutes.

1. If using charcoal baskets, when the coals in the chimney are lightly coated in white ash, wear protective gloves and carefully empty the coals into the baskets. Position the baskets in the center of the grill.

2. Alternatively, using a charcoal rake or long tongs, spread the coals into a tightly packed single layer across one-half to two-thirds of the charcoal grate. This is known as a two-zone fire and is ideal for grilling foods with a lot of surface area, like porterhouse steaks.

3. Put the cooking grate in place. If it has hinged sides, position the hinges over the charcoal. This makes it easier to add more coals later, if needed.

4. Close the lid, making sure all vents are open. Let the cooking grate preheat for 10 to 15 minutes, until the temperature on the lid's thermometer registers more than 500°F. This makes the grate easier to brush clean.

5. Uncover the grill and brush the cooking grate clean. Wait until the temperature reaches the correct zone for the recipe before placing food on the grate directly over the coals. Continue as directed in the recipe.

INDIRECT HEAT

When you give food a little buffer from the heat, either moving it away from the flame or shielding it in some manner, you are using indirect heat. For example, if the coals are burning on opposite sides of the grill and your food is cooking in the middle, you are using indirect heat. Indirect is the preferred heat for large cuts of meat or other large foods—whole chicken or turkey, pork loin, pork ribs, prime rib—that need to cook for more than 20 minutes.

1. Divide the coals into two equal piles on opposite sides of the charcoal grate, creating two zones for direct heat and one zone between them for indirect heat (known as a three-zone split fire). If using charcoal baskets, add coals to the baskets, then position them on opposite sides of the grate.

2. If you expect the food to drip a lot of fat, place an aluminum-foil drip pan between the coals. Put the cooking grate in place. If it has hinged sides, position the hinges over the charcoal. This makes it easier to add more coals later, if needed.

COMBINATION HEAT
Some foods are more high maintenance than others. For example, it's wise to cook bone-in chicken thighs with both direct and indirect heat. Start them over direct heat to sear and brown the exterior and then finish them over indirect heat until opaque at the center. Cooking them over direct heat only will probably yield a burnt exterior and a raw interior. The combination of two types of heat results in beautifully browned skin and a thoroughly cooked interior.

3. Close the lid, making sure all the vents are open. Let the cooking grate preheat for 10 to 15 minutes, until the temperature on the lid's thermometer registers more than 500°F. This will make the cooking grate easier to clean.

4. Uncover the grill and brush the cooking grate clean. Wait until the temperature reaches the correct zone for the recipe before placing food on the grate between the piles of coals. Continue as directed in the recipe.

Maintaining Temperature

Keeping the temperature consistent on a charcoal kettle grill is slightly more involved than on a gas grill. Some kettle grills have a built-in thermometer, but if yours does not, you can purchase a grill thermometer to check the temperature through the vent in the lid. Success in maintaining temperature in your charcoal grill comes down to regulating the flow of oxygen and adding charcoal when needed.

OPEN VENTS WIDER TO RAISE TEMPS

KEEP VENTS CLEAR OF ASH
Charcoal ash can clog or block the intake vents on the bottom of the grill, starving the fire of oxygen. Use the damper blades to sweep those vents clear of ashes about once an hour.

Use the vents to control the oxygen. A charcoal fire gets the oxygen it needs mostly through the vents on the bottom of the bowl. The vent (damper) on the lid allows some hot air to escape through the top, creating a vacuum that is filled by fresh air entering from the bottom. This airflow moves heat and smoke around the food continuously. The bigger the openings in the vents, the greater the airflow and the higher the temperatures.

Once you are in the desired temperature range, keep the lid closed as much as possible and use the vents on the lid to fine-tune the temperature. Remember, more oxygen leads to higher temperatures and less oxygen to lower temperatures.

Temperature drops with time. In a kettle grill, a fully lit chimney of charcoal briquettes will start off with screaming-hot heat (at least 500°F). If that's too high, just wait, as the temperature will drop gradually. You can leave the lid on and let it drop slowly, or remove the lid to allow more airflow so the fire burns out faster.

Add charcoal to increase heat. If the heat dips too low, you will need to add more charcoal. You can add unlit coals to the pile and wait about 15 minutes for the temperature to rise again, or you can light more charcoal in a chimney starter outside the grill and then add the hot coals to the embers of the existing fire for an almost-instant heat infusion.

Other variables that can affect how food cooks on a charcoal grill include the weather (we can't do much about that), the type of charcoal used (now we're talking; see box, opposite), and the distance between the charcoal and the food (we've got this!).

ADD CHARCOAL GENTLY
Hastily dumping hot coals onto the burning embers can send charcoal ash into the air and onto your food. Also, adding too much charcoal at once could smother your well-built fire.

HERE ARE THE TEMPERATURES TO AIM FOR:

VERY LOW HEAT	(225° TO 250°F)
LOW HEAT	(250° TO 350°F)
MEDIUM-LOW HEAT	(300° TO 350°F)
MEDIUM HEAT	(350° TO 450°F)
MEDIUM-HIGH HEAT ...	(400° TO 450°F)
HIGH HEAT	(450° TO 550°F)

TYPES OF CHARCOAL

Briquettes are the most popular form of charcoal in North America for two reasons: they're inexpensive and available everywhere. Standard briquettes are compressed black pillow-shaped blocks packed with sawdust and coal, along with binders and fillers. Some are presoaked in lighter fluid for easier starting, but those can impart a chemical taste to the food if the lighter fluid isn't fully burned off before grilling. Pure (or "all-natural") hardwood briquettes have the same pillow shape but burn at higher temperatures. Considered the charcoal gold standard by expert grillers, they are usually made of crushed hardwoods bound together with natural starches. Lump charcoal (or "charwood") is essentially burnt wood sold in bags. This type of charcoal burns out faster than briquettes, making it more challenging to control, but it does have its uses (see page 35). Briquettes produce a predictable, even heat over a long period of time. A chimney starter full of charcoal (80 to 100 briquettes) will last 30 to 60 minutes—starting at high heat and gradually cooling to medium and low heat—which is plenty of time to grill most foods without having to replenish the fire.

CHARCOAL BRIQUETTE QUANTITIES

Using a chimney starter and lighter cubes is the best and fastest way to start your charcoal. See below for how much charcoal you should use to start, and how much you should add during grilling to maintain the correct temperature.

Grill Diameter	DIRECT HEAT		INDIRECT HEAT (QUANTITIES SHOWN ARE NUMBER OF BRIQUETTES PER SIDE OF GRILL.)			
	Weber Briquettes	Standard Briquettes	Weber Briquettes (first hour)	Weber Briquettes (each hour after)	Standard Briquettes (first hour)	Standard Briquettes (each hour after)
Go-Anywhere portable	12	16	4	2	8	2
14 inch	25	30	5	3	9	6
18-inch compact	30	40	10	5	20	7
18 inch	30	40	10	5	20	7
22 inch	40	50	15	7	25	8
26 inch	65	80	25	8	40	9
37 inch	115	150	45	18	75	22
Summit Charcoal (24 inch)	48	60	48	8	30	8

TIME

Step two toward grilling success is to understand the importance of time and its relationship with temperature. With just about anything you grill, the goal is the same: to create tasty browning (or even a crust) on the food's surface and succulent tenderness inside. How you achieve this balancing act depends largely on the nature of what you are cooking and, of course, timing.

HOT & FAST

Thin, tender foods like hamburgers call for hot and fast grilling to create the crust quickly, but the interiors change from undercooked to overcooked in a matter of minutes, so be vigilant.

LOW & SLOW

Big, tough foods like pork shoulder call for a low and slow approach over the course of hours. It takes that kind of time (at the right temperature) to get both the inside and outside right where you want them to be.

TIMING ON THE GRILL

Heat, Energy, and Time

Heat is simply energy. When you are grilling, fast-moving molecules from the fire are colliding with slow-moving molecules in the raw food. As these two sets of molecules swirl around in an increasing frenzy, the food changes color, new flavors are created, the outside dries out, and the structure of the food inside begins to break down.

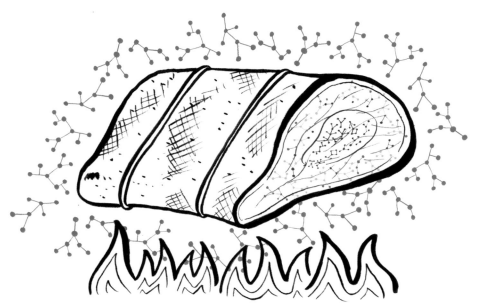

GREEN — SUPER FAST MOLECULES
YELLOW — SLOWER MOLECULES
RED — SUPER SLOW MOLECULES

Our four T's are team players, especially temperature and time. This is why you should consider them together. Food grilled over strong radiant direct heat will take much less time to cook. For example, a steak grilled over direct heat will take much less time than one grilled over indirect heat, and you'll get that flavorful sear. If using indirect heat, give the food more time—it's worth it.

The heat of a grill is a lot like the heat of the sun. It radiates from a source (gas or charcoal), heats the air, and then the air heats the food. On the grill, the outside of the food is almost always cooking faster than the inside. Your job as the griller is to control the temperature and timing so the outside and inside are done simultaneously.

If you're working with direct heat, the outside of the food will cook much, much faster than the inside. This is fantastic if you are cooking something small like shrimp. With direct high heat, assuming the timing is right, the outside of the shrimp will develop some good color and flavor before the inside is overcooked and dry.

Now, if you're grilling something big and tough like pork spareribs, direct high heat would torch them on the outside long before the inside was even close to palatable. That's why such foods call for indirect heat, sometimes very low indirect heat (about 250°F), sometimes for hours. The outside is still cooking faster than the inside, but not so much faster that it gets too dark.

There's some nuance to this direct-equals-short and indirect-equals-long arithmetic, and the ideal combinations of time and temperature are about as infinite as the number of foods you may want to grill. That's not meant to scare you. Instead, it's meant to segue smoothly to the handy Grilling Guides you'll find on pages 24 to 29, covering all those time, temp, and food variables.

RESTING

Consider a typical workweek. You have five highly productive days on and then two very necessary, battery-recharging days off. Grilled food operates similarly. It often needs some resting time off the heat before it should be cut. A little science will explain why.

Food is mostly water, but protein and fat are often part of the picture, too. The protein molecules in uncooked food are tightly coiled. These wound-up molecular springs hold onto water, which is why juices don't run when we cut into raw meat. When you grill a raw steak, however, the proteins "denature," or unwind. This process pushes the water molecules around and, in the case of cooked meat cut too soon, right out onto your cutting board. Letting meat rest after cooking allows the proteins to cool and recoil somewhat, thus grabbing back onto the water molecules they had previously displaced.

GUIDE TO RESTING TIMES

The ideal resting time depends mostly on how big the food is. The larger the food, the longer it should rest. Here are some guidelines for what needs a quick break versus a long weekend.

BEEF	**Steaks:** 3 to 5 minutes
	Roasts: 15 to 30 minutes
PORK	**Chops:** 3 to 5 minutes
	Roasts: 15 to 30 minutes
POULTRY	**Small parts:** 3 to 5 minutes
	Whole chicken: about 15 minutes
	Whole turkey: about 30 minutes
FISH	**Small fillets or seafood:** no resting
	Whole fish: 5 to 10 minutes

GRILLING GUIDES

The cuts, thicknesses, weights, and grilling times found in the following charts are meant to be guidelines rather than hard-and-fast rules. Cooking times are affected by all kinds of things, such as altitude, wind, and outside temperature. Two rules of thumb: Grill steaks, chops, and kebabs using the direct method for the time given on the chart or to your desired doneness, turning once. Grill roasts and thicker cuts using the indirect method for the time given on the chart or until an instant-read thermometer registers the desired internal temperature. Let roasts, whole poultry, or larger cuts of meat, and thick steaks or pork chops rest for 5 to 10 minutes (or more, see page 23) before carving because the internal temperature of the meat will rise 5 to 10 degrees during this time.

GRILLING BEEF

CUT	THICKNESS / WEIGHT	APPROXIMATE GRILLING TIME
Steak: New York strip, porterhouse, rib-eye, T-bone, or filet mignon (tenderloin)	¾ inch thick	**4–6 minutes** direct high heat
	1 inch thick	**6–8 minutes** direct high heat
	1¼ inches thick	**8–10 minutes** direct high heat
	1½ inches thick	**10–14 minutes:** sear 6–8 minutes direct high heat, grill 4–6 minutes indirect high heat
Beef, ground	¾ inch thick	**8–10 minutes** direct medium-high heat
Flank steak	1½–2 pounds, ¾ inch thick	**8–10 minutes** direct medium heat
Flat iron steak	1 inch thick	**8–10 minutes** direct medium heat
Hanger steak	1 inch thick	**8–10 minutes** direct medium heat
Kebab	1-inch cubes	**4–6 minutes** direct high heat
	1½-inch cubes	**6–7 minutes** direct high heat
Rib roast (prime rib), boneless	5–6 pounds	**1¼–1¾ hours** indirect medium heat
Rib roast (prime rib), with bone	8 pounds	**2–3 hours:** sear 10 minutes direct medium heat, grill 2–3 hours indirect low heat
Skirt steak	¼–½ inch thick	**4–6 minutes** direct high heat
Strip loin roast, boneless	4–5 pounds	**50 minutes–1 hour:** sear 10 minutes direct medium heat, grill 40–50 minutes indirect medium heat
Tenderloin, whole	3½–4 pounds	**35–45 minutes:** sear 15 minutes direct medium heat, grill 20–30 minutes indirect medium heat
Top sirloin	1½ inches thick	**10–14 minutes:** sear 6–8 minutes direct high heat, grill 4–6 minutes indirect high heat
Tri-tip	2–2½ pounds	**30–40 minutes:** sear 10 minutes direct medium heat, grill 20–30 minutes indirect medium heat
Veal loin chop	1 inch thick	**6–8 minutes** direct high heat

All cooking times are for medium-rare doneness except ground beef (medium).

STANDARDS FOR DONENESS

DONENESS	CHEF STANDARDS	USDA
Pork, ground	160°F	160°F
Pork, chops or roasts	145° to 150°F	145° to 160°F
Poultry	160° to 165°F	165°F
Red meat: rare	120° to 125°F	n/a
Red meat: medium rare	125° to 135°F	145°F
Red meat: medium	135° to 145°F	160°F
Red meat: medium well	145° to 155°F	n/a
Red meat: well done	155°F +	170°F

For optimal safety, the United States Department of Agriculture (USDA) recommends cooking red meat to 145°F (final temperature) and ground red meat to 160°F. The USDA believes that 145°F is medium rare, but virtually all chefs today believe medium rare is closer to 130°F. The chart above compares chef standards with USDA recommendations. Ultimately, doneness decisions are your choice.

GRILLING LAMB

CUT	THICKNESS / WEIGHT	APPROXIMATE GRILLING TIME
Chop: loin or rib	¾ inch thick	**4–6 minutes** direct high heat
	1 inch thick	**6–8 minutes** direct high heat
	1½ inches thick	**8–10 minutes** direct high heat
Lamb, ground	¾ inch thick	**8–10 minutes** direct medium-high heat
Leg of lamb, boneless, rolled	2½–3 pounds	**30–45 minutes:** sear 10–15 minutes direct medium heat, grill 20–30 minutes indirect medium heat
Leg of lamb, butterflied	3–3½ pounds	**30–45 minutes:** sear 10–15 minutes direct medium heat, grill 20–30 minutes indirect medium heat
Rack of lamb	1–1½ pounds	**15–20 minutes:** sear 5 minutes direct medium heat, grill 10–15 minutes indirect medium heat

All cooking times are for medium-rare doneness except ground lamb (medium).

TYPES OF RED MEAT FOR THE GRILL

TENDER CUTS FOR GRILLING

Beef New York strip steak

Beef porterhouse steak

Beef rib steak/rib-eye steak

Beef T-bone steak

Beef tenderloin (filet mignon) steak

Lamb loin chop

Lamb rib chop

Veal loin chop

MODERATELY TENDER CUTS FOR GRILLING

Beef flank steak

Beef flat iron steak

Beef hanger steak

Beef skirt steak

Beef top sirloin steak

Lamb shoulder blade chop

Lamb sirloin chop

Veal shoulder blade chop

BIGGER CUTS FOR SEARING AND GRILL-ROASTING

Beef standing rib roast (prime rib)

Beef strip loin roast

Beef tri-tip roast

Beef whole tenderloin

Leg of lamb

Rack of lamb

Rack of veal

TOUGHER CUTS FOR BARBECUING

Beef ribs

Brisket

GRILLING PORK

CUT	THICKNESS / WEIGHT	APPROXIMATE GRILLING TIME
Chop, boneless or bone in	¾ inch thick	**6–8 minutes** direct medium heat
	1 inch thick	**8–10 minutes** direct medium heat
	1¼–1½ inches thick	**10–12 minutes:** sear 6 minutes direct medium heat, grill 4–6 minutes indirect medium heat
Loin roast, boneless	3½ pounds	**28–40 minutes:** sear 8–10 minutes direct high heat, grill 20–30 minutes indirect high heat
Loin roast, bone in	3–5 pounds	**1¼–1¾ hours** indirect medium heat
Pork, ground	½ inch thick	**8–10 minutes** direct medium heat
Pork shoulder (Boston butt), boneless	5–6 pounds	**5–7 hours** indirect low heat
Ribs, baby back	1½–2 pounds	**3–4 hours** indirect low heat
Ribs, country-style, boneless	1½ inches thick	**12–15 minutes** direct medium heat
Ribs, country-style, bone in	1 inch thick	**45–50 minutes** indirect medium heat
Ribs, spareribs	2½–3½ pounds	**3–4 hours** indirect low heat
Sausages, fresh	3-ounce link	**20–25 minutes** direct medium heat
Sausages, precooked	3-ounce link	**10–12 minutes** direct medium heat
Tenderloin	1 pound	**15–20 minutes** direct medium heat

The USDA and most chefs agree that ground pork should be cooked to a safe internal temperature of 160°F. They also agree on cooking pork chops and roasts to 145° to 150°F, when the meat still has some pink in the center and all the juices haven't been driven out. Of course, the doneness you choose is entirely up to you.

TYPES OF PORK FOR THE GRILL

TENDER CUTS FOR GRILLING	MODERATELY TENDER CUTS FOR GRILLING	BIGGER CUTS FOR GRILL-ROASTING	TOUGHER CUTS FOR BARBECUING
Center-cut chop	Ham steak	Center loin roast	Baby back ribs
Loin or rib chop	Shoulder blade steak	Center rib roast	Shoulder (Boston butt)
Tenderloin	Sirloin chop	Country-style ribs	Spareribs
		Cured ham	
		Rack of pork	

GRILLING POULTRY

CUT	THICKNESS / WEIGHT	APPROXIMATE GRILLING TIME
Chicken breast, bone in	10–12 ounces	**23–35 minutes:** 3–5 minutes direct medium heat, 20–30 minutes indirect medium heat
Chicken breast, boneless, skinless	6–8 ounces	**8–12 minutes** direct medium heat
Chicken drumstick	3–4 ounces	**26–40 minutes:** 6–10 minutes direct medium heat, 20–30 minutes indirect medium heat
Chicken thigh, bone in	5–6 ounces	**36–40 minutes:** 6–10 minutes direct medium heat, 30 minutes indirect medium heat
Chicken thigh, boneless, skinless	4 ounces	**8–10 minutes** direct medium-high heat
Chicken thigh, ground	¾ inch thick	**12–14 minutes** direct medium heat
Chicken, whole	4–5 pounds	**1¼–1½ hours** indirect medium heat
Chicken, whole leg	10–12 ounces	**48 minutes–1 hour:** 40–50 minutes indirect medium heat, 8–10 minutes direct medium heat
Chicken wing	2–3 ounces	**35–43 minutes:** 30–35 minutes indirect medium heat, 5–8 minutes direct medium heat
Cornish game hen	1½–2 pounds	**50 minutes–1 hour** indirect high heat
Duck breast, boneless	10–12 ounces	**9–12 minutes:** 3–4 minutes direct low heat, 6–8 minutes indirect high heat
Duck, whole	5½–6 pounds	**40 minutes** indirect high heat
Turkey breast, boneless	1½–2 pounds	**45–60 minutes** indirect medium heat
Turkey, whole, not stuffed	10–12 pounds	**2½–3½ hours** indirect medium-low heat

Cooking times yield the USDA-recommended doneness temperature of 165°F.

GRILLING SEAFOOD

TYPE	THICKNESS / WEIGHT	APPROXIMATE GRILLING TIME
Fish, fillet or steak: halibut, red snapper, salmon, sea bass, swordfish, and tuna	½ inch thick	**6–8 minutes** direct high heat
	1 inch thick	**8–10 minutes** direct high heat
	1–1¼ inches thick	**10–12 minutes** direct high heat
Fish, whole	1 pound	**15–20 minutes** indirect medium heat
	2–2½ pounds	**20–30 minutes** indirect medium heat
	3 pounds	**30–45 minutes** indirect medium heat
Clams (discard any that do not open)	2–3 ounces	**6–8 minutes** direct high heat
Lobster tail	6 ounces	**7–11 minutes** direct medium heat
Mussels (discard any that do not open)	1–2 ounces	**5–6 minutes** direct high heat
Oysters	3–4 ounces	**5–7 minutes** direct high heat
Scallops	1½ ounces	**2–4 minutes** direct high heat
Shrimp	1½ ounces	**2–4 minutes** direct high heat

The general rule of thumb for grilling fish is 8 to 10 minutes per 1-inch thickness.

TYPES OF SEAFOOD FOR THE GRILL

FIRM FILLETS AND STEAKS	MEDIUM-FIRM FILLETS AND STEAKS	TENDER FILLETS	WHOLE FISH	SHELLFISH
Arctic char	Halibut	Cod	Branzino	Clams
Grouper	Mahimahi	Striped bass	Grouper	Lobster
Salmon	Monkfish	Trout	Red snapper	Mussels
Swordfish	Red snapper		Striped bass	Oysters
Tuna			Trout	Scallops
				Shrimp
				Squid

GRILLING VEGETABLES

TYPE	THICKNESS / SIZE	APPROXIMATE GRILLING TIME
Artichoke hearts	whole	**14–18 minutes:** boil 10–12 minutes; cut in half and grill 4–6 minutes direct medium heat
Asparagus	½-inch diameter	**6–8 minutes** direct medium heat
Beet	whole, 6 ounces each	**1–1½ hours** indirect medium heat
Bell pepper	whole	**10–12 minutes** direct medium heat
Carrot	1-inch diameter	**7–11 minutes:** boil 4–6 minutes, grill 3–5 minutes direct high heat
Corn, husked		**10–15 minutes** direct medium-high heat
Corn, in husk		**20–30 minutes** direct medium heat
Eggplant	½-inch-thick slices	**7–9 minutes** direct medium-high heat
Garlic	whole	**45 minutes–1 hour** indirect medium heat
Mushroom, button or shiitake		**8–10 minutes** direct medium heat
Mushroom, portabello		**8–12 minutes** direct medium heat
Onion	halved	**35–40 minutes** indirect medium heat
	½-inch-thick slices	**8–12 minutes** direct medium heat
Potato, new	halved	**20–30 minutes** indirect medium-high heat
Potato, russet	whole	**45 minutes–1 hour** indirect medium heat
	½-inch-thick wedges	**15–25 minutes** direct medium heat
Potato, sweet	whole	**45 minutes–1 hour** indirect high heat
	½-inch-thick wedges	**15–25 minutes** direct medium heat
Scallion	whole	**3–4 minutes** direct medium heat
Squash, acorn	halved, 1½ pounds total	**40 minutes–1 hour** indirect medium heat
Tomato, garden or plum	whole	**8–10 minutes** direct medium heat
	halved	**6–8 minutes** direct medium heat
Zucchini	½-inch-thick slices	**4–6 minutes** direct medium heat

Just about everything from artichoke hearts to zucchini tends to cook best over direct medium heat. The temperature on the grill's thermometer should be somewhere between 350° and 450°F.

GRILLING FRUIT

TYPE	THICKNESS / SIZE	APPROXIMATE GRILLING TIME
Apple	whole	**35–40 minutes** indirect medium heat
	½-inch-thick slices	**4–6 minutes** direct medium heat
Apricot	halved lengthwise	**4–6 minutes** direct medium heat
Banana	halved lengthwise	**3–5 minutes** direct medium heat
Nectarine, Peach, Pear, Plum	halved lengthwise	**6–8 minutes** direct medium heat
Pineapple	½-inch-thick slices or 1-inch wedges	**5–10 minutes** direct medium heat
Strawberry	whole	**4–5 minutes** direct medium heat

Just about everything from apples to strawberries tends to cook best over direct medium heat. The temperature on the grill's thermometer should be somewhere between 350° and 450°F.

TECHNIQUES

Now that you understand how to control the temperature and timing of your grilling, let's explore some techniques that can elevate your results even more. If you are a football fan, think of these as the skills you develop on the field to dodge an opponent, to throw an incredible pass, or to catch a pass in the corner of the end zone. Touchdown!

Smoke Signals.

Respond to

Keep a Lid on it.

DO THIS!

Play with New Ideas!

Season like you mean it!

Match the Heat with the Meat.

Crowd The Grill.

Have Just One Zone.

Fiddle So Much.

DON'T DO THIS!

Just Guess. ??? ??? ???

Start with a Cold, Dirty Grate.

GRILLING TECHNIQUES

Top Tips for Ultimate Grilling Success

Here are some simple techniques that will help you take charge of the fire versus the fire taking charge of you.

1. Don't start with a cold, dirty grate. A grill needs at least 15 minutes to get the grate hot enough to sear food properly. Preheat every time, and always give the hot grate a thorough once-over with a stiff-bristle brush before adding food. A hot, clean grate will brown food better, with less chance of sticking.

2. Season like you mean it. Salt is more important to great taste than any other ingredient. First, oil the food (not the grate), then sprinkle generously with salt, pepper, and/or other seasonings from edge to edge and on all sides. The oil will hold seasonings on the surface and prevent food from sticking to the grate.

3. Don't have just one zone. More heat zones mean more flexibility for times when something is cooking too fast or your food is flaring up or you are grilling two very different foods at the same time. At the very least, give yourself the advantages of two zones, one for direct heat and one for indirect heat.

4. Match the heat to the meat. Not everything should be grilled at the same temperature. Generally speaking, thin and tender foods do better over high temperatures, while thicker and tougher items often do better over less intense temperatures, sometimes in the form of indirect heat.

5. Don't crowd the grill. Packing too much food onto the cooking grate restricts your ability to be nimble and responsive. You should leave at least one-fourth of the grate clear, with plenty of space around each item of food; that way you can get your tongs in there and move the pieces from one area to another.

6. Keep a lid on it. Keeping the grill lid down as much as possible is especially important for maintaining even temperatures, controlling flare-ups, and capturing the fragrant smokiness that grilling generates.

7. Don't fiddle so much. Never poke and prod food more than you need to, or you'll lose flavors and color. You might also tear the surface of the food if you try to turn it too often. Turn most foods just once or twice. When in doubt, wait it out—assuming flare-ups are not an issue.

8. Respond to smoke signals. The quality of smoke from your grill could make or break your dinner. If it is black and dense, something is wrong (and maybe sooty). The food might be on fire, or the fire itself might not be getting enough air. What you want to see are wispy streams of clean, whitish smoke. Be ready to move your food, open the air vents, or add more fuel at the appropriate times.

9. Don't just guess. Knowing when food is done shouldn't be a guessing game. Sometimes color can tell you a lot. Sometimes texture provides clues. But with most meats, poultry, and fish, a thermometer is essential. Invest in a reliable one. It will make you right time after time (see pages 46 and 47).

10. Play with new ideas. There was a time when grilling meant one thing: meat (and only meat) charred over open flames. Today, grillers play with a much wider range of ingredients. The methods vary, too. Grilling now also means using outdoor fires to roast, smoke, bake, simmer, and stir-fry, among other techniques.

TAME THE FLAME

Flare-ups are flames that shoot above the cooking grate. Most of them are caused by too much fat or oxygen at the heat source and happen within the first few seconds of putting food on the grill or immediately after turning food. Flames that don't rise up through the cooking grate are not a problem. Stand back and let them run their course. These mild flare-ups also often go away after closing the lid, which reduces the oxygen reaching the flames. But if the flames threaten to burn your food, take action, especially if the food is covered in a sugary spice rub or sauce that can quickly turn bitter. If you are cooking on a charcoal grill, you might see the flames through the vents and hear the sputtering sounds. That's when you need to jockey the food to a safety zone where it may continue to drip fat but it won't ignite. Once the fat is no longer dripping and the flames have died down, you can move the food back over direct heat.

Direct-Coal Cooking

Want to impress friends and family with a new grilling skill? Go grateless. In this method, the food is cooked right on live coals for a remarkable sear and brag-worthy memories. Direct-coal cooking has been around for some time (not counting our prehistoric ancestors), and it was said to be President Eisenhower's favorite way to cook a steak.

1. Heap the chimney to brimming with lump charcoal (see box, opposite). Lump charcoal does not fit as compactly as briquettes, so the overflow will compensate for the difference. You need enough charcoal to spread into an even bed about 2 inches thick. Ignite the charcoal (do not use lighter fluid with direct-coal cooking, or ever, really).

2. Lump charcoal has a well-deserved reputation for burning very hot—and then burning down fairly quickly. As soon as the coals turn white, turn them out onto the charcoal grate. Use long-handled tongs to spread the coals into as even a layer as possible.

3. Use a sheet pan to fan any loose ashes off the coals, then immediately put the meat or vegetables on the coals while they are glowing orange and at the peak of their heat cycle.

4. If the coals stick to the food when turning, just shake them off or remove them with long tongs or a basting brush.

LUMP CHARCOAL

No substitutes here: lump charcoal is the only choice for direct-coal cooking because you and your guests will be eating the food right from the coals. Don't ever use briquettes (not even the hardwood "championship" variety) because the additives aren't safe for consumption. Plus, the ashes from briquettes can be gritty, while lump charcoal burns to a fine ash. An exception can be made if you're peeling away the food's outer layer, such as corn in the husk, before eating it.

You want the coal bed to be as even as possible, so use a charcoal rake or sturdy tongs to smash any very large charcoal chunks into smaller pieces before building the fire.

BEST FOODS FOR DIRECT-COAL COOKING

Steaks about 1 inch thick are great choices for direct-coal cooking. Thinner steaks will cook so quickly they won't get the chance to pick up substantial browning. Thicker steaks would spend too much time on the coals, overcooking their surfaces.

Corn in the husk has been cooked this way for centuries. Soak the ears in water for about 30 minutes and then ember-roast them long enough to turn the outer husk black and to create steam to cook the kernels, usually 5 to 10 minutes.

Sturdy vegetables, such as potatoes, yams, and onions, are ideal for this technique. Bury the unpeeled vegetables in the burning coals and let them cook until tender, usually 30 to 60 minutes. It is okay if the skins burn. Just let cool slightly and peel before serving. If you prefer to keep the charring to a minimum, wrap the vegetables individually in aluminum foil before burying them in the coals.

To avoid serious flare-ups, never oil the food and never cook meat with excess fat. Trim off nearly all the fat around the perimeter of steaks and avoid marinades or brines, as the moisture they add will dampen the coals and create a cold, ashy mess. Spice rubs that don't contain sugar sing in direct-coal cooking; the heat toasts the spices to bring out extra flavor.

SMOKING

Top Tips for Ultimate Smoking Success

Think of smoke as a complex range of flavors that you achieve by burning wood. This heady mix of tastes is typically associated with big hunks of meat that can withstand the steady stream of good, long smoking. But why should pork shoulders and briskets have all the fun? A whisper of smoke can add sweet, subtle fragrance to more delicate foods, such as salmon, too.

1. Start at the beginning. Many of the flavor compounds in smoke are fat and water soluble, which means the food you are cooking will absorb the smokiness best when raw. Start smoking at the beginning. As the surface dries out, the smoke cannot penetrate as well.

2. Match the heat to the meat. The way to make sinewy meats moist and tender is to cook them over low indirect heat with wood smoke. But don't miss easy opportunities to add sweet wood aromas to foods grilled over a hot fire for just minutes, like steaks, shrimp, and even vegetables.

3. Harness the water. Big fluctuations in smoking temperatures can dry out foods. Whenever you cook for longer than an hour, consider using a pan of water to help stabilize the heat and add some humidity. Use a large disposable foil pan, place it beside the burning embers, and don't forget to refill it.

4. Choose the wood. Smoking woods range from mild to strong in flavor: apple and cherry are mild, pecan and hickory are medium, and mesquite is the strongest. Pair the wood with the flavor of the food. For example, use apple wood with salmon and hickory or mesquite with brisket. Woods come in two forms: chips and chunks. Chips are coarsely chopped wood ideal for smoking over short intervals; soak for 30 minutes in water to cover before using. Chunks are larger pieces of wood ideal for smoking over longer intervals.

5. Know when to stop. A common mistake is to add too much wood, to the point where the food tastes bitter.

It's best to smoke food for no longer than half its cooking time, then see how it tastes, adding more next time if needed. Smoke should flow in a gentle stream, not billow out as if from a train engine.

6. Watch for smoke signals. Clean streams of whitish smoke can layer your food with the intoxicating scents of smoldering wood. But if your grill lacks enough ventilation or the wood is too wet, you'll get blackish smoke that can taint your food with soot. Soft, resinous woods, and even hardwoods that are freshly cut, also often burn with sooty smoke. Don't use them.

7. Let it flow. Airflow is essential for smoking success, so keep the vents on your grill lid open a little. The open vent will draw smoke from the charcoal and wood below, so it swirls over your food and out the top properly. Keep the vents on the bottom open, too, unless the fire gets too hot, then close them as needed to lower the temperature.

8. Mind your fire. Although smoking is relatively low-maintenance cooking, you must always remain mindful and safe. Never leave a lit fire unattended, and check the temperature every hour or so, adjusting the bottom vents or adding more charcoal if needed.

9. No peeking. Every time you open the grill, you lose heat and smoke, two critical elements for making a great meal. Open the lid only if you need to tend to the fire, the water pan, or the food, and ideally all three of them at once.

10. Develop a bark. Barbecued meat should glisten with a dark mahogany

crust, or bark, that borders on black. It is the delicious consequence of fat and spices sizzling with smoke on the food's surface and developing a caramelized crust. Before you remove the meat or wrap it, make sure the bark is dark.

11. Remember your priorities. The main ingredient in any smoked recipe should be your top priority. Don't overwhelm your centerpiece with an overly potent marinade, heavy-handed seasonings, or thick coats of sauce.

WHAT IS SMOKE?

The swirling plumes of smoke you see in the air are made up of tiny solid particles, droplets of liquid, and invisible gases, with the latter deserving the biggest tip of the hat. These gases hold the aromatic wood compounds that infuse food with delectable flavor.

When you smoke food, you are working to harness the invisible gases but not necessarily the visible wisps. If you see dark smoke coming from the vents, the solid and liquid particles are too big. These oversized particles will pile up on the surface of the meat and give it a sooty taste. But if a fire has plenty of oxygen (from airflow through vents), temperatures rise to the point that you get lovely aromatic compounds in tiny particles.

Smoking in a Charcoal Grill

If you are a barbecue fanatic, you probably use a special smoker that is designed to hold low temperatures for long hours. If you have a kettle grill instead, you can still smoke foods beautifully; just use these tips for smoking.

1. Soak the desired number of wood chips in water for at least 30 minutes before lighting the charcoal. Well-soaked chips will smolder and smoke, rather than flaming up like a second, unwanted heat source.

4. Use a drip pan when grilling foods that require more than 30 minutes of cooking time. The pan will catch rogue drippings and will help absorb and evenly redistribute heat inside the grill. Place the pan in the center of the charcoal grate and fill it three-fourths full with warm water.

5. Think long term. If your recipe calls for cooking more than 30 minutes, you'll likely need to refuel at some point. Light another batch of charcoal now and set the chimney aside in a safe spot (for example, on top of cinder blocks) so the coals will be fully lit when the fire needs more fuel.

6. Put the cooking grate in place to preheat. If it has hinged sides, position at least one of the hinged sides over the charcoal so it will be easy to add more charcoal later. Then close the lid and open the top vents completely.

2. Sweep away any ashes that have accumulated on the bottom of the grill, which can prevent enough air from getting to the fire. Make sure to leave the vents open on the grill bottom. Every hour or so, give the vents a gentle sweep to clear the ashes.

3. For larger foods, like ribs or brisket, arrange the coals on one side of the grill, leaving about two-thirds to three-quarters of the grill free for cooking. For smaller foods, use the three-zone split fire (see page 17).

7. Patience, griller. Wait until the temperature reaches the specified range for the recipe you are making, keeping in mind that as the charcoal burns, the temperature will drop. It may take a while to get there, but expertly smoked food is worth the wait.

8. A thermometer on the grill lid is the most reliable way to check the temperature. If your grill lid doesn't have one, use the "feel the heat" method: Spread out your fingers, palm down, about 5 inches above the charcoal grate. If you have to move your hand in 2 to 4 seconds, you've got high heat; 5 to 7 seconds, medium heat; 8 to 10 seconds, low heat; and 11 to 12 seconds, very low heat.

TENDING THE FIRE

The average chimney starter full of charcoal will give you 30 to 60 minutes of grilling time. Any foods requiring more than that will need backup (see step 5). If you are using standard charcoal briquettes, add them when they are fully lit so the additives have been burned off and won't affect the taste of your food. All-natural briquettes and lump charcoal, which are additive-free, can be added to the fire unlit or lit. Smaller pieces of lump charcoal will burn out quickly, so you will need to add them more often. Larger lumps will take a little more time to get hot, but they will last longer.

Like charcoal, you may want to replenish wood chips if the first batch has burned out. Plan to have some presoaked chips at the ready to scatter over the embers. Be sure all the charcoal is fully lit when you add wood chips. Damp chips and weak coals spell the end of a fire.

The grill vents are critical to tending the fire. The more air flowing into the grill, the hotter the fire will grow and the more frequently you will have to replenish it. To minimize additions, keep the lid closed as much as possible and (almost always) leave the vents on the bottom of the grill open. To slow the rate of a fire's burn, position the top vents as much as three-quarters closed.

Smoking in a Water Smoker

A water smoker allows you to smoke foods at consistent temperatures below 300°F for several hours. The upright bullet-shaped unit is made up of three sections: The charcoal burns in the bottom; the water sits in a pan in the middle, keeping the temperature low and preventing fat from dripping into the coals; and the meat sits on one or two racks in the middle section. The top section is the lid.

1. If you are using a 22½-inch smoker, fill the chimney starter with charcoal and light the charcoal in a safe way (see step 5, page 38). If you are using an 18-inch smoker, fill the chimney starter only three-quarters full with charcoal.

4. Make sure the water pan is empty and suspended inside the middle section and the charcoal access door is closed. Set the middle section over the bottom section and immediately fill the pan three-quarters full with water. Set the two cooking grates in place inside the middle section.

5. Place the lid on top of the smoker. A water smoker has vents on the bottom section and on the lid. At this point, open the top vents completely and close the bottom vents halfway. Wait until the smoker reaches its ideal temperature range of 225° to 275°F.

6. Open the charcoal access door and, using tongs or insulated gloves, add as many (dry) wood chunks as the recipe suggests. Close the charcoal access door and wait for a few minutes for the smoke to stream out of the top vents.

2. Remove the middle and top sections from the bottom section. Lay the charcoal grate in the bottom section and set the charcoal ring on top of the grate. Add enough unlit charcoal to the ring to fill it three-quarters full and spread it out evenly.

3. When the briquettes are lightly covered with white ash, carefully pour the lit charcoal over the unlit charcoal, spreading it out evenly. Over time, the unlit charcoal will burn and extend the life of the fire.

REGULATING THE HEAT
The easiest way to regulate the smoker's temperature is by adjusting the vents. The less air you allow into the smoker, the lower the temperature. To raise the temperature, open the vents wider.

You can also raise the temperature by adding charcoal through the access door, though this is rarely necessary for recipes that cook in less than 6 hours.

A third option involves the water pan. Water regulates the temperature by absorbing heat and releasing it gradually. The more water in the pan, the lower the temperature will be.

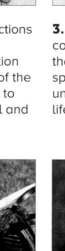

7. Remove the lid and arrange the food on the cooking grates, starting with the bottom grate. If you're using both grates, remember that whatever is on the top grate will drip onto what is on the bottom grate. If it is a pork shoulder above a prime rib, it would likely be fine; if it is salmon fillets above pork ribs, it would not.

8. Replace the lid on the smoker. Wait for 10 to 15 minutes to see if the temperature returns to the ideal range. The addition of meat will often bring down the temperature. If the temperature remains too low, open the bottom vents a bit more. If the temperature is too high, close the top vents as much as halfway, but never close them all the way.

To soak or not to soak?
Soaking wood chips extends their burn time, which translates into more of their desirable aromas in your food. Wood chunks last longer naturally and do not need to be soaked.

Smoking in a Gas Grill

Smoking is a snap if your gas grill is equipped with a built-in smoker box. Even without one, you can get big smoke aromas with little effort.

1. Soak wood chips in water for at least 30 minutes. Any less time and they are likely to give you more flames than smoke (check the recipe to see how much you need).

3. Using long-handled tongs, open the lid of the smoker box. Grab some of the soaked wood chips with the tongs, let the excess water drain off, and drop the chips into the box. Spread them out so they cover the bottom of the box, exposing as many chips as possible to the burner below. Continue to add as many chips as the recipe suggests. Close the lid of the smoker box, then close the grill lid. Wait for a few minutes for smoke to pour out of the grill.

4. Arrange the food in the middle of the cooking grate, over the unlit burner(s). Close the grill lid as soon as possible and let the food cook. Keep the lid closed as much as possible.

5. You can control how quickly the chips smoke by turning the knob of the smoker box's dedicated burner higher or lower. The burner should usually be set to the lowest setting so the chips smolder slowly. If you need to add more wood chips to the box, do it before the smoldering chips have burned up. Smoldering chips will help light the new chips.

2. In most cases, you will be smoking with indirect (low) heat. Turn off the burner(s) in the middle of the grill and turn down the outside burners to the temperature the recipe suggests. For now, keep the burner under the smoker box turned to high so the chips will smoke quickly.

CONTROLLING THE TEMPERATURE

In most cases, controlling the temperature on a gas grill during cooking involves only adjusting one or two of the main burners. The exception is if you want to smoke at very low temperatures (below 250°F). Then you must turn off all but one of the main burners. That's it.

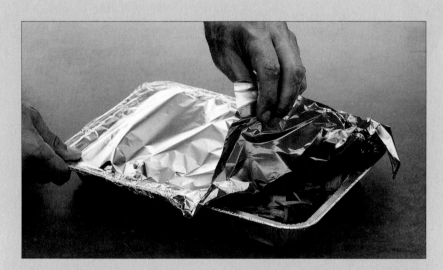

MAKE YOUR OWN SMOKER BOX

If your gas grill doesn't have a built-in smoker box, you can make one. Place presoaked and drained wood chips in a foil pan and cover the pan with aluminum foil. Poke holes in the bottom of the pan and in the foil cover to allow the smoke to escape. Place the pan directly on the bars over an unlit burner or two, preferably in a back corner of the cooking box. Put the cooking grates in place over the pan. Turn on all the burners to high and close the lid. Add food when the grill is fully smoking, adjusting the temperature as needed. The only down side is that your homemade box doesn't allow you to add more chips as you go. You can also buy a smoker box with a hinged lid designed to sit on top of the cooking grates, which makes replenishing wood chips easy.

TOOLS

For the great painters of the world, the brush is an extension of the artist. Similarly, your grilling tools are the instruments you use to make your meal a masterpiece.

ESSENTIALS

You don't need every tool imaginable, but imagine flipping burgers without a spatula or turning chicken pieces with bare fingers. These are our essential tools for grilling.

NICE TO HAVE

It is much easier to be a better griller, deftly
handing all types of ingredients and techniques,
when you use what the experts use. weber

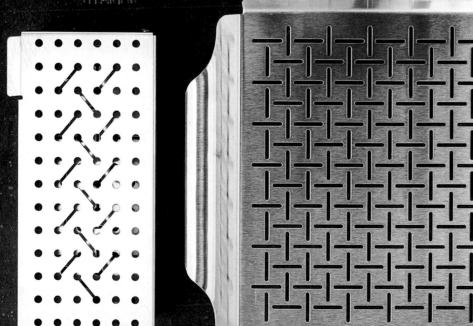

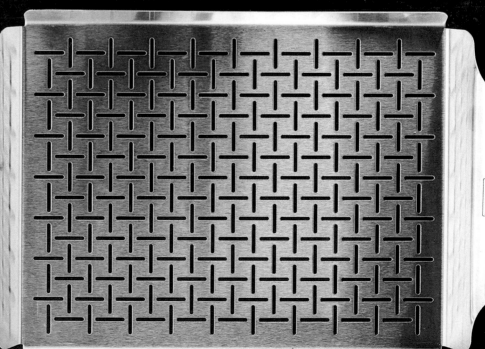

The Essential Tools

Tongs Every single time—that's how often you will use tongs to grill. Have a few pairs of durable, spring-loaded tongs that are long enough to protect your hands and arms from the heat. Have one pair for loading raw food on the grill and moving it around and a second pair (or clean first pair) for when it's time to remove food. Dedicate a third pair to rearranging charcoal.

Spatula Tongs are essential—but not for flipping burgers. You'll need a spatula for that and other things like fish fillets. Look for a long-handled one with a bent (offset) neck, so the blade is set lower than the handle. That makes it easier to lift food off the cooking grates.

Brush If you don't clean your cooking grates, you will sabotage your meal. The surest way to clean the bars is to use a solid, long-handled brush with securely anchored stainless-steel bristles and apply a good deal of pressure.

Chimney starter Simple, efficient, and inexpensive, this is the best tool for lighting charcoal (see page 14). A chimney is also an excellent place to hold your lit backup coals for fire replenishing.

The Nice-to-Haves

Insulated gloves Pouring coals out of a chimney starter, arranging coals inside any cooker, and lifting hot grates are not tasks you can do bare-handed. Wear gloves that are thick, insulated, and long enough to cover your forearms.

Instant-read thermometer This is the most accurate way to check many foods for perfect doneness. If you have one that includes a probe that remains in the food and sends the internal temperature to your smartphone or tablet, use it (see box, opposite).

Perforated grill pan Food too small or delicate for the cooking grates finds a safe cooking haven on a perforated grill pan.

Basting brush If bastes and sauces are part of your repertoire, you will want one of these, preferably one with heat-resistant silicone bristles and a long handle.

Charcoal baskets Ever attempted to move a pile of burning charcoal one coal at a time? These baskets are big sanity savers as you're mastering the art of indirect grilling. Armed with tongs, pick up a basket and put it where you need it.

Smoker box If your gas grill doesn't have a built-in smoker box, go portable. Filled with your favorite wood chips, it sits right on the cooking grates and can be easily reloaded with chips as your food cooks. (You can even make your own, see page 43.)

Cedar plank A natural cedar plank delivers fragrant aromas with minimal effort. Submerge it in water for at least 1 hour before putting it on the grill. Otherwise you are asking for flames.

Charcoal rake Fanatics of live-fire cooking will appreciate the ease with which this long-handled tool can push or pull hot coals from one area of the charcoal grate to another. It does only one thing, yes, but it does it very well.

Lights If you cannot see it, it will probably burn—or worse. A light on a grill handle, or placing the grill in a well-lit area, is essential. Because when natural light goes, it goes fast.

Fish basket Adjustable steel-wire baskets keep fish just above the grate, where the sticking happens. The fish still gets direct exposure to the flavors of the grill, but you get to turn the fish with peace of mind (and with tongs, of course).

Poultry roaster A poultry roaster perches a bird upright on the cooking grate, allowing the heat to flow around the meat evenly. Some of these roasters have a cup that can be filled with beer or other liquid if you like to steam the bird from the inside.

Rib rack This clever item saves space on your cooker by standing racks of ribs upright rather than laying them flat. Now you can smoke three or four racks of ribs where only two once reasonably fit.

Timer A timer is the fail-safe that we busy, easily distracted folks need. It never forgets when to check the coals or turn the meat. You might want two of them for multitasking.

Spray bottle Fill one of these little bottles with apple juice and vinegar for keeping smoked meats moist.

WEBER iGRILL

Hello, Digital Age. Nice to meet you! As outdoor cooks, we like the primordial satisfaction of grilling over flickering fires. A big part of the gratification lies in doing something natural and non-techy—something close to what generations of grillers have always done. Our grandparents weren't using digital devices to grill, so why bother with this technology now?

Here are two good reasons why: better food and peace of mind. The grilling experience is essentially the same as it has been for decades. It's just that now a probe is inserted into whatever you are cooking. That probe is communicating the internal temperature of your food to a digital base next to your grill, and the digital base is communicating to your phone (via Bluetooth).

You can be on the other side of your yard or on the other side of your house and still have constant access to what's happening to the food on the grill. You can set the app on your phone to notify you when your food has reached whatever temperature you prefer. You can even monitor a few cuts of meat at the same time. And you can use a sensor to monitor the ambient temperature inside your grill or smoker. Whoa! That means no more surprises. That means perfect doneness every time. We think our grandparents would have appreciated that.

Transform Your Grill

GRIDDLE

With this workhorse tool, you can do everything from making a bacon-and-eggs breakfast to baking a bread pudding. It also comes in handy for items too small (little vegetables) or delicate (thin-cut fish) for the cooking grates. You will use this more than you think.

TOP TIPS FOR GRIDDLES

Choose cast iron. Buy a cast-iron griddle that fits your grill and the number of people you like to feed. Weber makes a convenient 12-inch round griddle, but larger sizes are out there, too. It's nice if it covers one-third to one-half of the cooking grate, so you still have space to grill directly on the grate.

Preheat the griddle. Cast iron is dense, so it takes at least 10 minutes to preheat. Make sure the griddle is nice and hot before you set food on it.

Oil the griddle first. If you are concerned the food might stick, coat the griddle first with some oil, but be stingy, as too much can cause dangerous sputtering and flare-ups.

PIZZA STONE

For every frozen pizza we consume, a resident of Naples, Italy, weeps. Or maybe not. But in the spirit of peace and international unity, we highly recommend using a pizza stone. This solid stone slab placed on the grill evenly retains and distributes heat, which fills each pizza with light, doughy air pockets and toasts the bottom into a crackling, golden brown crust—just like in Naples.

TOP TIPS FOR PIZZA STONES

Position it on the grate. In many cases, you can set a pizza stone right on top of the grill grate, often in a metal frame that makes it easy to move the stone on and off the grill. On some grills you can remove the center circular cooking grate insert and replace it with the pizza stone in its frame.

Preheat the stone. You will need to prepare your charcoal or gas grill for indirect high heat and preheat the stone for at least 15 minutes. The temperature of the grill should rise to at least 500°F.

Use it for more than pizza. Depending on how hot the fire is and how you configure it (direct versus indirect heat), you can also cook such foods as bread and crostata (see recipe on page 326).

WOK

Traditionally, the focal point of a typical Chinese kitchen was a round hole over a firebox of burning wood and embers, with a wok resting snugly in the hole. You can embrace the ancient art of live-fire stir-frying with a wok placed directly on your gas or charcoal grill. Ideally, choose a wok made of enamel-coated cast iron, which retains heat well without reacting to acidic ingredients. Some sit on top of the cooking grate, but better ones fit into a round hole in the center of the cooking grate, resting closer to the heat.

TOP TIPS FOR WOKS

Choose utensils wisely. A wooden spatula with a shovel-like shape that fits the sloped sides of a wok is kind to enamel coatings and ideal for scooping up sauce on the wok bottom.

Work quickly. No beer breaks here; stir-frying happens in a short burst of time. Prepare your ingredients, sauces, and garnishes and place them and serving dishes near the grill before you start cooking. Cut the ingredients into uniform pieces so they cook evenly.

Preheat the wok. Heat the wok for 10 to 15 minutes. Authentic stir-fried tastes and textures require a screaming-hot wok. When you flick a few drops of water into the hot wok, they should dance and evaporate almost on contact.

Even protein, even searing. Quickly spread pieces of meat or other protein so they are in direct contact with the hot surface. Then wait, without moving it, for 20 to 30 seconds to give the food a chance to sear.

Don't add too much at once. If you overcrowd the wok, the temperature will drop, and the food will steam rather than sear and brown. Make sure vegetables are dry so they don't steam.

Happy Hour

Italian Bruschetta, recipe on page 68; **Asparagus and Lemon Pizza**, recipe on page 89; **Maple-Bourbon Chicken Wings**, recipe on page 56; **Roasted Carrot Hummus with Pita Chips**, recipe on page 72

STARTERS

BBQ GENIUS

Maple-Bourbon Chicken Wings RECIPE ON PAGE 56

CHICKEN WINGS

What was once deemed the least desirable part of a chicken—except in barrooms and fraternity houses—is now flying high as a crispy crowd-pleasing appetizer that is equally at home with American barbecue sauces, Asian ingredients, or really whatever flavors you like. Great wings depend on mastering the techniques that deliver the ideal textures and tastes. We cover all that on pages 54 and 55.

Q & A

everything chicken wings

Q: What kind of wings should I buy?

A: Today, supermarkets sell both whole wings and wing parts, and choosing one of the smaller parts can sometimes be the thing to do. For example, if you are all about crispy chicken skin, you might prefer the narrow, pointed tips, as they are mostly just skin and bone. If you appreciate a little meat on the bones, look for the center section of the wing, known as the "flat" or "wingette." The third section, which is closest to the breast, has a little less skin than the tip and a little less meat than the flat. It is usually called the "drumette" and looks like a small drumstick. That said,

FIVE WAYS TO RUIN CHICKEN WINGS

1. Grill them straight from the freezer.

2. Marinate them in sweet barbecue sauce that will burn.

3. Grill them over briquettes soaked in lighter fluid.

4. Pour good beer on crispy wings.

5. Overcook them to the point that the meat is parched.

you can still grill whole wings with great success. Think of them as a sampler platter of everything wings have to offer.

Q: How should I get them ready for the grill?

A: There are many options for seasoning wings. We lean toward spice rubs because they work faster than marinades and are dry. Anything wet will reduce your chances of turning out a batch of crisp wings. They might taste delicious after soaking in a bath of your favorite marinade, but you will have a hard time cooking off the liquid so the skin can turn crispy. Stick with spice rubs. And before you season the wings with spices, always pat them dry with paper towels to absorb any surface moisture.

Q: How should I grill them?

A: Our preferred approach is to use a combination of direct and indirect heat. We like to brown wings first over direct medium heat, keeping them there as long as possible to develop the flavors and crispiness. When the skin begins to look quite dark (almost burned), we move them to indirect heat. The less-in-

tense circulating heat penetrates down to the bones without scorching the skin.

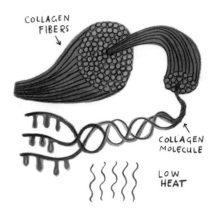

Q: What if I want my wings to be super tender?

A: In that case, we suggest you cook the wings entirely over indirect heat, which allows you to do more to break down the chewy elasticity of the skin. That stretchy texture comes from collagen, a series of microscopic coiled protein ropes present in the skin and tough connective tissue. If your grill heat is low enough— around 300°F—you can leave wings over indirect heat for 1½ to 2 hours. That will yield a soft texture that you can almost slurp.

Q: Why is the skin on my chicken wings so flabby?

A: It's probably the sauce. Coating wings on the grill with tomato- and vinegar-based sauces, both with high water contents, will soften the skin in a Nashville hot second. Sauces or toppings with a lower water content, like Buffalo sauce or seasoned lard, yield only slightly better results. If you value a crunchy texture, serve your finished, perfectly crisp wings with the sauce on the side.

Q: Why are my wings burning?

A: Barbecue sauce or another sugary coating could be the problem. The optimal range for grilling wings is 300° to 400°F, the temperature range at which the Maillard reaction takes place. Named after a mustachioed French chemist who died in the 1930s, this chemical reaction is the delicate dance between the amino acids and the sugars in our food that yields the much-coveted browning. But to make that happen, we have to keep a close eye on those naturally occurring sugars. If we add to them (with sauce) and they are allowed to get too hot for too long, the oxygen, nitrogen, and hydrogen that are released will turn into bitter-tasting carbon and ash.

Keeping a spray bottle of water handy to cool surface temperatures quickly when things start to get out of hand is helpful, as is moving the meat away from the direct heat source, be it a pile of coals or a gas flame. When in doubt, use slightly lower heat toward the end of cooking. The internal reactions will continue to take place but the surface sugars won't get torched.

GRILL SCIENCE

Baking Powder: Not Just for Baking

Baking powder is amazing. You probably thought it was just for aerating baked goods like cakes and muffins, but it can also help you make browner, crispier chicken wings. In fact, it can improve the overall browning of all kinds of ingredients. That's because it makes whatever it is applied to more alkaline. Remember the high-school science class in which you learned that everything is on a pH scale from very acidic to very alkaline? Well, the baking soda (bicarbonate of soda) in baking powder will make the skin of chicken wings much more alkaline. That speeds up the browning process and also helps to make the skin crispy. If you have time, season each pound of chicken wings with ½ teaspoon baking powder, ½ teaspoon kosher salt, and ¼ teaspoon ground black pepper. Set a wire rack on a baking sheet, arrange the wings in a single layer on the rack, and put the pan, uncovered, in the refrigerator overnight. By the next day, the salt will have pulled some water from the skin on the wings and the baking powder will have made the skin more alkaline. Now your wings are primed for ultimate browning and crispiness.

Maple-Bourbon Chicken Wings

12 chicken wings,
about 3 pounds total

Extra-virgin olive oil

**CHIPOTLE-OREGANO
RUB**

1 teaspoon kosher salt

1 teaspoon dried oregano

½ teaspoon ground cumin

½ teaspoon chipotle
chile powder

¼ teaspoon ground
black pepper

**MAPLE-BOURBON
BBQ SAUCE**

¾ cup ketchup

¼ cup maple syrup

¼ cup bourbon

2 tablespoons cider vinegar

¼ teaspoon chipotle
chile powder

Here, you brown the wings first over direct heat without any sauce. That's when the skin gets crispy. Then you move the wings over indirect heat, where it is safe to layer on the sweet sauce without the threat of it scorching.

1. The chicken wing is made up of three sections: the drumette (attached to the chicken body), the wingette (or "flat"; the middle section), and the tip. Each section has a bone ball socket, or joint. Flex each section to find the joint.

2. Using the tip of a boning knife, and keeping the joint extended to expose the socket, cut through the ball socket connecting the drumette and wingette and then through the socket connecting the wingette and tip. Discard the wing tips or save for stock (they tend to burn on the grill).

5. Brush the cooking grates clean. Grill the wingettes and drumettes over **direct medium heat**, with the lid closed as much as possible, for 10 minutes, turning once or twice and watching closely for flare-ups that could scorch the skin.

6. Brush the chicken pieces with sauce on all sides and move them over **indirect medium heat**. Continue to cook, with the lid closed as much as possible, until the meat is no longer pink at the bone, 10 to 15 minutes. During this time, stay vigilant, as the sugars in the sauce could burn. Remove from the grill and serve warm.

SERVES **4–6**

PREP: **20 MIN**

COOK: **12–15 MIN (SAUCE)**

GRILL: **20–25 MIN**

3. Brush the chicken wings very lightly with oil. In a small bowl mix together all the rub ingredients, then season the wings evenly with the rub. Set aside at room temperature while you prepare the grill. Prepare the grill for direct cooking and indirect cooking over medium heat (350° to 450°F).

4. In a small saucepan combine all the sauce ingredients. Bring to a boil over high heat on the stove, then reduce the heat to a simmer and cook until slightly thickened, 12 to 15 minutes, stirring occasionally. Remove from the heat and set aside.

VARIATIONS

HONEY-MUSTARD SAUCE

In a small bowl mix together ¼ cup honey, ¼ cup Dijon mustard, 2 tablespoons mayonnaise, and 2 teaspoons fresh lemon juice. Brush the wings occasionally with this sauce after moving them from direct to indirect heat.

BUFFALO SAUCE

In a small saucepan over medium heat, stir together ⅓ cup hot sauce (such as Frank's RedHot® or Crystal), ¼ cup unsalted butter, 2 teaspoons distilled white vinegar, ½ teaspoon garlic powder, and ½ teaspoon Worcestershire sauce. Cook until the butter has melted, stirring occasionally. Brush the wings occasionally with this sauce after moving them from direct to indirect heat.

Smoked Chicken Wings with Hoisin Glaze

FIVE-SPICE RUB

2 teaspoons
granulated garlic

1½ teaspoons
Chinese five spice

1 teaspoon ground
coriander

1 teaspoon kosher salt

½ teaspoon ground
black pepper

12 chicken wings,
about 3 pounds total

Extra-virgin olive oil

HOISIN GLAZE

1 tablespoon toasted
sesame oil

1 teaspoon grated garlic

1 teaspoon peeled, finely
grated fresh ginger

¼ cup hoisin sauce

2 tablespoons soy sauce

2 tablespoons packed light
brown sugar

2 tablespoons honey

1 tablespoon rice vinegar

2 scallions, white and light
green parts only, thinly
sliced on the diagonal
(optional)

The melt-in-your-mouth quality of these slow-cooked wings goes seamlessly with their smoky Asian flavors. For top-notch texture, never allow the temperature of your grill or smoker to go higher than 300°F. Small wings need only about 1½ hours to cook. Larger wings will take about 2 hours.

SERVES **4**

PREP: **20 MIN**

GRILL: **1½–2 HOURS**

SPECIAL EQUIPMENT:
**3 OR 4 SMALL
CHERRY OR APPLE
WOOD CHUNKS
(OR 3–4 HANDFULS
CHIPS, SOAKED IN
WATER 30 MIN)**

1. Prepare the grill or smoker for indirect cooking over low heat (250° to 300°F). In a small bowl mix together all the rub ingredients. Brush the chicken wings lightly with olive oil. Season them evenly with the rub.

2. Brush the cooking grates clean. Add the wood chunks to the coals (or drain and add the wood chips to the grill) and close the lid. When smoke appears, arrange the wings, skin side down, on the grates and grill over **indirect very low heat**, with the lid closed, for 1 hour.

3. Meanwhile, make the glaze: In a small saucepan warm the sesame oil over medium heat on the stove. Add the garlic and ginger and cook 30 to 60 seconds, stirring constantly. Add the remaining glaze ingredients, mix well, and cook until simmering, 1 to 2 minutes. Set aside off the heat.

4. After the first hour of cooking the wings, cut into one at the joint to check for doneness. The meat should no longer be pink at the bone. If it is pink, let the wings cook for another 30 minutes before you glaze them.

5. Brush the wings all over with the glaze and cook until the glaze has penetrated the surface of the wings, about 30 minutes. Transfer the wings to a platter and garnish with the scallions. Serve warm.

A NOTE ON GARLIC

Granulated garlic and garlic powder are marginally different versions of dried garlic. The granulated version is coarser, like fine cornmeal, while powdered is finer, almost like flour. A teaspoon of garlic powder will contain a slightly larger amount of garlic than a teaspoon of granulated garlic, but the difference won't ruin your spice rub, so use whichever one you have, assuming it is not as old as your oldest pair of shoes. Both versions lose flavor over time.

Tarragon-Mustard Shrimp Skewers

1½ pounds medium shrimp (26/30 count), peeled and deveined, tails left on (see steps 2 and 3, pages 274 and 275)

MUSTARD PASTE

3 tablespoons extra-virgin olive oil

3 tablespoons Dijon mustard

1 tablespoon dried tarragon, crushed between your fingertips

1 teaspoon dried dill, crushed between your fingertips

½ teaspoon kosher salt

¼ teaspoon ground black pepper

1 lemon, cut into wedges

Dijon mustard and dried herbs are considered pantry staples for good reason: they are all-star ingredients that work wonders on all sorts of recipes, including this easy mustard paste for grilled shrimp. Crushing the dried herbs helps to release their flavors and distribute them more evenly in the paste.

1. Divide the shrimp into four equal portions. Thread the shrimp onto the skewers in the following way: Begin by skewering 1 shrimp through both the head and tail ends.

2. Skewer the second shrimp through the head end only, with the tail end facing in the opposite direction.

3. Skewer the remaining shrimp just like the second one, with the tails facing the same way. Choose shrimp that are the same size so you can nestle them together with no space between them. This keeps the shrimp from spinning and prevents them from drying out on the grill. Repeat with the remaining shrimp.

4. In a small bowl whisk together all the paste ingredients. Brush the paste on both sides of the shrimp. Prepare the grill for direct cooking over high heat (450° to 550°F). Brush the cooking grates clean.

5. Grill the skewers over **direct high heat**, with the lid closed, until the shrimp are firm to the touch and just turning opaque in the center, 2 to 4 minutes, turning the skewers once and moving them to a clean area of the cooking grates. Serve warm with the lemon wedges.

Ground Lamb Kefta with Yogurt Sauce

KEFTA

Extra-virgin olive oil

2 pounds ground lamb

6 garlic cloves, minced or pushed through a press

½ small yellow onion, grated, with juices (about ¼ cup)

¼ cup chopped fresh cilantro leaves and tender stems

¼ cup chopped fresh mint leaves

1 tablespoon ground cumin

1 tablespoon ground coriander

1½ teaspoons kosher salt

1 teaspoon sweet paprika

½ teaspoon cayenne pepper

½ teaspoon ground black pepper

YOGURT SAUCE

1 cup plain whole-milk Greek yogurt

1 tablespoon chopped fresh mint leaves

1 garlic clove, minced or pushed through a press

¼ teaspoon kosher salt

¼ teaspoon ground black pepper

¼ teaspoon hot sauce, such as Tabasco®

2 teaspoons extra-virgin olive oil

1½ tablespoons chopped fresh mint leaves

1½ tablespoons chopped fresh cilantro leaves

About ¾ cup (8 ounces) harissa, store-bought

Kefta are essentially Middle Eastern meatballs that are cooked in a variety of ways. They are best when shaped lightly by hand, seared deeply on a grill, and accompanied by a bold, tangy, flavor-rich sauce. Refrigerating the raw meatballs first improves their texture and prevents sticking.

1. Lightly oil a large baking sheet. In a large bowl combine all the remaining kefta ingredients and mix gently with your hands until evenly distributed. Divide into 18 equal portions (about 2 ounces each) and arrange on the prepared pan.

2. With damp hands and a light touch, form each portion into an oval about 3 inches long and 1½ inches wide. Insert a skewer into each portion. Cover loosely with plastic wrap and refrigerate for at least 1 hour or up to 8 hours to firm up.

3. When ready to cook, prepare the grill for direct cooking over medium-high heat (400° to 450°F). While the grill heats, let the kefta sit at room temperature. In a small bowl whisk together all the yogurt sauce ingredients. You should have about 1 cup. Cover and refrigerate until serving.

4. Lightly brush the kefta all over with olive oil. Grill the kefta over **direct medium-high heat**, with the lid closed, until browned on all sides and cooked through, 8 to 12 minutes, turning occasionally.

5. Arrange on a serving platter, drizzle with the olive oil, and garnish with the mint and cilantro. Serve with the harissa and yogurt sauce.

Bruschetta with Marinated Peppers
RECIPE ON PAGE 66

BRUSCHETTA

An inspired Italian antipasto, bruschetta is simply toasted bread with a topping. But to serve it properly, the bread should be toasted on a grill. The word *bruschetta* comes from *bruscare,* which means "cooked over coals" in Roman dialect. On the following pages, we'll show you our favorite method for making this crowd-pleasing appetizer, with plenty of fresh ideas for toppings.

Bruschetta with Marinated Peppers

MARINATED PEPPERS

2 large bell peppers, red, yellow, and/or orange, each about 8 ounces

2 tablespoons extra-virgin olive oil

2 teaspoons red wine vinegar

2 teaspoons finely chopped fresh rosemary leaves

1 garlic clove, crushed

¼ teaspoon kosher salt

Pinch of crushed red pepper flakes

6 to 8 large fresh basil leaves

6 center-cut slices from 1-pound loaf rustic Italian or French bread, each ½ inch thick

Extra-virgin olive oil

6 ounces Fontina cheese, coarsely grated (about 1½ cups)

This recipe calls for grilling the bread on both sides so the cheese melts on a toasted top. For the variations on the following pages, you may prefer instead to toast just one side, which results in a chewier texture. The bread will also be less likely to shatter when you bite into it.

1. Prepare the grill for direct cooking over high heat (450° to 550°F). Brush the cooking grates clean. Grill the bell peppers over **direct high heat**, with the lid closed, until blackened and blistered all over, 15 to 20 minutes, turning occasionally.

2. Place the peppers in a medium bowl and cover with plastic wrap to trap the steam. Let stand for 10 to 15 minutes.

6. Prepare the grill for direct and indirect cooking over medium heat (350° to 450°F). Lightly brush both sides of the bread slices with the oil.

7. Brush the cooking grates clean. Toast the slices on one side over **direct medium heat**, with the lid closed, until golden brown on the first side, about 2 minutes. Transfer the slices, grilled side up, to a baking sheet.

SERVES **6**

PREP: **20 MIN**

MARINATE: **1–2 HOURS OR UP TO 2 DAYS**

GRILL: **20 MIN**

3. Cut away the stem and core from 1 pepper, then slit the pepper lengthwise, spread it open, and remove the seeds and white membranes. Peel away and discard the charred skin. Repeat with the remaining pepper.

4. Cut the peppers lengthwise into ⅓-inch-wide strips. In a bowl combine the pepper strips, oil, vinegar, rosemary, garlic, salt, and red pepper flakes. Cover and let stand at room temperature for 1 to 2 hours, or cover and refrigerate for up to 2 days (let stand at room temperature for 1 hour before serving).

5. Just before grilling the bread, finely chop the basil and add it to the marinated peppers.

8. Top the bread slices with the Fontina, dividing it evenly. Using a fork, remove the peppers from the marinade, letting the excess marinade drip back into the bowl, and arrange on the bread slices, dividing the peppers evenly.

9. Grill the bruschetta over **indirect medium heat,** with the lid closed, until the cheese is just melted, about 2 minutes. Transfer to a platter and serve right away.

FLAVOR BOMB
your
BRUSCHETTA

We still love the classic topping of diced fresh tomatoes, basil, and olive oil, but how nice that an Italian idea can wear so many other delicious international styles. The toppings can be sweet or savory, meaty or not, home cooked or straight from a jar.

PLOUGHMAN

Substitute walnut bread for the rustic Italian bread. Core and thinly slice 1 Granny Smith apple. Coarsely grate 3 ounces sharp cheddar cheese (about ¾ cup). Grill the bread as directed in the recipe on page 66, toasting on one side only. Top the grilled side of each bread slice with 3 or 4 apple slices, then 2 tablespoons cheese. Grill as directed to melt the cheese. Transfer to a platter and top with 1 teaspoon each fruit chutney and crumbled cooked bacon.

SPANISH

Grill the bread as directed in the recipe on page 66, but toast on both sides. Rub one side of each slice with a peeled garlic clove. Halve 3 large plum tomatoes lengthwise. Coarsely grate the cut side of each tomato half into a bowl and discard the skin. Top each bread slice with about 2 tablespoons of the grated tomato. Drizzle with extra-virgin olive oil and sprinkle with flaky sea salt.

ITALIAN

Cut 8 ounces (2 balls) fresh buffalo mozzarella into 12 slices total. Grill the bread as directed in the recipe on page 66, toasting on one side only. Spread the grilled side of each bread slice with 1 tablespoon basil pesto and top with 2 mozzarella slices. Grill as directed to melt the cheese. Transfer to a platter and top each with 1 prosciutto slice and some arugula leaves. Drizzle with extra-virgin olive oil and sprinkle with ground black pepper.

CALIFORNIA

Peel and pit 2 large avocados. Add to a bowl with 2 teaspoons fresh lemon juice, ½ teaspoon kosher salt, and ¼ teaspoon ground black pepper. Mash with a fork until slightly chunky. Grill the bread as directed in the recipe on page 66, but toast on both sides. Spread the avocado mixture on the toasts. Drizzle with extra-virgin olive oil and sprinkle with crushed red pepper flakes.

SUMMERTIME

Grill the bread as directed in the recipe on page 66, but toast on both sides. Spread 2 tablespoons ricotta cheese on each piece and season with kosher salt and ground black pepper. Arrange a sliced, grilled peach half (see Steps 2 and 3, page 75; brush with olive oil in place of the dressing before grilling) over the ricotta on each toast. Drizzle with honey and sprinkle with chopped fresh thyme leaves.

RUSTIC

Grill the bread as directed in the recipe on page 66, but toast on both sides. Spread 2 tablespoons fresh goat cheese and then 2 teaspoons fig jam on each piece. Finish with finely chopped fresh rosemary leaves (or small sprigs) and ground black pepper.

Grilled Onion and Sour Cream Dip

GRILLED ONIONS

3 medium yellow onions, about 1½ pounds total

2 tablespoons extra-virgin olive oil

1 teaspoon fresh thyme leaves, roughly chopped

½ teaspoon kosher salt

DIP

1 cup sour cream

4 ounces (½ cup) cream cheese, softened

¼ cup mayonnaise

1 garlic clove, minced or pushed through a press

1 teaspoon kosher salt

1 teaspoon Worcestershire sauce

½ teaspoon ground black pepper

¼ teaspoon hot sauce, such as Tabasco®

2 tablespoons finely chopped fresh chives, divided

Sturdy potato chips or pita chips

Pass up that store-bought packet of onion dip mix. This classic party dip deserves an update. Our modern version begins by charring the onions on the grill and then chopping them to a chunky finish. The resulting coarse texture and naturally bold flavors will wean you off that packet for good.

SERVES **6–8**

PREP: **15 MIN**

GRILL: **25–35 MIN**

SPECIAL EQUIPMENT:
**LARGE PERFORATED
GRILL PAN**

1. Prepare the grill for direct cooking over medium heat (350° to 450°F). Brush the cooking grates clean. Cut the onions in half lengthwise, then slice into ¼-inch-thick half-moons.

2. In a large bowl combine the onions, oil, thyme, and salt and toss to coat the onions evenly.

3. Spread the onion mixture in an even layer on a large perforated grill pan.

4. Set the grill pan over **direct medium heat** and cook the onions, with the lid closed, until soft and golden brown, 25 to 35 minutes, stirring about every 5 minutes.

5. Remove the grill pan from the grill and let the onions cool to room temperature. Discard any onion bits that have turned black (to avoid any unwanted bitter flavors).

6. In a food processor combine all of the dip ingredients except the chives. Process until blended. Add the onions and pulse to a dip consistency with some onion pieces remaining. Add all but ½ teaspoon chives and pulse once. Transfer to a bowl, sprinkle with the reserved chives, and serve with the chips.

Roasted Carrot Hummus with Pita Chips

HUMMUS

1 pound carrots, peeled and ends trimmed

½ cup plus 1 tablespoon extra-virgin olive oil, divided

1¾ teaspoons kosher salt, divided

2 garlic cloves

1 can (15 ounces) chickpeas, drained and rinsed

½ cup tahini

½ cup water

6 tablespoons fresh lemon juice

1½ teaspoons ground cumin

1 teaspoon ground coriander

½ teaspoon smoked paprika

¼ teaspoon ground black pepper

PITA CHIPS

2 whole-wheat or white pita breads, each about 7 inches in diameter

4 tablespoons (½ stick) unsalted butter, melted

1 teaspoon smoked paprika

1 teaspoon ground cumin

½ teaspoon kosher salt

Extra-virgin olive oil, for drizzling

Smoked paprika, for dusting

For a sweet, satisfying makeover of traditional hummus, roast carrot sticks on the grill until tender enough to pulverize easily in a food processor. It helps if they are all cut the same thickness to start. Toast thin pita wedges on a grill pan over indirect heat so they get crisp without burning.

SERVES **4–6**

PREP: **20 MIN**

GRILL: **40 MIN**

SPECIAL EQUIPMENT:
**LARGE PERFORATED
GRILL PAN**

1. Prepare the grill for indirect cooking over medium heat (350° to 450°F). Cut the carrots crosswise in half and then lengthwise into evenly sized sticks each about ⅓ inch thick.

2. Coat the carrots with the 1 tablespoon oil and season with ½ teaspoon salt. Brush the cooking grates clean. Arrange the carrot sticks perpendicular to the grate bars so they won't fall between them.

3. Grill the carrots over **indirect medium heat**, with the lid closed, until lightly charred and very tender and soft, about 30 minutes, turning once or twice. Remove from the grill and let cool to room temperature.

4. In a food processor pulse the garlic until minced, then add the carrots and pulse until finely chopped. Scrape down the bowl and add all the remaining hummus ingredients, including the ½ cup oil and 1¼ teaspoons salt. Process until very smooth, 2 to 3 minutes, scraping the bowl as needed. Transfer to a serving bowl.

5. Split each pita bread into two thin rounds. In a small bowl stir together the melted butter, paprika, cumin, and salt. Brush both sides of each pita round with the butter mixture. Stack the rounds and cut like a cake into 8 wedges (for a total of 24 wedges). Transfer the wedges to a large perforated grill pan.

6. Set over **indirect medium heat** and cook, with the lid closed, until the wedges are crisp, 10 to 12 minutes, turning occasionally. Watch closely so they do not burn. Transfer to a platter with the bowl of hummus. Garnish the hummus with a drizzle of oil and a dusting of paprika. Serve with the chips.

Grilled Peach Salad with Goat Cheese

VINAIGRETTE

1 small shallot, minced
(about 1 tablespoon)

1½ tablespoons white
balsamic or champagne
vinegar

2 tablespoons fresh
lemon juice

¾ teaspoon kosher salt

¼ teaspoon ground
black pepper

⅓ cup extra-virgin olive oil

3 firm but ripe peaches,
halved and pitted

¼ cup skin-on sliced
almonds

1 head red leaf or Boston
lettuce, leaves separated
and roughly torn

2 tablespoons chopped
fresh mint leaves, plus a
few small whole leaves

½ cup crumbled fresh goat
cheese, such as chèvre
(about 3 ounces)

Ripe peaches for a salad need only a brief stint on the grill. Too much time turns them into charred mushiness, so keep an eye on them. The simple vinaigrette here both makes this salad and is ideal for brushing on the peaches before grilling to prevent them from sticking to the grates.

SERVES **4**

PREP: **15 MIN**

GRILL: **5–7 MIN**

SPECIAL EQUIPMENT:
**10-INCH CAST-IRON
SKILLET OR GRIDDLE**

1. In a small bowl whisk together the shallot, vinegar, lemon juice, salt, and pepper. Add the oil in a slow, steady stream while whisking constantly to emulsify. Prepare the grill for direct cooking over medium heat (350° to 450°F). Brush the cooking grates clean.

2. Place a cast-iron griddle or skillet on one side of the grill, leaving space for the peaches. Close the lid and preheat for about 3 minutes. Lightly brush the peaches all over with some of the vinaigrette.

3. Grill the peaches, starting cut side down and turning once when they are nearly ready, directly on the grates over **direct medium heat**, with the lid closed, until lightly charred and beginning to soften but not mushy, 5 to 7 minutes. Use a wooden skewer to test doneness.

4. While the peaches are grilling, toast the nuts on the griddle or skillet, stirring occasionally, until golden brown, 2 to 4 minutes. Transfer to a plate and let cool to room temperature.

5. When the peaches are ready, transfer them to a cutting board and let cool completely. Cut into wedges. If the skins come off, they may be chopped and added to the salad or discarded. Just before assembling the salad, whisk the dressing again to emulsify.

6. Combine the lettuce and chopped mint in a wide, shallow serving bowl. Scatter the peaches, goat cheese, and almonds over the greens and drizzle with as much of the remaining dressing as you like. Arrange the mint leaves over the top of the salad and serve immediately, passing any extra dressing separately.

BBQ Buffalo Chicken Chopped Salad

BLUE CHEESE DRESSING

¼ cup buttermilk

¼ cup plain whole-milk Greek yogurt

2 tablespoons cider vinegar

2 tablespoons mayonnaise

¼ teaspoon kosher salt

⅛ teaspoon ground black pepper

⅓ cup crumbled blue cheese (about 1½ ounces)

BUFFALO SAUCE

⅓ cup cayenne pepper sauce, such as Frank's RedHot®

2 tablespoons unsalted butter

1 teaspoon kosher salt

1 teaspoon sweet paprika

½ teaspoon ground black pepper

2 boneless, skinless chicken breast halves, each 6 to 8 ounces

Kosher salt and ground black pepper

1 large ear corn, shucked and silk removed

Extra-virgin olive oil

1 head romaine lettuce or 2 romaine hearts, cut crosswise into bite-size strips (about 8 cups)

2 celery ribs, thinly sliced crosswise

1 medium carrot, peeled and coarsely grated

½ cup grape tomatoes, halved (or quartered if large)

2 tablespoons finely chopped fresh chives

This dinner salad is a healthy nod to the pub-grub favorite Buffalo wings. The recipe calls for boneless chicken breasts pounded to an even thickness, grilled, and then coated in a spicy, buttery Buffalo wing sauce. You'll taste a kick, but you won't break a sweat.

1. In a small bowl whisk together all the dressing ingredients except the blue cheese until well mixed. Stir in the cheese. Cover and refrigerate until ready to assemble the salad.

2. In a small saucepan, stir together all the Buffalo sauce ingredients over low heat on the stove until the butter melts. Remove from the heat and let cool for a few minutes. Prepare the grill for direct cooking over medium heat (350° to 450°F).

3. Place the breasts between two large sheets of plastic wrap. Using the bottom of a small, heavy skillet or the flat side of a meat mallet, pound the breasts to an even ½-inch thickness. Divide the Buffalo sauce in half. Reserve half for the salad and use the other half to coat the breasts evenly. Season with salt and pepper.

4. Brush the cooking grates clean. Lightly brush the corn with oil. Grill the corn over **direct medium heat**, with the lid closed, until slightly charred and softened a bit, about 10 minutes, turning occasionally. Meanwhile, grill the chicken over **direct medium heat** until firm to the touch and opaque to the center, 6 to 8 minutes, turning once.

5. Transfer the chicken to a cutting board and cut into bite-size pieces. Lay the ear of corn flat on the cutting board and, using a sharp knife, slice along the length to remove the kernels, rotating the ear after each cut until all the kernels are removed.

6. Combine the corn, lettuce, celery, carrot, and tomatoes in a serving bowl. Add about ½ cup of the dressing and toss to combine. Mound the chicken in the center of the salad and drizzle with some of the dressing and Buffalo sauce. Garnish with the chives and serve with the remaining dressing and sauce on the side.

Vietnamese Skirt Steak Salad

DRESSING

3 scallions, white and light green parts only, roughly chopped (about ⅓ cup)

⅔ cup soy sauce

Finely grated zest of 2 limes

¼ cup fresh lime juice (from 2 to 3 limes)

2-inch piece fresh ginger, peeled and cut into chunks

4 garlic cloves, smashed

2 tablespoons Asian fish sauce

2 tablespoons toasted sesame oil

MARINADE

¼ cup canola or peanut oil

2 tablespoons packed light brown sugar

1½ pounds beef skirt steak, about ½ inch thick, trimmed of excess fat

SALAD

4 to 6 ounces rice vermicelli (rice sticks)

8 ounces English cucumber, halved lengthwise and cut crosswise into thin half-moons (about 2 cups)

1 large carrot, peeled and coarsely grated (about 1¼ cups)

2 scallions, white and light green parts only, thinly sliced on the diagonal (about ½ cup)

1 cup bean sprouts

½ cup lightly packed fresh mint leaves

½ cup lightly packed fresh cilantro leaves

½ cup roughly chopped salted roasted peanuts

1 red jalapeño chile pepper, thinly sliced crosswise

A balancing act of opposites, this salad is soft and crunchy, fresh and cooked, sweet and spicy. You'll need to allow time for marinating, but it will be time well spent. Grill the meat to at least medium rare, as rare skirt steak can be tough. If you like, use kitchen shears to cut the noodles to shorter lengths.

1. In a food processor combine all the dressing ingredients and process until smooth, about 30 seconds.

2. Pour ½ cup of the dressing into a baking dish large enough to hold the steak pieces in a single layer and add the marinade ingredients. Whisk to dissolve the sugar. Set aside the rest of the dressing for serving.

3. Cut the steak crosswise into large sections that are easy to turn on the grill and so each has a uniform thickness. Put the steak pieces in the marinade and turn to coat evenly. Cover and refrigerate for 2 to 4 hours.

4. Soften the vermicelli in warm water, following the package instructions. Drain well. Transfer to a large serving bowl, moisten with some of the reserved dressing, and mix to coat well. Add the cucumber, carrot, scallions, and bean sprouts and enough dressing to coat the ingredients lightly, mixing well.

5. Prepare the grill for direct cooking over high heat (450° to 550°F). Brush the cooking grates clean. Lift the steak pieces from the marinade, allowing the excess marinade to drip back into the dish. Grill over **direct high heat**, with the lid closed, until cooked to your desired doneness, 4 to 6 minutes for medium rare.

6. Transfer the steak to a cutting board and let rest for about 5 minutes. Cut the meat across the grain into ⅓-inch-thick slices. Add the meat and any accumulated juices to the noodle mixture. Scatter the mint, cilantro, peanuts, and jalapeño over the salad and toss to mix. Serve with any remaining dressing.

BBQ GENIUS

Classic Tomato, Mozzarella, and Basil Pizza

RECIPE ON PAGE 86

PIZZA

Remember this rule of thumb: the fewer the ingredients in a recipe, the better quality each one needs to be. For this classic pizza Margherita that means three things: springing for supple fresh mozzarella cheese, not the waxy, bland stuff; pureeing drained whole canned tomatoes to a make a thick sauce with an intense tomato flavor; and hunting down a bunch of fragrant fresh basil.

everything
pizza

Q: Can you really make pizza on a grill?

A: Sure you can, and it's terrific! There are at least two distinct ways to make pizza on a grill, one challenging, one not so challenging. For the first option, press the dough into a round and oil it on both sides. Next, grill one side of the dough round by itself just until it is toasted and firm (usually a few minutes). Then, flip the dough so it is toasted side up and arrange your toppings on the toasted side. Finally, cook the pizza until the bottom is crisp and the cheese has melted. This

FIVE STEPS TO GREAT PIZZA

1. Let the dough relax before shaping, especially if chilled.

2. Use your hands to pull the dough gently into shape; never use a rolling pin.

3. Choose ingredients that complement one another.

4. Make sure the pizza isn't stuck to the pizza peel before sliding it onto the hot stone.

5. Grill over indirect heat until browned and bubbly.

way works, provided your timing is perfect, your fire is not too hot, and your toppings need only a few minutes of cooking. If that sounds exhausting, read on.

The other way, the one you'll find on the following pages, is to use a pizza stone set directly on the grill grate. This easy work-around all but guarantees a touch of Neapolitan magic.

Q: What are the elements of great pizza?

A: In Naples, Italy, the widely acknowledged birthplace of pizza, pies are baked in special wood-burning ovens that reach screaming-hot temperatures. It takes only about a minute in one to achieve a light, airy crust with a bubbly section of charred dough. Good news: outdoor grills can make pretty amazing facsimiles.

While a great crust is the foundation of a great pizza, there are also other elements to consider. A savory sauce, melty cheese, and other flavorful ingredient combinations can make or break an amazing pie. You can add just about anything you want to a pizza, and we'll share some of our best combinations in the coming pages, but keep in mind

that you don't want to overwhelm your pizza with too many toppings. A heavy hand with the sauce can result in a soggy pie. The best pies offer a light mix of ingredients.

Q: What tools do I need to make classic pizza on the grill?

A: You'll get the best results using a pizza stone (round or rectangular) and a pizza peel (paddle). Other bread-making tools, such as a bench knife and a kitchen scale, will come in handy but are not essential.

Q: Can I use refrigerated store-bought dough?

A: Sure you can, as long as the dough is still "alive" with yeast. You'll get about three 12-inch pizzas out of 2 pounds of dough. Cut it into equal pieces and shape each piece into a ball.

Then allow the dough to rest at room temperature, covered loosely with plastic wrap, for at least 2 hours before shaping the crusts. This gives the dough time to "proof," or puff up a bit, which is a sign that lets you know the yeast is alive and working. Also, letting the dough rest relaxes the gluten, making it easier to coax it into a thin round.

Q: Why is it so hard to shape cold pizza dough? What does temperature have to do with elasticity?

A: Think about a major-league pitcher warming up in a bullpen. In the absence of those pregame practice pitches, the arm muscles are stiff, tough to operate, and, worse, at risk of tearing. The proteins that make up wheat gluten operate similarly. They bind together

82 ULTIMATE GRILLING

and get stretched out during kneading, giving the dough its structure and lift in the process. But when chilled, the proteins constrict and cling to one another, cutting down on elasticity and increasing the likelihood of tearing. By allowing dough to come to room temperature—basically, to do a bullpen warm-up—you're giving the proteins the opportunity to relax and spread out. And from there on, it's all perfect pizza games all the time.

Q: How do I set up the grill?

A: Set it up for indirect high heat. That means the heat will be radiating from opposite sides of the grill. If there is too much heat directly under the stone, the bottom of the pizza will burn before the top of the crust has a chance to brown and bubble. For a charcoal grill, we recommend using two charcoal baskets spread apart on the cooking grate (see Step 1, page 17). For effects similar to a wood-fired oven, add a couple of small wood chunks (not soaked) to the charcoal. If you have a gas grill, light the outside burners on high and preheat the stone over indirect heat for at least 10 minutes.

GRILL SCIENCE

Do I need a pizza stone? Can't I use a baking sheet?

Where a stone differs from a baking sheet is in its mass. Just as a lightweight pan will burn or inconsistently heat food on a stove top, a flimsy surface on the grill will yield unsatisfactory crusts.

Pizza stones, which come in a variety of natural materials—clay, tile, firebrick—and are primarily sold unglazed, hold a lot of heat and are able to distribute it uniformly across the top. That means when the dough is placed on the stone, it cooks steadily, evenly, and, best of all, quickly, turning out the much-coveted thin, crisp crust.

Additionally, moisture from the pizza leeches into the stone, adding to its conductive properties. Think about traditional Neapolitan pizzas cooked in brick or stone ovens: they are ready in a flash and perfectly cooked because of the even, well-distributed heat of the cooking surface, the convection properties channeled by the oven's shape, and the fire's energy. The grill, in all its approachable dexterity, offers the same characteristics when the lid is closed.

Homemade Pizza Dough

1½ cups warm water (110° to 115°F)

1 teaspoon active dry yeast

1 teaspoon sugar

1¼ pounds (about 4 cups) all-purpose flour, plus more as needed

2 teaspoons kosher salt

3 tablespoons extra-virgin olive oil

A food processor makes quick work of whirling dough ingredients into a ball. However, for a crust that rises and bubbles up the way a great crust should, the key is kneading the ball long enough—until soft and supple—and adding just enough flour so the surface is slightly tacky yet not sticky.

1. To make the dough in a food processor: Pour the warm water into a bowl or liquid measuring pitcher, add the yeast and sugar, and whisk gently. Let stand until a little frothy, about 5 minutes.

2. In a food processor fitted with the plastic blade (a sharp metal blade can cut the dough), combine the flour and salt. With the motor running, add the warm water mixture and the oil through the feed tube.

5. Turn the dough out onto a work surface and knead by hand, adding more flour as needed, until the dough is soft and smooth, 5 to 8 minutes.

6. Lightly coat a large bowl with oil. Shape the dough into a ball, put it into the bowl, and turn to coat with the oil. Cover the bowl with plastic wrap or a kitchen towel.

MAKE-AHEAD DOUGH

If you like, you can make the dough a day ahead and refrigerate it overnight. Let the dough rise as directed in Step 7. Then form it into balls, cover loosely, and refrigerate for up to 24 hours. Let the dough stand at room temperature for 1 to 2 hours to take the chill off before you stretch, top, and grill it.

3. Process until a soft but not sticky dough clumps up and rides on the top of the blade (there might be some crumbles of dough, too). If the dough is sticky, dust with 1 to 2 tablespoons flour. If it is too dry, sprinkle with 1 to 2 tablespoons water. Process briefly, check the dough again, and repeat until the texture is correct.

4. To make the dough by hand: In a large bowl whisk together the warm water, yeast, sugar, and oil and let stand until a little frothy, about 5 minutes. Stir in the flour and salt with a wooden spoon and then work them in by hand until a stiff dough forms, adding flour or water until the consistency is correct (see Step 3).

7. Let stand in a warm, draft-free place until the dough is doubled in volume, about 2 hours.

8. Divide the dough into three equal pieces. Form each piece into a ball. Place the dough balls on a floured baking sheet and cover loosely with plastic wrap. Let stand in a warm, draft-free place until the dough is puffy and doubled in volume, about 1 hour.

Classic Tomato, Mozzarella, and Basil Pizza

Homemade Pizza Dough (page 84), or 2 pounds store-bought pizza dough

TOPPINGS (PER PIZZA)

All-purpose flour, for dusting the work surface

⅓ to ½ cup high-quality store-bought pizza or marinara sauce

3 to 4 ounces fresh mozzarella cheese, hand sliced into ⅓-inch-thick rounds, then torn into pieces

3 to 4 tablespoons freshly grated pecorino romano cheese

5 or 6 large fresh basil leaves, torn into small pieces

Extra-virgin olive oil, for drizzling (optional)

Direct from your grill, here is a Naples-style pizza sporting a crispy, chewy crust with a few superb ingredients on top. We have provided a dough recipe, but to save time, you can purchase a couple of pounds of dough from a pizzeria or even your local supermarket.

1. To make the pizza, prepare the grill for indirect cooking over high heat (500° to 525°F). Position the pizza stone on the grate. Preheat the stone with the lid closed while you shape the pizza.

2. Lightly flour your hands and dust a pizza peel with flour, coating it thoroughly. On a lightly floured work surface, using your fingers, gently press and stretch one dough ball into an 8- or 9-inch round. (Do not use a rolling pin, as it will press too much air out of the dough.)

6. Shake the peel horizontally (just a jiggle) to be sure the pizza will slide. If it sticks, scatter some flour under the offending area. Do not top the dough with too much sauce or cheese or it will weight it down, making it hard to slide it onto the stone. As the cheese melts, it will spread over the surface.

7. Quickly slide the pizza off the peel onto the stone. Grill over **indirect high heat**, with the lid closed.

3. Pick up the dough at one edge with both hands, spacing your hands about 1 inch apart. Letting the dough droop onto the work surface, gently but quickly rotate the dough in one direction, as if turning a wheel, until you have a uniformly thin round.

4. If necessary, drape the dough over the backs of your hands and move them apart to stretch the dough further into a 12-inch round. Let gravity do most of the work of stretching the dough into shape.

5. Position the dough on the floured peel. If there are any holes, pinch them closed. Stretch the dough back into shape. Using the underside of a soupspoon, spread the sauce onto the dough, leaving a ½-inch border uncovered. Top evenly with the mozzarella and then the pecorino romano.

8. Cook until the pizza bottom is crisp and has a scattering of dark brown spots and the topping is bubbling and browned, 7 to 9 minutes, checking the underside after 5 minutes to be sure it is browning but not burning. If the pizza is browning too quickly, use the peel to rotate it 180 degrees on the stone.

9. Using the peel and tongs, transfer the pizza to a cutting board. Sprinkle with the basil and then drizzle with oil, if desired. Using a pizza wheel or large knife, cut the pizza into wedges and serve. Repeat the steps to shape, top, and cook the remaining pizzas.

FLAVOR BOMB *your* PIZZA

Plain cheese pizza? Maybe some other time. These recipes are for the flavor maximalists among us. The ingredient amounts provided are for one pizza only. Consider this license to try many options at once—and create a pizza party for the record books.

MUSHROOM AND GARLIC

Omit the basil and use freshly grated Parmigiano-Reggiano® cheese in place of the pecorino romano. For each pizza, in a large skillet heat 1 tablespoon olive oil over high heat. Add 2 cups thinly sliced cremini or button mushrooms and cook for 3 minutes. Add 2 garlic cloves, finely chopped, and 1 teaspoon minced fresh rosemary and cook, stirring occasionally, until the mushrooms are tender but not browned, about 2 minutes more. Let cool. Top the pizza with the sauce and cheeses as directed, then spoon on the mushroom mixture. Grill the pizza according to the recipe on page 86.

ARTICHOKE AND OLIVE

Omit the basil. For each pizza, top with the sauce and mozzarella as directed, then scatter ½ cup thawed, well-drained, and coarsely chopped frozen artichoke hearts and ⅓ cup coarsely chopped pitted Kalamata olives over the top. Sprinkle with 1 teaspoon dried oregano and the pecorino romano cheese. Grill the pizza according to the recipe on page 86. Just before serving, season with a large pinch of crushed red pepper flakes.

ASPARAGUS AND LEMON

Omit the sauce, pecorino romano cheese, and basil. For each pizza, snap off and discard the tough ends from 16 thin asparagus spears (about 4 ounces), then cut into ½-inch lengths to measure about ¾ cup. Bring a saucepan of salted water to a boil over high heat, add the asparagus, and cook until crisp-tender, 2 to 3 minutes; drain, rinse with cold water to cool, and pat dry. Thinly slice 3 ounces fresh mozzarella cheese, arrange the slices evenly over the dough, top with the asparagus, and finish with 2 tablespoons freshly grated Parmigiano-Reggiano® cheese. Grill the pizza according to the recipe on page 86. Just before serving, sprinkle with the finely grated zest of 1 small lemon.

FONTINA AND PESTO

Omit the mozzarella and basil. For each pizza, top with the sauce as directed, then top with 1 cup shredded Fontina cheese, preferably Fontina Val d'Aosta (4 ounces). Drop ¼ cup jarred pesto in 10 small mounds on top of the dough, then sprinkle the pecorino romano cheese on top. Grill the pizza according to the recipe on page 86.

Carne y Vino
Lamb Rib Chops with North African Spices, recipe on page 150; **Steak Fries with Chipotle Ketchup and Aioli,** recipe on page 314; **Porterhouse Steaks with Board Sauce,** recipe on page 126; **Portabello Mushrooms with Chard and Feta,** recipe on page 302

BEEF & LAMB

Classic American Cheeseburger

RECIPE ON PAGE 96

BURGERS

Even allowing for differences in personal taste, the burgers on the following pages approach perfection. At first bite, meaty juices will run across your tongue, and the flavors will remind you just how gratifying an old-fashioned burger can be. Here are our favorite ways to create burger nirvana.

Q: My store sells different types of ground beef. Should I buy the one labeled "hamburger" or something else?

A: The short answer is something else. Prepackaged "hamburger" is often made with beef scraps, making the taste and consistency of that meat questionable at best. We want to keep you happy, so we think you are better off with ground meat labeled with a particular cut of

FIVE WAYS TO RUIN A BURGER

1. Cook frozen patties straight from the freezer. They'll steam and turn to mush before developing flavor.

2. Press on the burger when it's on the cooking grate, releasing juices and probably causing flare-ups.

3. Overload a burger with too many toppings, burying the main attraction.

4. Use sliced bread with holes as the "bun," allowing condiments and juices to seep out.

5. Finish it in a microwave because it was undercooked. That drains it of juiciness and turns the bun to the consistency of wet paper towels.

beef, like chuck or round. Even "ground beef" is better than "hamburger" because by law, the former can't include fat scraps.

Q: What does all that other information on the label mean? What's up with numbers like 80/20?

A: Package labels like 80/20 describe the ratio of lean meat to fat. In this case, it is an ideal combination. Fat is important to making burgers juicy and delicious, so definitely embrace it. You can instead opt for 85/15 for burgers, but if you reach for anything hovering near 90/10, you're in Mojave-dry territory. That 10 percent fat virtually melts away during grilling, leaving you with dry, crumbly pucks.

Q: What about seasoning the meat?

A: Yes. Do this. Salt and pepper do taste good together. For each 1½ pounds of meat (enough for four burgers) you will need about 1 teaspoon kosher salt and ½ teaspoon ground black pepper. Either gently

mix the seasoning into the meat before making the patties or sprinkle the seasoning evenly on both sides of the patties. Both methods work. If you sprinkle on the outside, refrigerate the patties for 30 minutes or less to let the seasoning mingle and distribute its flavor throughout the meat . . . but no longer. Salt can draw moisture out of the meat, just as it does with cured bacon or sausages. But burgers are not meant to have the firm, bouncy texture of good sausages. To keep the salt from pulling out moisture, grill those patties within 30 minutes of shaping.

Q: How big should I make my burgers?

A: If you start with a handful of meat about the size of a tennis ball, you will have roughly 6 ounces. That's a fairly generous amount for a patty that will fit the standard 4-inch-wide hamburger bun. If the buns are wider, you will need more ground beef to avoid the dreaded all-bun-no-burger bite. Patties always shrink as they cook, so start with burgers that are about ½ inch wider than the buns. That means the ideal patty for the average bun, after "dimpling" (see below), is about 4 inches wide and ¾ inch thick. If in a hurry, you can flatten the patties to less than ¾ inch and they'll cook a little faster.

Q: Any tips for shaping the patties?

A: Don't overwork them. Super-squashed, packed-down patties lack the miniscule air bubbles necessary for creating good burger texture and collecting the sublime melting fat and juices. Without the bubbles, all that goodness runs right out of the burger. Gentle handling is the name of the game here.

Q: What's up with making a "dimple" in each burger?

A: Burgers tend to puff up in the middle as they cook, making the tops rounded and thus not so great for stacking toppings or cooperating with buns. To avoid this bulge, use your thumb or the back of a spoon to make a shallow well, or indentation, about 1 inch wide and ⅓ inch deep in the center of each raw patty. As each patty cooks, this "dimple" will fill in and flatten out, giving you a level surface.

Q: How often should I flip the burgers?

A: Flipping often is expected with gymnasts but is to be avoided with burgers. We endorse turning the patties only once or twice during grilling. There should be an audible hiss as the burgers hit your sizzling-hot grate. When you hear that noise, close the lid and do nothing. Really, nothing. Resist all urges to open the lid and fiddle with the burgers. Premature fiddling leads to common but avoidable problems like meat sticking to the grate and patties falling apart. Let a crust form on the underside because this is what will release the burger from the grate. Oh, and it tastes good, too.

GRILL SCIENCE

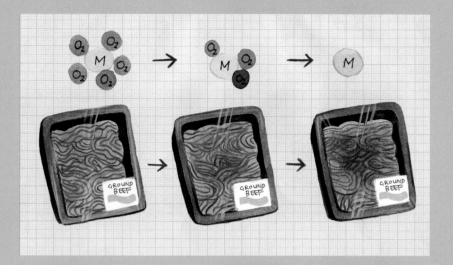

Sometimes the meat looks a little brownish in the package? Is it okay to buy that?

You're right to be cautious. Brown meat might be fine, but "might" doesn't inspire much confidence, does it? The only surefire way to know if the brown is gonna get you down is if you can smell the meat, which isn't really an option with prewrapped supermarket meat. Save yourself a lot of heartache (and possibly other ache) and buy only reddish meat, which is always superior. Here's why. Beef gets its red color from an iron-containing protein called myoglobin. Myoglobin stores oxygen in the muscle tissue, which the muscle needs when it does its job: move. Beef coming fresh out of a meat grinder is purplish red and chock-full of myoglobin. Wrapping the ground meat in plastic deprives it of oxygen, which in the course of a couple of days will turn the surface at first redder and then to an unfortunate brownish color. It can look bad, and sometimes smells worse. Typically, ground beef doesn't go bad as soon as it goes brown. It is usually fine for a couple of more days in your fridge. Always buy bright red meat at the store, and if it turns brown at home, give it the sniff test before using it.

Classic American Cheeseburger

1½ pounds ground chuck (80% lean)

1 teaspoon kosher salt

½ teaspoon ground black pepper

4 thin slices mild cheddar cheese

4 sesame hamburger buns, split

Mayonnaise, ketchup, and/or mustard

4 to 8 slices ripe tomato, each about ¼ inch thick

12 dill pickle chips

4 leaves iceberg lettuce, torn to fit buns

A good burger will restore your faith in, well, everything. Meaty, rich, and charred with a flavor-packed crust, these burgers will reward you for your attention to the details, such as not turning the patties more than once or twice and not squashing them with a spatula on the grill!

1. Prepare the grill for direct cooking over medium-high heat (400° to 450°F). In a bowl, using your hands, gently mix together the ground chuck, salt, and pepper.

2. Divide the meat into four equal portions in the bowl.

6. Turn the patties only when enough crust has developed on the surface of the meat to ensure they will release easily—without sticking—from the grates.

7. During the final minute of grilling time, place a cheese slice on each patty to melt.

3. Gently form four patties of equal size, each about ¾ inch thick.

4. Using your thumb or the back of a spoon, make a shallow indentation about 1 inch wide in the center of each patty. This will prevent the patties from forming a dome as they cook.

5. Brush the cooking grates clean. Grill the patties over **direct medium-high heat**, with the lid closed, until cooked to medium (160°F), 8 to 10 minutes, turning once or twice.

8. As soon as you've added the cheese, toast the buns, cut side down, over direct heat.

9. To build each burger, spread the bottom half of the bun with mayonnaise, top with a patty, and then layer with 1 or 2 tomato slices, 3 pickle chips, and lettuce. Spread the top half of the bun with ketchup and/or mustard and close the burger. Serve at once.

GREEK

Omit the cheddar and use toasted ciabatta buns. Spread the bottom half of each toasted bun with 1 tablespoon mayonnaise and top each with 6 to 8 baby spinach leaves. Add a patty, followed by 1 to 2 tablespoons store-bought olive tapenade and 1 to 2 tablespoons crumbled feta cheese.

MUSHROOM

Swap out the cheddar for Swiss cheese. Sauté 3 cups thinly sliced mushrooms and ½ cup finely chopped yellow onion in some olive oil with 1 teaspoon each Worcestershire sauce and dried thyme. Spread both halves of each toasted bun with Dijon mustard. Top each bottom bun with a Swiss-topped patty, followed by mushrooms and onions.

BARBECUE

Spread both halves of each toasted bun with your favorite homemade (page 336) or store-bought barbecue sauce. Top the bottom half of each bun with the cheddar-topped patty, followed by grilled onion slices (see Steps 1 to 5, page 71), crisp-cooked bacon, and dill pickle slices. Add more sauce as you like.

RED CHILI

Omit the cheddar slices. Warm 1 cup red chili and 1 cup sauerkraut separately. Spread the bottom half of each toasted bun with ¼ cup of the sauerkraut. Add the patty and spoon ¼ cup of the red chili over it. Top with grated cheddar cheese and spread the top half of each bun with yellow mustard.

FLAVOR BOMB
your
BURGER

These combos are an easy way to wow the crowd. Make the toppings from scratch or use your favorite purchased version. Start with the Classic American Cheeseburger recipe on page 96 and let your imagination run wild.

BREAKFAST
Spread both halves of each toasted bun with ketchup. Top the bottom half of each bun with the cheddar-topped patty, followed by thick grilled tomato slices, crisp-cooked bacon, and a fried egg.

MEXICAN
Swap out the cheddar slices for pepper jack cheese. Top each patty with 1 to 2 tablespoons guacamole, 1 tablespoon pico de gallo (page 340), 1 to 3 slices pickled jalapeño pepper, and some chopped fresh cilantro.

HAWAIIAN
Swap out the cheddar for provolone cheese. Spread each toasted bun half with mayonnaise. Top the bottom half of each bun with the provolone-topped patty, drizzle with store-bought teriyaki sauce, and then finish with a thin ham slice and a thin grilled pineapple slice (see Step 4, page 244).

Griddle-Smashed Burgers with Special Sauce

SPECIAL SAUCE

⅓ cup mayonnaise

3 tablespoons tomato ketchup

2 tablespoons minced dill pickle

1 tablespoon spicy yellow mustard

¼ teaspoon hot sauce

SEASONING SALT

1 teaspoon kosher salt

½ teaspoon sugar

¼ teaspoon ground black pepper

¼ teaspoon onion powder

1½ pounds ground round (85% lean)

Vegetable oil

4 sesame hamburger buns, split

4 slices Vidalia or other sweet onion, each ⅛ inch thick

4 slices ripe tomato, each about ¼ inch thick

4 large leaves iceberg or romaine lettuce, torn to fit buns

A tiny bit of sugar in this homemade seasoning salt goes a long way toward browning the top and bottom of the burgers. This recipe is an exception to the rule never to smash the patties with a spatula. Here, the griddle captures the juices and uses them to flavor the meat.

SERVES **4**

PREP: **20 MIN**

GRILL: **6–8 MIN**

SPECIAL EQUIPMENT:
**LARGE CAST-IRON
GRIDDLE**

1. In a medium bowl stir together all the sauce ingredients. In a small bowl stir together all the seasoning-salt ingredients. Prepare the grill for direct cooking over medium-high heat (400° to 450°F).

2. Brush the cooking grates clean. Place a cast-iron griddle over direct heat, close the lid, and preheat until very hot, 5 to 10 minutes. Shape the ground round into four balls of equal size.

3. Using your hands, press each patty firmly and evenly to flatten it into a 4-inch round about ½ inch thick. Season both sides evenly with the seasoning salt.

4. Lightly brush the hot griddle with vegetable oil. Place the patties on the griddle, spacing them well apart so you can turn them easily later. Using a spatula, smash each patty to flatten it to about ⅓ inch thick. This will help create a deliciously browned crust. Cook over **direct medium-high heat**, with the lid closed, for 3 to 4 minutes.

5. Using a clean spatula, scrape the patties from the griddle, keeping the browned crust on the underside as intact as possible, and flip them over. Cook, with the lid closed, until the second side is browned and the patties are cooked to medium (160°F), 3 to 4 minutes.

6. During the final minute of grilling time, toast the buns, cut side down, on the area around the griddle. To build the burgers, spread the bottom half of each bun with the sauce, top with a patty, then layer with an onion slice, a tomato slice, and lettuce. Spread the top half of the bun with more sauce and close the burger. Serve at once.

Monday Night Flank Steak

SPICE PASTE

3 tablespoons extra-virgin olive oil

1 teaspoon sweet paprika

1 teaspoon kosher salt

½ teaspoon dried oregano

½ teaspoon ground coriander

½ teaspoon granulated garlic

¼ teaspoon ground black pepper

1 flank steak, 1¾ to 2 pounds and about ¾ inch thick, trimmed of excess fat

HORSERADISH SAUCE

1 cup sour cream

2 tablespoons well-drained prepared horseradish

1 tablespoon Dijon mustard

2 teaspoons Worcestershire sauce

½ teaspoon kosher salt

¼ teaspoon ground black pepper

Flank steak is a weeknight warrior. It's versatile, it's quick to grill, and it's relatively inexpensive. To ensure the flavorful meat retains all its beefy juices, let it rest for a full 10 minutes before slicing it across the grain. The horseradish sauce is not only easy but also great with any cut of beef.

SERVES **4–6**

 PREP: **15 MIN**

 GRILL: **8–10 MIN**

 REST: **10 MIN**

1. In a small bowl mix together all the spice-paste ingredients. Brush the paste evenly over both sides of the flank steak. Let stand at room temperature while you preheat the grill and prepare the sauce.

2. Prepare the grill for direct cooking over medium-high heat (400° to 450°F). In a medium bowl whisk together all the sauce ingredients.

3. Grill the flank steak over **direct medium-high heat**, with the lid closed, until cooked to your desired doneness, 8 to 10 minutes for medium rare, turning just once for a deep sear.

4. Transfer the steak to a cutting board and let rest for 10 minutes.

5. Cut the steak across the grain into ¼-inch-thick slices. Taste the meat and season with more salt and pepper if needed. Serve warm with the sauce.

VARIATION

FLANK STEAK WITH CHERRY TOMATOES AND ARUGULA

Omit the sauce. Grill the steak with the paste. In a bowl combine 3 cups (3 ounces) firmly packed baby arugula and 2 cups (10 ounces) cherry tomatoes, cut in half. Just before serving, drizzle 1 tablespoon extra-virgin olive oil and 1 teaspoon balsamic vinegar over the arugula and tomatoes and mix well. Season to taste with salt and pepper. Serve with the sliced steak.

Spiced Skirt Steak Fajitas

SPICE RUB

1½ teaspoons kosher salt

1½ teaspoons prepared chili powder

1 teaspoon granulated garlic

½ teaspoon ground coriander

½ teaspoon ground cumin

2 pounds skirt steak, about ½ inch thick, trimmed of excess fat and cut crosswise into pieces about 8 inches long and of uniform thickness

Olive oil

VEGETABLES

1 medium red bell pepper, seeded and cut lengthwise into ½-inch-wide strips

1 medium yellow bell pepper, seeded and cut lengthwise into ½-inch-wide strips

1 medium orange bell pepper, seeded and cut lengthwise into ½-inch-wide strips

1 medium white onion, halved lengthwise and cut into ⅓-inch-thick half-moons

2 tablespoons extra-virgin olive oil

1 teaspoon dried oregano

½ teaspoon kosher salt

FOR SERVING

12 (7-inch) flour tortillas

1 cup shredded Monterey Jack cheese

Guacamole (page 340)

Pico de Gallo (page 340)

1 cup sour cream

Lime wedges

For nicely browned peppers and onions, preheat a grill pan for 5 to 10 minutes before you add the vegetables. If your grill is big enough, grill the vegetables and skirt steak at the same time. Most of the optional garnishes (see page 107) require no cooking at all.

1. In a bowl stir together all the spice rub ingredients. Lightly coat the steak on both sides with oil. Season the steak evenly on both sides with the spice rub. Cover and refrigerate until ready to grill.

2. Prepare the grill for direct cooking over medium-high heat (about 450°F). Remove the steak from the refrigerator. In a large bowl toss the peppers and onion with the oil, oregano, and salt to coat well.

3. Brush the cooking grates clean. Place a large perforated grill pan over direct heat, close the lid, and preheat for 5 to 10 minutes. Spread the vegetables on the preheated grill pan.

4. Cook the vegetables over **direct medium-high heat**, with the lid closed, until tender and lightly browned but still a bit crisp, 12 to 15 minutes, stirring a few times. Remove the grill pan of vegetables and set aside while you grill the steak.

5. Grill the steak over **direct medium-high heat**, with the lid closed, until cooked to your desired doneness, 6 to 8 minutes for medium rare, turning once or twice.

6. When the steak is done, transfer to a cutting board (preferably with a well, to collect the juices) to rest for a few minutes. >

Skirt Steak Fajitas

7. While the meat is resting, brush the cooking grates clean again, then heat the tortillas on the grates over **direct medium-high heat** for 10 to 20 seconds on each side just to warm them (don't let them get crisp). As soon as a batch comes off the grill, wrap them in a kitchen towel to keep them warm while you heat the remaining tortillas.

8. Return the vegetables in the grill pan to the grill and warm them over **direct medium-high heat** for a few minutes, stirring occasionally.

9. Cut the steak into thin strips across the grain (cutting across the grain yields more tender meat that isn't chewy).

10. Arrange the sliced steak on a platter with the vegetables and drizzle the steak with the juices from the cutting board. Serve right away. Invite your guests to fill the warm tortillas with some steak and vegetables and with cheese, guacamole, pico de gallo, sour cream, and a squeeze of lime as they like.

Let's Have a Fajita Party

SLICED PICKLED
JALAPEÑOS

HOT SAUCE

LIMES

PICO DE
GALLO

GUACAMOLE

SOUR
CREAM

TOMATILLA
SALSA

SHREDDED
MONTEREY
JACK CHEESE

FRESH
CILANTRO

BBQ GENIUS

Charred Rib-Eye Steaks with Mushrooms
RECIPE ON PAGE 112

RIB-EYE STEAKS

Whether the choice is bone-in or boneless, we think rib-eye steaks occupy hallowed ground in the grilling world, so we often grill them simply and leave them alone in their majesty. Or if we are inclined to embellish them, we drape them in something equally special, like a heady mix of mushrooms and crispy pancetta. For more of our favorite top-shelf steak toppings, see pages 114 and 115.

Q & A

everything rib-eye steaks

Q: What's the easiest way to grill a great rib eye?

A: These days, chefs and cookbooks are full of complicated ways to finesse steaks to greatness. From using *sous vide* machines to multiple flipping techniques, we've seen and tried them all. But grilling steaks does not need to be complicated: Preheat the grill on high, lightly oil the rib eyes, and season them with salt and pepper. Grill them for 3 to 4 minutes per side, depending on their thickness and your preferred doneness, and then eat them. Wasn't that easy?

Q: What else should I know?

A: Okay, let's back up for a moment and talk shopping strategy. Your final results will depend to a huge degree on what you buy. When considering your options, look first at the marbling, those visible lines of milky-white fat running throughout the meat. Much of that fat will melt on the grill and saturate your steaks with juices. Fat not only has its own glorious flavors but also acts like a little pack mule for other flavors. That said, too much marbling—either around the outer edges of a steak or in large clumps within a steak—can be trouble. Melting fat dripping into the fire can cause unwanted flare-ups, a sooty taste, and gristly bits. You can trim the perimeter fat to a thickness of about ¼ inch, but the larger clumps within the steaks are more challenging. You are better off passing up super-fatty steaks.

Q: How should I season them?

A: Salt and pepper are really all you need, but not just any salt and pepper. When your approach involves only steak, fire, and seasonings, the seasonings must be top-notch. Table salt falls pathetically short of kosher salt or sea salt in terms of function and taste: table salt is too fine and hard to distribute evenly, and often carries a metallic taste because of the presence of iodine. Pure flakes of salt don't completely dissolve into the meat, offering a bit of salty crunch when mixed with steak juices. We believe pepper is essential, too, preferably freshly ground. You will be in good shape if the pepper was ground within the last few days.

Q: How cold should the steaks be when they hit the grill?

A: We're all pressed for time, so we understand how sometimes steaks go directly from the fridge to the grill. But if you happen to think ahead, you will be rewarded.

Salting steaks and letting them sit at room temperature for 20 to 30 minutes will give the salt some time to work its way into the meat. Also, the steaks will lose some of their chill during that time, which means they will cook a bit faster and probably end up juicier as a result.

Q: Why do steak-house steaks turn out so great?

A: Quality matters. Steak houses typically buy prime steaks, which represent a big step above the choice steaks most supermarkets sell. Prime steaks have a lot more intramuscular marbling. Steak houses also tend to have the infrastructure and wherewithal to dry-age their meat, something most of us grillers aren't equipped to do. A great steak house will let steaks sit in humidity-controlled aging rooms for three to four weeks, which makes a big difference in taste.

Q: Will searing the steaks seal in the juices?

A: Sorry, searing does not do that. There is an old myth still circulating that a good sear will create an impenetrable crust that prevents moisture from escaping. Not true. Instead, searing produces a quick rate of moisture loss, but that's okay. The flavors in the crust are worth some moisture loss. The key here is to start with steaks that can afford some moisture loss and to get them off the grill before they are overdone.

Q: What happens if I cut into grilled steaks too soon?

A: We know. Sometimes you want to cut into hot steaks right away to see how they look, but we still can't advocate for this practice. A cooking steak is a hotbed of activity: proteins uncoiling and moving moisture around; melting fat lubricating the proteins; seasonings, sugars, and smoke causing various surface reactions.

Even after pulling meat off the grill, the party rages on. Cutting into the steak at this point effectively shuts off the action—like flicking on the house lights at last call—and releases those precious juices onto the cutting board. Instead, let the steak rest to allow the juices time to settle down and redistribute throughout the meat.

Q: So how will I know when my steaks are done?

A: The surest way to know is with an instant-read thermometer. As long as the sensor is right in the middle of the steak (not touching bone), you will get an accurate reading. See page 25 for internal temperatures that correspond to each level of doneness. If you don't have a thermometer, you can press the surface of the steak with a fingertip. The meat will get firmer as it cooks. When it has the same firmness as the base of your thumb, your steak has reached your preferred doneness.

GRILL SCIENCE

What's this about salting steaks minutes or even hours before grilling? What does this do? And how long is too long?

Indulge us in this bromide about chloride. That tiny ion, one-half of a salt molecule, acts as a powerful cellular spelunker, carving out paths and clearing the way for the movement of moisture. This is why salt is added to sports drinks: it keeps nutrients, minerals, and water flowing freely throughout our bodies, especially when we sweat.

A liberal sprinkling of salt on the surface of meat will draw out some moisture, but its greatest gift is what it does on the inside. When meat is heated, the proteins actively unwind, tossing water molecules out in the process. Chloride clears the room, so to speak, making more space for water molecules so they don't all get chucked out. More moisture retained in the meat means a more tender end product.

Oh, did we mention the flavor? As the chloride ion travels inward, it brings all of the taste-boosting properties of salt with it. When to salt the meat depends on the cut: a thick roast can stand for a full 24 hours, while a standard rib eye does well with 10 to 30 minutes.

Charred Rib-Eye Steaks with Mushrooms

4 boneless rib-eye steaks, each about 12 ounces and 1¼ inches thick

4 teaspoons extra-virgin olive oil

1½ teaspoons kosher salt

1 teaspoon ground black pepper

MUSHROOMS

2 tablespoons extra-virgin olive oil

4 ounces pancetta, cut into ¼-inch dice (about ⅔ cup)

12 ounces large cremini mushrooms, cleaned, stem ends trimmed, and sliced ⅓ inch thick

1 tablespoon capers, rinsed and drained

1 to 2 large garlic cloves, minced or pushed through a press

1 teaspoon chopped fresh thyme leaves, or ½ teaspoon dried thyme

Kosher salt and ground black pepper

2 tablespoons chopped fresh Italian parsley

Rib eyes top our steak short list for their distinctive combination of flavor and tenderness. This recipe ups the ante with a topping of seared pancetta and mushrooms, both cooked hot and fast to achieve rich browning. If you want to skip the mushrooms, see pages 114 and 115 for other great toppings.

1. To help prevent flare-ups, trim the fat along the edge of each steak to no more than ¼ inch. Rub both sides of each steak with the oil, then season evenly with the salt and pepper. Let the steaks stand at room temperature for 15 to 20 minutes to warm slightly. This step helps them cook more evenly.

2. Meanwhile, prepare the grill for direct cooking over high heat (450° to 550°F). Brush the cooking grates clean. Place a large cast-iron griddle or skillet over direct heat on half the grill, close the lid, and preheat for 10 to 15 minutes.

5. Add the oil and pancetta to the griddle and cook until the pancetta is lightly browned, 1 to 2 minutes, stirring occasionally. Add the mushrooms, spreading them out in an even layer, and cook, with the lid closed as much as possible, until seared golden brown and tender, 6 to 8 minutes, stirring occasionally.

6. Add the capers, garlic, and thyme and stir until the garlic is fragrant, 30 to 60 seconds. Remove from the heat. Season to taste with salt and pepper if needed. Divide the steaks among four serving plates and top with the mushroom mixture. Drizzle with any accumulated juices from the platter. Garnish with the parsley and serve.

SERVES **4**

PREP: **15 MIN**

GRILL: **15–20 MIN**

SPECIAL EQUIPMENT:
**12-INCH CAST-IRON
SKILLET OR GRIDDLE**

3. Grill the steaks on the grates over **direct high heat**, with the lid closed, until they have nice grill marks and are cooked medium rare (125°F), 6 to 8 minutes, turning once or twice. Transfer the steaks to a platter and let rest while you prepare the mushrooms.

4. While grilling the steaks, if a flare-up occurs that lasts longer than a few seconds, slide the steaks to a cool section of the grill and wait for the fire to burn down before moving them back.

VARIATION

BONE-IN STEAKS

Steaks with or without the bones? Steak fanatics will gnash their teeth on this issue for days. Really, both boneless and bone-in rib eyes are great, though we like the bones for various reasons. First of all, they look awesome, and it's gratifying to gnaw on them as the main course winds down. Second, in most grilling scenarios, the meat near the bone will be a little less cooked than the rest of the steak because the bone is an insulator from the heat. This works out nicely, we think. It's a welcome bit of variety. If you too decide to grill bone-in steaks, keep in mind the insulating effect; it often means your steaks will take just a little longer (about a minute) than the boneless versions.

FLAVOR BOMB *your* RIB-EYE STEAK

A rib eye is a pretty swanky cut of meat all by itself. We think any accompaniments should be of an equally high level. For example, they should be profoundly rich, super crispy, wonderfully earthy, or loaded with umami flavors. Take your pick.

BLUE CHEESE CRUMBLES WITH TARRAGON

In a small bowl mix together ½ cup crumbled blue cheese (2½ ounces), 2 teaspoons chopped fresh tarragon, and ½ teaspoon finely grated lemon zest. Let stand for at least 30 minutes (or refrigerate for up to 2 days) before serving. Spoon on top of warm steaks.

CRISPY FRIED SHALLOTS

Heat 3 cups canola oil in a large saucepan over medium heat until it begins to shimmer (350°F on a deep-frying thermometer). Carefully stir in 2 cups thinly sliced shallots and cook until golden and crisp, 10 to 15 minutes, stirring occasionally. Use a slotted spoon to transfer the shallots to a paper towel–lined baking sheet to drain. Season with kosher salt. Scatter on top of warm steaks.

CORN AND BLACK BEAN SALSA

Shuck and remove the silk from 3 ears corn, rub with olive oil, and grill over direct medium heat (350° to 450°F), with the lid closed, until browned in spots and tender, 10 to 15 minutes. Remove from the grill and let cool for a few minutes. Cut the kernels from the cobs and mix in a bowl with 1 cup drained and rinsed canned black beans, ¼ cup roughly chopped fresh cilantro, 1 tablespoon minced jalapeño chile pepper, 1 tablespoon fresh lime juice, 1 tablespoon extra-virgin olive oil, ¼ teaspoon ground cumin, and ¼ teaspoon kosher salt. Spoon over warm steaks.

HOISIN-GINGER STEAK SAUCE

In a small saucepan heat 2 teaspoons toasted sesame oil over medium heat. Add 4 teaspoons minced, peeled fresh ginger and cook for 45 seconds, stirring. Add ⅔ cup hoisin sauce, 2 tablespoons reduced-sodium soy sauce, 5 teaspoons seasoned rice vinegar, and ⅓ cup water. Bring to a boil, then reduce to a simmer and cook until slightly thickened, about 3 minutes. Remove from the heat and stir in 2 tablespoons thinly sliced scallions, white and light green parts only. Spoon over warm steaks.

Reverse-Seared Rib-Eye Steaks

4 rib-eye steaks, each about 1 pound and 1½ inches thick

1½ tablespoons extra-virgin olive oil, plus more for drizzling (optional)

2 teaspoons kosher salt

1½ teaspoons ground black pepper

Steak tastes best when it has a crust of charred flavors on the outside and a wide swath of juicy, evenly cooked meat inside. How do you get that combo? Roast the steaks over indirect low heat for about 20 minutes and then finish with about 2 minutes of charring on each side.

1. Prepare the grill for indirect cooking over low heat (about 300°F). To help prevent flare-ups, trim the fat along the edge of each steak to no more than ¼ inch. Rub the oil into both sides of the steaks and then season evenly with the salt and pepper. Set aside at room temperature while the grill heats.

2. Brush the cooking grates clean. Grill the steaks over **indirect low heat**, with the lid closed, until an instant-read thermometer inserted into the center of a steak registers 100°F, about 20 minutes. Transfer the steaks to a platter.

3. Raise the heat of the grill for direct cooking over high heat (450° to 550°F). Return the steaks to the grill and cook over **direct high heat**, with the lid closed, until the thermometer inserted into the center of a steak registers 125° to 130°F for medium rare, 4 to 5 minutes, turning once.

4. Remove the steaks from the grill and let rest for about 5 minutes; during that time, the internal temperature will rise 5 to 10 degrees. Serve whole or cut across the grain into ½-inch-thick slices. Drizzle any accumulated juices over the top, then, if desired, drizzle with a little oil.

MUSCLE MATTERS

Many people think of a rib eye as single piece of marvelous meat. True, it is marvelous, but there are actually two muscles held together in each steak. We refer to them casually as the "eye" and the "cap." The eye is the center section that is well-known and appreciated for its flavor and tenderness. The cap is the C-shaped outer section and has an even more luxurious level of buttery tenderness and beefier flavor gloriously saturated with fat.

Strip Steaks with Gorgonzola Butter
RECIPE ON PAGE 120

STRIP STEAKS

This especially handsome cut comes from a muscle that doesn't do much. The *longissimus dorsi* muscle is therefore pretty soft, which means you can grill strip steaks over high heat and still enjoy a tender result. Strip steaks are not quite as tender as rib eyes or beef tenderloin steaks, however. They are typically more finely grained, usually without a lot of fat or connective tissue. Here are some tips for success.

Top Tips for the Ultimate Strip Steaks

1. Purchase steaks that bend easily. You can judge how tender your strips steaks will be on the plate by how soft they are when raw. If you pick up a steak by one end, it should bend and dangle almost as much as a boneless chicken breast.

2. Consider the crosshatch. Diamond-shaped grill marks look especially good on strip steaks. Here is how to achieve them: Imagine the steaks on clock faces lying flat on your grill grate. Then imagine each steak has a clock hand at ten o'clock. Sear each steak in that position for at least a couple of minutes, just long enough to create grill marks in one direction.

Then rotate each steak so the clock hand points to two o'clock. Sear each steak in that position for a couple of minutes. Now, flip the steaks over and admire your handiwork. You can do the same thing on the second side, but because the marks are only for show, one side is enough.

3. Swap positions. Here's one way to help make sure your steaks will cook evenly: Swap their positions on the grill grate when you turn them. For example, move the steaks in the center to the outside and the steaks on the outside to the center. This way, they each get a turn in the middle.

4. Give them a rest. Strip steaks are leaner and firmer than some other steaks from the short loin (middle section) of a cow, so it is especially important to let them rest fully after grilling to allow the juices to redistribute throughout the meat. We think they should be served warm, too, so resting for no more than 3 to 5 minutes at room temperature should deliver both results.

5. Slice with intention. The tenderness of a steak depends in part on how thinly it is sliced. Thinner slices are easier to chew and enjoy. Also, if you want to exaggerate that effect, slice the steak on the diagonal to give each slice a wider section of rosy red meat.

6. Brown the fat. Every strip steak features a luscious band of fat along one side. Set over direct heat, it has the potential to turn golden, crispy, and irresistible. During the last few minutes of grilling, using tongs, hold each steak upright so the fatty side is in direct contact with the hot grate, giving the fat a chance to render. But be vigilant to ensure you don't render so much fat that it causes excessive flames.

Strip Steaks with Gorgonzola Butter

GORGONZOLA BUTTER

1 medium garlic head

1 teaspoon extra-virgin olive oil

6 tablespoons (¾ stick) unsalted butter, softened

¼ cup (about 1½ ounces) crumbled Gorgonzola cheese (not dolce)

2 tablespoons finely chopped fresh Italian parsley leaves

¼ teaspoon kosher salt

4 strip steaks, each 10 to 12 ounces and 1 to 1¼ inches thick, trimmed of excess fat

2 tablespoons extra-virgin olive oil

1¼ teaspoons kosher salt

1 teaspoon ground black pepper

Steak likes butter almost as much as cake likes ice cream. Here, we mix roasted garlic and Gorgonzola into softened butter, chill it, and then melt a dollop on each hot steak. Easy to make, flavored butters will keep refrigerated for 3 days or frozen for up to 1 month.

1. Preheat the grill for indirect cooking over medium heat (350° to 450°F). Cut about ½ inch off the top of the garlic head to expose the cloves. Stand the garlic, cut side up, on a piece of aluminum foil and drizzle the oil on top.

2. Wrap the foil around the garlic and seal tightly. Roast the garlic over **indirect medium heat**, with the lid closed, until soft, 40 to 60 minutes.

6. Thirty minutes before grilling, lightly coat the steaks with the oil, then season with the salt and pepper. Let stand at room temperature to warm slightly. Take the compound butter out of the refrigerator if it's been chilling for longer than 1 hour.

7. Raise the heat of the grill for direct cooking over high heat (450° to 550°F). Brush the cooking grates clean. Grill the steaks over **direct high heat**, with the lid closed, until cooked to your desired doneness, 7 to 9 minutes for medium rare (125° to 130°F), turning once or twice. Remove from the grill and let rest for about 5 minutes.

SERVES **4**	PREP: **20 MIN**	CHILL: **ABOUT 1 HOUR (BUTTER)**	GRILL: **ABOUT 1 HOUR**	REST: **5 MIN**

3. Remove the garlic from the grill and let cool to the touch, then squeeze the garlic pulp out of the skin into a small bowl; discard the skin. You should have about 1½ tablespoons roasted garlic.

4. Add all of the remaining butter ingredients to the bowl and mash together with a fork to mix well.

5. Scrape the gorgonzola butter out of the bowl onto a sheet of waxed paper and shape into a rough log. Roll the butter in the paper and shape by hand into a smooth log about 5 inches long. Chill until firm, at least 1 hour.

8. Cut the butter log crosswise into eight equal slices. Top each steak with two slices of the butter and serve right away.

COOKING EVENLY

When grilling over charcoal, the heat varies from one area of the cooking grate to another, even when it appears that you have an even bed of charcoal under the food. For example, the steaks that cook near the edge of the bed don't get as much heat as the steaks right over the center. To make sure your steaks cook evenly, swap their positions after turning them, moving the steaks in the center to the outside, and the outside steaks toward the center.

Spicy Thai Strip Steaks a la Plancha

4 strip steaks, each about 10 ounces and 1 to 1¼ inches thick, trimmed

2 tablespoons soy sauce

2 tablespoons Shoaxing wine (Chinese rice wine) or mirin

2 tablespoons vegetable oil

2 garlic cloves, grated

1 tablespoon finely grated fresh ginger (about 1½-inch piece)

THAI DRESSING

¼ cup fish sauce

2 tablespoons toasted sesame oil

3 tablespoons packed dark brown sugar

3 tablespoons fresh lime juice

3 tablespoons thinly sliced shallot

2 tablespoons finely chopped fresh cilantro leaves

2 tablespoons finely chopped fresh mint leaves

1 teaspoon crushed red pepper flakes or to taste

1 tablespoon toasted sesame oil

6 cups mesclun salad greens

⅓ cup thinly sliced English cucumber

⅓ cup shredded carrot

⅓ cup bean sprouts

1 lime, cut into wedges

It's the steak of many names—New York strip, Kansas City strip, top sirloin, top loin—and many virtues. Here, its singular flavor comes alive quickly on a hot metal plate (aka griddle or *plancha*). We marinate these steaks at room temperature for just 1 hour—but no longer for food safety.

SERVES 4–6

 PREP: 15–20 MIN

 MARINATE: 1 HOUR

 GRILL: 5–7 MIN

 REST: 5 MIN

SPECIAL EQUIPMENT: LARGE CAST-IRON GRIDDLE

1. Place the steaks in a single layer in a 13-by-9-inch baking dish. In a small bowl whisk together the soy sauce, wine, oil, garlic, and ginger. Pour over the steaks, then turn the steaks to coat with the marinade. Cover and let stand at room temperature for 1 hour.

2. In a small bowl combine all the ingredients for the dressing, using up to 2 teaspoons red pepper flakes if you prefer a spicier dressing. Whisk until the sugar dissolves. Set aside to allow the flavors to develop.

3. Prepare the grill for direct cooking over high heat (450° to 550°F). Brush the cooking grates clean. Place a large cast-iron griddle over direct heat, close the lid, and preheat for 10 to 15 minutes. When the griddle is smoking hot, place the steaks on the griddle.

4. Grill the steaks over **direct high heat**, with the lid closed, until the meat is deep brown and cooked to your desired doneness, 5 to 7 minutes for medium rare (125° to 130°F), turning once. Transfer the steaks to a cutting board and let rest for 5 minutes.

5. Thinly slice the meat across the grain. Arrange the meat on a platter and spoon all but 1 tablespoon of the dressing over the top.

6. In a medium bowl whisk together the reserved 1 tablespoon dressing and the sesame oil. Add the greens, cucumber, carrot, and bean sprouts and toss to coat. Serve the salad alongside the steak and pass the lime wedges at the table.

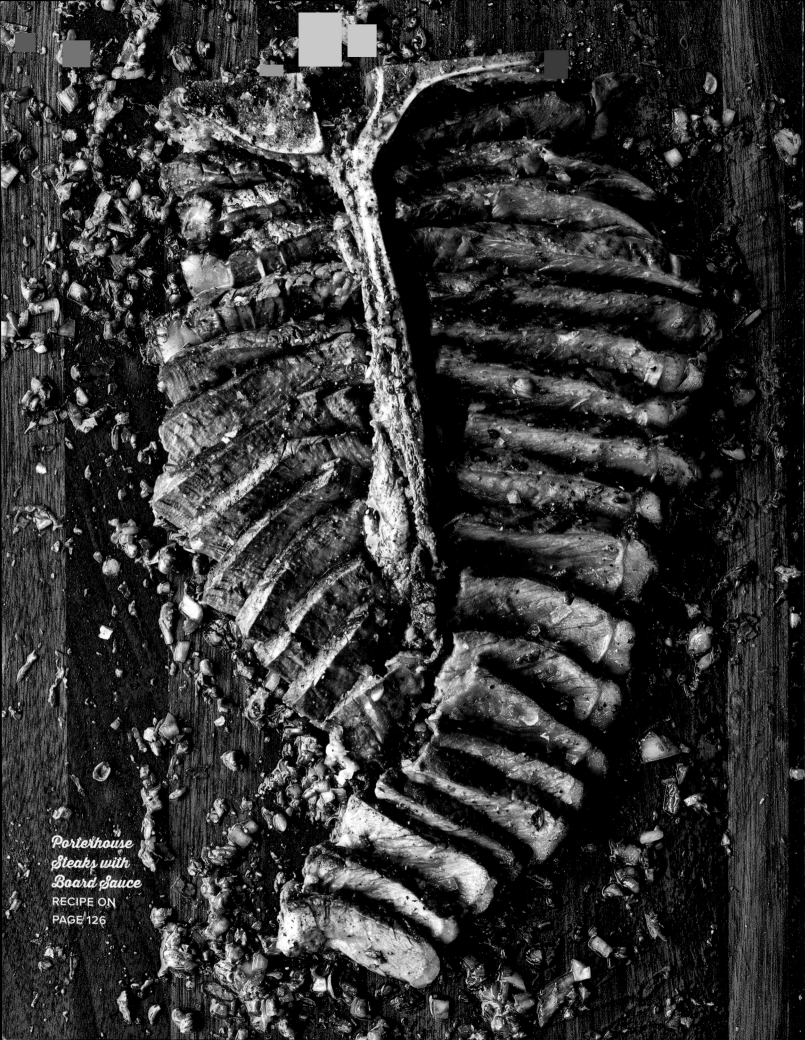

Porterhouse Steaks with Board Sauce
RECIPE ON
PAGE 126

PORTERHOUSE STEAKS

Maybe you have been fortunate enough to find yourself in a live-fire restaurant or in the backyard of someone who has learned the art of grilling big, marbled porterhouse steaks over flickering flames. If you haven't already mastered what you saw and envied, here are some tips to point you on your way.

Top Tips for the Ultimate Porterhouse

1. Look for large tenderloins. The first feature to seek out is the width. What defines a porterhouse steak, which is essentially a filet mignon and a strip steak separated by a bone, is the width of the tenderloin section. If the filet mignon is less than 1½ inches wide, you are looking at a T-bone steak.

2. Find thick, marbled steaks. Porterhouse steaks are meant to be meaty and juicy. If they are cut too thinly or are too lean, they will overcook quickly and turn out dry. For memorable results, look for steaks at least 1 inch thick and generously marbled with milky-white fat.

3. Avoid fatty flare-ups. As much as we love fat, wide streaks of it, particularly around the edges of a steak, can melt and cause unwanted

flare-ups. Choose your steaks well and trim any perimeter fat to about ¼ inch thick.

4. Take the chill off. Super-cold steaks cook more slowly than those you pull from the refrigerator 30 to 60 minutes before grilling. The longer they cook, the more they dry out, so let them warm up a bit before they hit the fire.

5. Season twice. Season raw steaks with more salt than you think, preferably pure kosher salt or sea salt to amplify the flavors below the surface. After grilling, lightly season the cut slices all over.

6. Sear the tenderloin less. The tenderloin section cooks faster than the strip section. To even out the overall doneness, position the tenderloin section along the outer edge of direct heat (almost over indirect heat). That way, while you are searing the meat, the tenderloin will absorb a little less heat and cook more slowly.

7. Sear and slide. Searing alone could burn these thick steaks. For impressive grill marks and char without over-cooking the tops and bottoms, sear the steaks over direct high heat for a few minutes on each side and then slide the steaks to indirect heat to finish cooking.

Porterhouse Steaks with Board Sauce

2 well-marbled, top-quality porterhouse steaks, each about 1 pound and 1¼ to 1½ inches thick

2 tablespoons extra-virgin olive oil

2 teaspoons kosher salt

BOARD SAUCE

2 small shallots, about 2½ ounces total, minced (generous ⅓ cup)

2 tablespoons capers, rinsed, drained, and finely chopped

Finely grated zest of 1 lemon

¼ cup finely chopped fresh basil leaves

1 teaspoon minced fresh rosemary leaves

2 tablespoons high-quality extra-virgin olive oil

1 tablespoon balsamic vinegar, preferably 10 years old

1 teaspoon ground black pepper, divided

Imagine how easy dinner could be if you mixed—right on a cutting board—a handful of raw ingredients that play well together, and then dragged your steaks through that spontaneous "sauce." Feel free to substitute your favorite fresh herbs and types of oil and vinegar.

1. Place the steaks in a single layer on a baking sheet and pat dry with a paper towel. Rub the oil into both sides of the steaks and then season them evenly with the salt. Let stand while you prepare the board sauce and the grill.

2. Arrange all the board sauce ingredients, including ½ teaspoon of the pepper, in a pile in the center of a large cutting board, putting the oil and vinegar in the center of the pile. Let the pile stand while you preheat the grill and grill the steak, or for up to 1 hour.

6. Spread the board sauce into a layer large enough to accommodate both steaks side by side.

7. Use tongs to transfer the steaks to the cutting board, laying them flat on the sauce. Season the tops with the remaining ½ teaspoon pepper.

SERVES 4–6	PREP: **10–15 MIN**	 GRILL: **10–12 MIN**	REST: **3–5 MIN**

3. Prepare the grill for direct and indirect cooking over medium-high heat (400° to 450°F). Brush the cooking grates clean.

4. Grill the steaks over **direct medium-high heat**, with the lid closed, until cooked to your desired doneness, 10 to 12 minutes for medium rare (125° to 130°F), rotating and turning the steaks once or twice. To cook the steaks longer, slide them to the indirect heat side of the grill.

5. Meanwhile, use a wooden spoon to mix the sauce ingredients together gently on the board into a juicy, chunky mixture.

8. Use the tongs to move the steaks around so they pick up some of the sauce flavorings, then turn the steaks over. Let rest, uncovered, for 3 to 5 minutes.

9. Cut the meat away from the bone.

10. Next, cut the meat across the grain into 1/3-inch-thick slices. As you cut the meat, turn each slice back and forth in the board sauce until it is nicely coated with the flavorings. Season with salt and pepper if needed and serve right away.

T-Bones with Red Wine Cipollini Onions

RED WINE ONIONS

3 tablespoons unsalted butter, divided

1 pound medium cipollini onions (about 15), each 1½ to 1¾ inches in diameter, or 1 pound small sweet onions, halved

1 cup dry red wine, preferably Cabernet Sauvignon

½ cup low-sodium beef broth, plus ¼ cup if needed

⅓ cup balsamic vinegar

3 tablespoons packed light brown sugar

1 tablespoon finely chopped fresh thyme

1 bay leaf

¼ teaspoon kosher salt

¼ teaspoon ground black pepper

2 well-marbled T-bone or porterhouse steaks, each about 1 pound and 1½ inches thick

1 tablespoon extra-virgin olive oil

1½ teaspoons kosher salt

1 teaspoon ground black pepper

1 tablespoon finely chopped fresh thyme (optional)

It's rare when a vegetable threatens to outshine steak, but the onions here share the spotlight. To maximize their flavor, brown them deeply before adding the sauce ingredients and then simmer the liquids until syrupy. You'll wind up with a delectable savory onion jam—and a great steak, too.

SERVES **4–6**

 PREP: **30 MIN**

 GRILL: **ABOUT 45 MIN**

 REST: **3–5 MIN**

SPECIAL EQUIPMENT:
10-INCH CAST-IRON SKILLET OR GRIDDLE

1. Prepare the grill for direct cooking over medium heat (400°F). Brush the cooking grates clean. Preheat the griddle over **direct heat** for 10 minutes. Add 2 tablespoons butter and then the onions to the griddle and cook, with the lid closed, until deep golden brown and slightly caramelized, 8 to 10 minutes, turning occasionally.

2. Add the wine, ½ cup broth, vinegar, brown sugar, thyme, bay leaf, salt, and pepper to the onions and simmer, with the lid closed, until the liquid is reduced by more than half and the onions are tender when pierced with a fork, 15 to 20 minutes. (This step helps concentrate the flavors.)

3. If the onions are not yet tender, continue to cook until soft, about 5 minutes longer, making sure they do not burn. If most of the liquid has evaporated, add the ¼ cup broth to finish cooking the onions. When the onions are tender, remove the griddle from the grill; there should be ⅔ to ¾ cup liquid remaining.

4. Allow the steaks to stand at room temperature for 30 minutes before grilling. Raise the heat of the grill for direct and indirect cooking over high heat (450° to 550°F). Brush the oil into both sides of the steaks and then season evenly with the salt and pepper. Brush the cooking grates clean.

5. Grill the steaks over **direct high heat**, with the lid closed, until well marked on each side, about 8 minutes total, turning once. Move the steaks over **indirect high heat** and continue to cook, with the lid closed, to your desired doneness, 6 to 8 minutes for medium rare (125°F). Remove the steaks and let rest for 3 to 5 minutes.

6. Meanwhile, rewarm the onions until the liquid is syrupy, 1 to 3 minutes. Stir in the remaining 1 tablespoon butter, adjust the seasoning with salt and pepper, and remove from the heat. Remove the bay leaf. Cut the meat off the bone, then thinly slice across the grain. Serve with the onions, garnished with the thyme, if desired.

Coal-Cooked Porterhouse Steaks with Pesto

ARUGULA PESTO

3 tablespoons
pine nuts, toasted

1 garlic clove

2 cups packed baby
arugula leaves

1 cup packed fresh
basil leaves

¼ cup freshly
grated Parmigiano-
Reggiano® cheese

¼ teaspoon kosher salt

⅛ teaspoon ground
black pepper

⅓ to ½ cup extra-virgin
olive oil

2 well-marbled, top-quality
porterhouse steaks, each
1 to 1½ pounds and 1 to
1¼ inches thick

1 teaspoon kosher salt

½ teaspoon ground
black pepper

Maldon sea salt (optional)

Every now and again it's good to go grateless. Cooking steaks directly on burning embers yields flavor-packed, showstopping—and perfectly safe—results. Follow these precautions to prevent rising flames: trim the fat from the steaks, forgo any oil, and keep the grill closed as much as possible.

SERVES **4-6**

PREP:
15 MIN

GRILL:
6-8 MIN

REST:
3-5 MIN

SPECIAL EQUIPMENT:
**CHARCOAL GRILL, CHIMNEY STARTER,
ALL-NATURAL LUMP CHARCOAL,
CHARCOAL RAKE OR LONG TONGS,
LARGE GRILL PAN OR SHEET PAN,
SILICON BASTING BRUSH**

1. In a food processor pulse the pine nuts and garlic until minced. Scrape down the sides of the bowl. Add the arugula, basil, cheese, salt, and pepper and pulse until finely chopped. Scrape down the bowl again. With the motor running, add enough oil to create a smooth, emulsified sauce. Transfer to a serving bowl.

2. Trim off and discard nearly all of the fat around the perimeter of each steak. In a bowl stir together the salt and pepper, then season the steaks evenly on both sides with the mixture. (Unlike other recipes in this book, do not brush the steaks with oil.) Let stand at room temperature for 15 to 30 minutes before grilling.

3. Set the cooking grate or your grill aside; you will not be using it for this recipe. Place a large chimney starter on the charcoal grate and fill the starter to brimming (all the way above the top of the starter) with all-natural lump charcoal. Light the charcoal.

4. Once the coals are lightly covered with gray ash, using a charcoal rake or long tongs, spread the hot coals as evenly as possible on the grate. Break apart larger pieces of charcoal to create an even bed of coals. Use a large grill pan or sheet pan to fan any loose ashes from the coals. The coals should be glowing.

5. Place the steaks, flat side down, directly on the coals. Close the grill, open the top and bottom vents, and cook until the steaks are browned and cooked to your desired doneness, 6 to 8 minutes for medium rare (125°F), turning once and using a basting brush to clean off any coals or ashes that cling to the meat.

6. Remove the steaks from the grill and let rest for 3 to 5 minutes. Just before serving, season lightly with Maldon salt, if desired. Cut the steaks off the bone and thinly slice across the grain. Serve warm with the pesto.

Filet Mignon with Mushroom-Cognac Sauce

4 filets mignons or beef tenderloin steaks, each 6 to 8 ounces and 1¼ inches thick

Extra-virgin olive oil

Kosher salt and ground black pepper

MUSHROOM-COGNAC SAUCE

1 tablespoon extra-virgin olive oil

8 to 10 ounces cremini mushrooms, cleaned, stem ends trimmed, and cut into ¼-inch-thick slices

1 small garlic clove, minced

¼ cup Cognac or Calvados (apple brandy)

½ cup low-sodium beef broth, plus more if needed

1 tablespoon Dijon mustard

¾ cup heavy whipping cream

2 fresh rosemary sprigs, each about 5 inches long, plus about ½ teaspoon minced fresh leaves

¼ teaspoon kosher salt

⅛ teaspoon ground black pepper

Break out the white tablecloth—we're about to get fancy. Elegant, tender filet mignon meets its sophisticated match with this luxurious sauce. Give the mushrooms a hot sear to color them and strengthen their flavors before simmering them in brandy, broth, and cream. Maître d' not included.

1. Prepare the grill for direct cooking over high heat (450° to 550°F). Brush the steaks on both sides with oil and season evenly on both sides with salt and pepper. Let stand at room temperature while you prepare the mushroom sauce.

2. To make the mushroom-cognac sauce, warm the oil in a large (10- to 12-inch) skillet over medium-high heat on the stove. Add the mushrooms and sear until lightly browned, 3 to 5 minutes, stirring only once or twice.

3. Add the garlic and cook until fragrant, about 30 seconds, stirring occasionally. Turn off the exhaust fan, if using, and carefully add the Cognac (it may ignite, but it is fine if it doesn't).

4. Simmer, stirring to scrape up any browned bits, until reduced by about half; it should take less than 1 minute. Stir in the broth and mustard, then add the cream and rosemary sprigs.

5. Bring to a robust simmer, then reduce the heat to medium-low and simmer gently until thickened to a saucy consistency, 5 to 8 minutes, stirring frequently. Discard the rosemary sprigs and stir in the salt and pepper. Set aside and keep warm. If the sauce becomes too thick, thin with broth, 1 tablespoon at a time.

6. Brush the cooking grates clean. Grill the steaks over **direct high heat,** with the lid closed, until cooked to your desired doneness, 8 to 10 minutes for medium rare (125° to 130°F), turning once or twice. Remove from the grill and let rest for a few minutes. Top the steaks with the sauce, garnish with the minced rosemary, and serve.

Beef Tenderloin Roast with Red Wine Sauce

1 beef tenderloin roast, about 3 pounds, preferably center cut

1 tablespoon kosher salt

1 teaspoon ground black pepper

1 tablespoon juniper berries

3 garlic cloves

2 tablespoons packed fresh thyme leaves

2 tablespoons packed fresh rosemary leaves

2 tablespoons packed fresh mint leaves

2 tablespoons extra-virgin olive oil

RED WINE SAUCE

6 tablespoons (¾ stick) cold unsalted butter, divided

1 large shallot, minced (about ⅓ cup)

3 cups full-bodied red wine, such as Cabernet Sauvignon

1 cup unsalted or low-sodium beef broth

3 fresh thyme sprigs

1 bay leaf

1 teaspoon balsamic vinegar

1 teaspoon packed light brown sugar

Scant ½ teaspoon kosher salt

½ teaspoon ground black pepper

A whole beef tenderloin usually weighs 6 to 7 pounds and has odd-shaped ends. For this recipe, look for a more manageable 3-pound piece from the middle of the tenderloin. Called the "center cut," its cylindrical shape makes for consistent cooking. Use an instant-read thermometer for precise results.

1. Trim the tenderloin of excess fat and silver skin. If the tenderloin has the narrow (tail end) attached, fold it under the fillet for even cooking and truss with 12- to 15-inch lengths of butcher's twine every 2 inches. Season the meat evenly with the salt and pepper.

2. Using a mortar with a pestle, smash together the juniper berries and garlic until a paste forms. Finely chop the herbs and stir into the paste. Alternatively, pulse the juniper and garlic in a food processor until finely ground. Add the herbs and process until finely chopped. Mix in the oil.

3. Place the tenderloin on a baking sheet and rub all over with the herb mixture. Cover the pan with plastic wrap and refrigerate for at least 6 hours or up to overnight. Remove from the refrigerator 1 hour before grilling and let stand at room temperature while you make the sauce.

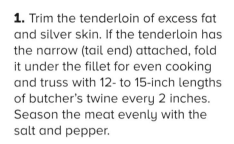

4. To make the red wine sauce, in a wide saucepan over medium heat on the stove, melt 1 tablespoon of the butter. Add the shallot and sauté until soft and translucent, 3 to 4 minutes. Add the wine, broth, thyme, and bay leaf, bring to a boil, and boil until the mixture is reduced to about 1 cup, 20 to 25 minutes.

5. Strain the sauce through a fine-mesh sieve into a small skillet or saucepan, pushing down on the solids to extract as much liquid as possible. You should have about ¾ cup. Bring to a simmer over medium heat, stir in the vinegar and sugar, and boil until slightly syrupy and reduced to a scant ½ cup, 3 to 5 minutes. Set aside.

6. Prepare the grill for direct and indirect cooking over medium heat (350° to 450°F). Brush the cooking grates clean. Sear the tenderloin over **direct medium heat** on all sides, with the lid closed as much as possible, 12 to 15 minutes, turning a quarter turn every 3 to 4 minutes. >

Beef Tenderloin Roast with Red Wine Sauce

7. Slide the meat over **indirect medium heat** and continue, with the lid closed, until an instant-read thermometer inserted into the thickest part registers 125°F for rare, 130°F for medium rare, or to your desired doneness, 15 to 35 minutes, depending on the thickness.

8. Transfer the beef to a cutting board and let rest for 10 minutes. Reheat the sauce gently over medium-low heat on the stove. Whisk in the remaining 5 tablespoons butter, 1 tablespoon at a time, until emulsified (do not boil or the sauce will "break"). Remove from the heat, stir in any juices from the cutting board, and season with the salt and pepper.

9. Cut the tenderloin across the grain into thick slices, divide them among the plates, and serve immediately with the sauce.

Simple Sauces for Beef Tenderloin

HERB-SHALLOT VINAIGRETTE

In a medium bowl whisk together ¼ cup extra-virgin olive oil; 3 tablespoons white wine vinegar; 3 tablespoons chopped fresh herbs, such as basil, chives, Italian parsley, or your favorite combination; 1 teaspoon minced shallot; ½ teaspoon Dijon mustard; ¼ teaspoon kosher salt; and ⅛ teaspoon ground black pepper until well combined.

BRANDY-MUSTARD SAUCE

In a medium skillet over medium heat, melt 1 tablespoon unsalted butter. Add 2 tablespoons minced shallot and cook until softened, 1 to 2 minutes, stirring often. Add 2 tablespoons Cognac or other brandy and cook until reduced to a glaze, about 30 seconds. Add ½ cup low-sodium beef broth, raise the heat to high, and bring to a boil. Cook until the broth reduces by half, 2 to 3 minutes. Add ¾ cup heavy whipping cream, bring to a simmer (not a boil), and adjust the heat to maintain a simmer. Whisk in 3 tablespoons whole-grain mustard and simmer until the sauce is reduced to ¾ cup and is thick enough to coat the back of a spoon, 3 to 5 minutes. Season with kosher salt and serve warm, garnished with chopped fresh chives.

COOL GREEN AVOCADO-HERB SAUCE

In a food processor or blender combine 1 medium ripe Hass avocado, pitted and peeled; one 2-inch-long piece English cucumber, peeled and roughly chopped; ¼ cup sour cream; ¼ cup thinly sliced scallions, white and green parts; ¼ cup chopped fresh dill; the juice of 1 lime; and ⅛ teaspoon hot sauce, or to taste, and puree until smooth. Season with kosher salt. Pour into a bowl, cover, and refrigerate until serving. Bring to room temperature and garnish with chopped fresh dill just before serving.

Rotisserie Rib Roast with Melted Onions

GARLIC-ROSEMARY PASTE

6 garlic cloves, smashed

1 cup packed fresh Italian parsley leaves and tender stems

2 tablespoons fresh rosemary leaves

1 tablespoon fresh thyme leaves

¼ cup Dijon mustard

2 tablespoons extra-virgin olive oil

1 boneless beef rib roast, 5½ to 6 pounds, trimmed of excess fat

2 teaspoons kosher salt

1½ teaspoons ground black pepper

MELTED ONIONS

3 large Vidalia or other sweet onions, about 2½ pounds total, thinly sliced

1 tablespoon extra-virgin olive oil

2 teaspoons Worcestershire sauce

¾ teaspoon kosher salt

½ teaspoon ground black pepper

This roast is the gift that keeps on giving. Not only is the meat delicious, but its dripping fat and juices rain precious flavor on the onions below. Be sure to center the roast on the spit and secure it well for even cooking. For juicier slices, let the meat rest for 30 minutes before carving.

1. In a food processor process the garlic until chopped and it sticks to the sides of the bowl. Scrape down the sides of the bowl. Add the parsley, rosemary, and thyme and pulse until finely chopped, occasionally scraping down the sides of the bowl. Add the mustard and oil and process just until blended.

2. Using 18-inch lengths of butcher's twine, tie the roast tightly in 2-inch intervals to give it as uniform and cylindrical a shape as possible. Trim the ends of the string. Place the roast on a baking sheet.

3. Season the roast evenly with the salt and pepper, then rub the paste all over the roast. Let stand at room temperature for 1 hour.

4. Meanwhile, combine the onions, oil, Worcestershire sauce, salt, and pepper in a large cast-iron skillet and toss until thoroughly combined. Remove the cooking grate(s).

5. Prepare the grill for indirect cooking over medium-low heat (350°F). Place the skillet in the area of the grill under where the roast will be on the rotisserie. Cook the onions over **indirect medium-low heat**, with the lid closed, for 30 minutes, stirring occasionally.

6. Meanwhile, set up the spit. Slide one pronged fork, with the tines facing inward, onto the spit about 10 inches from the end of the spit. Secure the fork but do not tighten it yet. Slide the spit through the roast as close to the center as possible and then gently push the meat onto the fork tines until they are deep inside. **>**

Rotisserie Rib Roast with Melted Onions

7. Add the other pronged fork to the spit with the tines facing inward and then push firmly into the meat. Secure the fork but don't tighten it yet. Place the spit into the rotisserie motor and center the roast over the skillet of onions. Tighten the forks. Stir the onions, then continue to stir them every 20 minutes as the roast cooks.

8. Drain the wood chips and scatter over the coals or add to the smoker box of a gas grill. Close the lid and turn on the rotisserie. Grill the roast over **indirect medium-low heat**, with the lid closed, until an instant-read thermometer inserted into the thickest part registers 120°F for medium rare, 1½ hours to 1¾ hours.

9. Wearing heavy, insulated gloves, carefully remove the spit from the grill. Gently loosen the forks and slide the roast off the spit and onto a cutting board. Let rest for about 30 minutes.

10. The onions are ready when they are caramelized, soft, and dark brown. If they are not, set the skillet over direct heat and continue to cook the onions over **direct medium-low heat**, with the lid closed, until they are browned, 10 to 20 minutes longer, stirring frequently. Remove from the grill.

11. Cut the roast into thick slices across the grain and serve with the onions.

Prime Rib Leftovers

Prime Rib Sandwiches with Caramelized Onions and Horseradish

In a 10-inch nonstick skillet heat 2 tablespoons olive oil over medium heat. Add 3 cups thinly sliced yellow onions, ½ teaspoon dried thyme, ½ teaspoon kosher salt, and ¼ teaspoon ground black pepper. Cook until the onions are very tender and deep golden brown, 20 to 30 minutes, stirring occasionally and adding water, a teaspoon at a time, if necessary to prevent burning. Remove from the heat.

In a small bowl stir together ½ cup mayonnaise, 2 tablespoons well-drained prepared horseradish, and 1 tablespoon Dijon mustard. Slice 1 pound leftover beef as thinly as possible and cut away any large clumps of fat. Use rolls or sliced bread to make sandwiches with the thinly sliced beef, caramelized onions, horseradish mayonnaise, and lettuce leaves.

Roast Beef Hash Browns

Peel and coarsely shred 1 pound russet potatoes (2 small). Put the potatoes in a large bowl of cold water, and mix to release the starch. Drain the potatoes and rinse under cold water. Transfer to a kitchen towel. Bring the corners together, shape the potatoes into a ball, and tighten the towel around the potatoes over the sink to squeeze out as much moisture as possible. Set aside. Cut 4 ounces leftover beef into ¼-inch pieces (1 cup).

Heat 2 tablespoons olive oil in a 10-inch nonstick skillet over high heat. Spread the beef in the skillet and fry until crispy, 2 to 3 minutes. Lower the heat to medium, add the potatoes, and season with ½ teaspoon kosher salt, ½ teaspoon granulated onion, and ¼ teaspoon black pepper. Stir together the ingredients to coat the pototoes with beef fat, then spread them out in an even layer. Cook until the underside is browned and crusty, 4 to 6 minutes. Using a spatula, carefully flip the potato mixture, then continue to cook until crispy and browned on the second side, 4 to 6 minutes, Serve warm.

Beef Fried Rice

In a small bowl stir together the sauce ingredients: 1 tablespoon soy sauce, 2 teaspoons toasted sesame oil, 2 teaspoons Asian fish sauce, and 1 teaspoon sugar. Cut 8 ounces leftover beef into ¼-inch pieces (about 2 cups). Prep 1 cup finely diced yellow onion; 1 tablespoon peeled, minced fresh ginger; and 1 tablespoon minced garlic.

Preheat a wok or very large skillet over high heat and add 2 tablespoons vegetable oil. Add the beef and ½ teaspoon crushed red pepper flakes and stir-fry until the edges of the beef are beginning to brown, 2 to 3 minutes. Add the reserved onion, ginger, and garlic and continue to stir-fry until the onions are beginning to brown, 2 to 3 minutes. Add 4 cups cold cooked short-grain rice, breaking up any clumps with the edge of a spoon. Stir-fry for 3 to 4 minutes. Add as much of the sauce as you like and mix well. Remove from the heat. Add ⅓ cup finely chopped fresh cilantro. Serve immediately.

Beef Chili Tacos

Make a simple guacamole by mashing the flesh of 2 large ripe Hass avocados with 2 teaspoons fresh lime juice, ¼ teaspoon kosher salt, and ⅛ teaspoon ground black pepper. Set aside. Thinly slice 4 to 6 ounces leftover beef, cutting away any large clumps of fat. Cut the beef slices into ¼-inch chunks (about 1½ cups).

In a medium saucepan heat 2 tablespoons olive oil over high heat. Add the beef and fry until brown and crispy, 2 to 3 minutes, stirring occasionally. Reduce the heat to medium, add 1 can (15 ounces) chili with beans, and cook until the chili is thickened and warmed through.

Meanwhile, warm 6 to 8 small flour or corn tortillas. Fill the tortillas with the beef mixture and guacamole. Garnish with chopped fresh cilantro. Serve warm.

Texas-Style Brisket
RECIPE ON PAGE 144

BRISKET

Welcome to big-league barbecue. Mastering your first brisket is like moving up from the minors to the majors. It's an amazing achievement, but you don't get there without paying attention. Allow us to walk you through some pointers and lingo.

Top Tips for the Ultimate Brisket

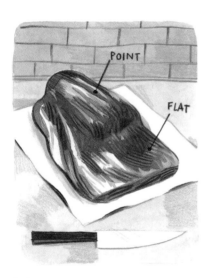

1. Buy a "whole packer." That is 'cue speak for a portion of the chest area that has two major muscles. First is the "point," or deckle, which is somewhat dome shaped on top. Under the point and extending away from it is the "flat," which is always leaner. Look for a flat that is at least 1 inch thick at the thinnest part; otherwise, it will dry out before the point is fully cooked. Finally, pick up the brisket and bend it. It should flop a little and not be stiff.

2. Set aside plenty of time for prep. Allow at least 30 minutes for trimming a whole brisket, and be sure to use a good, sharp knife. Trim the top layer of fat so it is no more than ⅓ inch thick and remove the silver skin from the underside of the meat.

3. Prepare for "the stall." If you are grilling your first brisket, you may start to panic after 4 to 5 hours of cooking. This is when the internal temperature of the meat will reach 150° to 160°F and plateau there, as if it has stopped cooking. That's "the stall," and it happens because moisture is evaporating and cooling the meat a bit. We recommend wrapping the meat in a sheet of butcher paper at this point to help retain some moisture and to push the internal temperature past the plateau.

4. Don't rush it. The most common mistake that people make is not cooking the brisket long enough. The meat might look done, and the internal temperature might be slightly over 200°F—both good signs—but touch is the most reliable test for doneness. The meat should be as soft as a marshmallow, which usually takes more time than you think. The second biggest mistake is not letting the meat rest long enough before cutting it. For optimal tenderness and juiciness, it should rest for a couple of hours (yes, hours).

PARTY TIMELINE

4 a.m. Wake up and start the charcoal.

5 a.m. Put the brisket on the smoker.

9 to 10 a.m. Wrap the brisket in butcher paper.

2 or 3 p.m. Take the brisket off and let it rest.

5 or 6 p.m. Slice and serve your succulent brisket.

Texas-Style Brisket

1 untrimmed whole beef brisket, 12 to 14 pounds, including both the flat and point sections (see page 147)

¼ cup coarsely ground black pepper

¼ cup kosher salt

SPRAY

½ cup cider vinegar

½ cup water

Hamburger buns, split, or bread slices (optional)

Cola Barbecue Sauce (page 336), Smoked Onion BBQ Sauce (page 336), or other homemade or store-bought sauce (optional)

Smoking a brisket is an all-day affair. While you don't have to be hunched over the grill that whole time, you need to stay close by. The difference between "pretty good" and "great" brisket will depend on how you handle the changing temperatures of the smoker and the cleanliness of the smoke.

1. Using a very sharp knife, round off the corners of the brisket. Make sure the brisket has no 90-degree angles. This will help the heat to move aerodynamically across the meat. Trim the fat on the fatty side of the brisket to about ⅓ inch thick but no less.

2. On the meatier side, remove the web-like membrane covering the meat so the coarsely grained meat underneath is visible.

6. Pour enough lit charcoal on top to fill the ring. Fill the water pan three-fourths full with water and assemble the smoker (see page 38). Wait until the temperature of the smoker reaches about 275°F, 20 to 30 minutes. At this point, you will see some light-colored smoke coming out of the vents. Brush the cooking grates clean.

7. Place the brisket, fat side up, on the top cooking grate and close the lid. Cook over **indirect very low heat**, with the lid closed as much as possible.

SERVES
ABOUT 12

PREP:
45 MIN

GRILL:
9–12 HOURS

REST:
2–4 HOURS

SPECIAL EQUIPMENT:
WATER SMOKER, 6–8 FIST-SIZE OAK AND/OR MESQUITE WOOD CHUNKS, BUTCHER PAPER, SPRAY BOTTLE, INSULATED COOLER (OPTIONAL)

3. Remove any hard clumps of fat on either side of the brisket. Note the section shaped like a wedge between the point and flat. Be sure to cut away most of that fat. If you don't, that fat will never melt (render).

4. In a small bowl stir together the pepper and salt. Season the bottom of the brisket first and the fatty side last, making sure you apply the rub evenly on all sides. Refrigerate the brisket until ready to smoke (you can do this up to 12 hours in advance).

5. Fill a chimney starter full of charcoal and light it. Add six to eight hardwood chunks to the smoker first and then cover them with unlit charcoal until the ring is about three-fourths full.

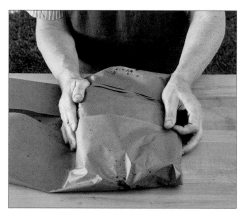

8. Cook until the surface color looks like it does in the above photo, 4 to 5 hours. Achieving that surface color indicates a good "bark" has been created and the brisket will no longer absorb much smoke. The temperature in the thickest part of the brisket will be around 150° to 160°F, but color is the primary indication of a good bark.

9. Arrange two sheets of 3-foot-long butcher paper side by side and overlapping. Fill a spray bottle with the vinegar and water and spray the brisket all over. Transfer the brisket, fatty side up, to the center of the paper. Fold one long side of the paper over the brisket, bring each side in and over, then roll it up until wrapped and sealed (like a burrito).

10. Place the wrapped brisket, fat side down, on the top cooking grate over **indirect very low heat**. Adjust the heat of the smoker as needed to maintain the temperature between 250° and 275°F. **>**

11. Cook, with the lid closed, until the meat is so tender that when you press it with your fingers through the paper it feels like a giant marshmallow or sponge. This will probably take 5 to 7 hours more.

12. At that point, the internal temperature should be 202° to 205°F in the flat and 208° to 211°F in the point, though tenderness is a more important indicator of doneness. The amount of time depends on the breed of cattle and other characteristics of the meat. A common mistake is taking the brisket off too early.

13. Transfer the brisket, still wrapped in butcher paper, to a dry, insulated cooler or turned-off oven. Close the cooler or oven and let the meat rest for 2 to 4 hours. Don't skip this step. It helps loosen the muscles and absorb moisture back into the brisket. The ideal serving temperature of the brisket is 140° to 145°F.

14. Unwrap the brisket and set it on a cutting board, being careful to keep the precious meat juices in the butcher paper. Starting with the flat, cut the brisket across the grain into thin slices.

15. The grain runs differently in the point section, so once you get to that portion of the brisket, you'll need to turn your knife. First, cut the point in half, then slice each portion across the grain. Serve the brisket warm on buns or bread with barbecue sauce, if using.

BRISKET PERFECTION

A properly cooked brisket is tender but not delicate. If a pencil-thick slice falls apart as you are slicing it, that's overcooked. If, on the other hand, that slice comes apart easily when you tug on it from opposite ends, that's sheer brisket perfection.

The Elements of Brisket

This massive hunk of meat from the chest of a steer combines two distinct but overlapping muscles. One is a lean, somewhat rectangular muscle called the flat. The slices in this photo are cut from the end of the brisket where only the flat is visible.

The other brisket muscle is a mounded collection of fatty meat and loosely bound stretches of collagen that, under low-and-slow barbecue conditions, will melt into something so spectacular that it could be called brisket butter. This muscle is called the point (or deckle). About halfway down the brisket, the point begins to overlap the flat beneath it. Its mounded shape extends all the way to the bottom edge of the meat in this photo.

Many barbecue joints sell brisket either lean or fatty. Lean meat is usually cut from the flat. Fatty (or moist) brisket usually comes from the point, sometimes with a layer of flat meat clinging to it.

The point is also the source of barbecue's greatest gift to carnivores: burnt ends. If you cut the crusty parts of the point into small cubes, toss them in a pan with a little barbecue sauce, and set the pan on the smoker for about half an hour, the meat surrenders any resistance, while the surface remains a little crusty. It is a smoky treasure that almost dissolves in your mouth, like a brisket foie gras.

Lamb Rib Chops with
North African Spices
RECIPE ON PAGE 150

LAMB CHOPS

Love them or leave them: that's what we think about lamb chops. We love the strong flavors of lamb, but we respect that some people just don't like them. We prefer the meat of young lamb raised in the United States, which is milder and sweeter than the meat imported from Australia, New Zealand, or Iceland. Plus, it has a real affinity for the char and smoke of a grill.

Top Tips for the Ultimate Lamb Chops

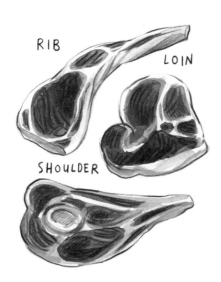

1. Know your cuts. Not all lamb chops are the same! While there are essentially three choices out there, we prefer rib chops or loin chops (shoulder chops are an economical choice but can be difficult to cook to tenderness).

Loin chops are the lamb equivalent of T-bone or porterhouse steaks. On one side of the bone you have the meltingly soft texture of the tenderloin, and on the other side the subtle chewiness of the loin back.

Tender rib chops are good looking (and expensive) with a smooth flavor. These are the chops that make up a rack of lamb, which is cut from the center rib cage. We prefer to have our butcher trim them for us.

2. Check the colors. Look for lamb chops with light red meat. They have a clean, buttery flavor. Avoid those with either pale pink or intensely dark meat. The fat around the chop should be bright white and not at all yellowish.

3. Get the thick ones. Most people prefer lamb cooked rare or medium rare. Getting that doneness with thin chops is challenging, as they can easily overcook. Buy either chops that are at least ¾ inch thick or double-cut chops.

4. Don't cook them cold. A chop taken straight from the fridge will not cook evenly. The outside will overcook before the center warms up. Let chops sit at room temperature (covered on the counter) for 15 to 20 minutes before grilling.

5. Don't go past medium rare. Lamb chops achieve their peak levels of taste and tenderness somewhere between rare and medium rare. Don't overcook them or the meat will be surprisingly dry and chewy.

6. Tame the game. When you are thinking about what to serve with lamb chops, either let them shine on their own (with just salt, pepper, and maybe some garlic) or pair them with something equally strong, such as an assertive spice rub, a bold pesto sauce, or a hearty tomato sauce.

Lamb Rib Chops with North African Spices

NORTH AFRICAN SPICE PASTE

2 to 3 garlic cloves, minced or pushed through a press

⅓ cup packed fresh cilantro leaves, very finely chopped (3 tablespoons)

⅓ cup packed fresh basil leaves, very finely chopped (3 tablespoons)

2 tablespoons sherry vinegar

1½ teaspoons sweet paprika

¾ teaspoon kosher salt

¾ teaspoon ground cumin

⅛ to ¼ teaspoon cayenne pepper or ground black pepper

⅓ cup extra-virgin olive oil

2 teaspoons ground cumin

1 teaspoon kosher salt

1 teaspoon ground black pepper

16 lamb rib chops, each about ¾ inch thick, meat and bones trimmed of excess fat

Extra-virgin olive oil

1 lemon, sliced (optional)

Yes, fat is fabulous, but too much can turn your lamb chops into a fireball. Trim the fat well and use only enough oil to help the spices stick. Lamb can handle a lot of flavor, so our spice paste is garlicky and tart and packed with the heady flavor of fresh herbs.

1. In a medium bowl whisk together all the ingredients for the paste until smooth and emulsified.

2. Alternatively, make the spice paste in a food processor. With the motor running, first add the whole garlic cloves. Then add the cilantro and basil leaves and all the remaining ingredients and process until smooth.

6. Brush the paste on both sides of each chop. Serve the chops warm. If desired, garnish with the lemon slices.

SERVES **4**

PREP: **20 MIN**

GRILL: **3–5 MIN**

3. In a small bowl mix together the cumin, salt, and pepper. Lightly rub the lamb chops on both sides with oil and season all over with the cumin mixture, pressing lightly to adhere. Let stand at room temperature for 15 to 20 minutes while you prepare the grill.

4. Prepare the grill for direct and indirect cooking over high heat (450° to 550°F.) Brush the cooking grates clean. Grill the chops over **direct high heat**, with the lid closed, until cooked to your desired doneness, 3 to 5 minutes for medium rare (125° to 130°F), turning once or twice.

5. If flare-ups occur, move the chops to **indirect high heat** until the flames subside and add a minute or so to the grilling time. Remove the chops from the grill, then whisk the paste to emulsify it again.

Rosemary Lamb Loin Chops with Feta

¼ cup extra-virgin olive oil

2 tablespoons finely chopped fresh rosemary leaves

2 teaspoons minced garlic

1½ teaspoons kosher salt

1 teaspoon ground black pepper

8 bone-in lamb loin chops, each 4 to 6 ounces and 1¼ to 1½ inches thick, trimmed of excess fat

2 ounces feta cheese, cold

2 tablespoons finely chopped fresh dill leaves

Lamb loin chops, like T-bone steaks, have big natural flavors, so they stand up well to pungent aromatics like rosemary and garlic. Refrigerate a little block of feta cheese, which will make it easier to grate over the chops for a final flourish of flavor.

SERVES **4**

PREP: **15 MIN**

GRILL: **10–12 MIN**

1. In a small bowl mix together the oil, rosemary, garlic, salt, and pepper. Lightly coat the chops on both sides with the rosemary mixture. Let stand at room temperature for 15 to 20 minutes while you prepare the grill.

2. Prepare the grill for direct and indirect cooking over medium-high heat (400° to 450°F). Brush the cooking grates clean. Grill the chops over **direct medium-high heat**, with the lid closed, until cooked to your desired doneness, 10 to 12 minutes for medium rare (125° to 130°F), turning once or twice.

3. If flare-ups occur, move the chops to **indirect medium-high heat** until the flames subside and add a minute or so to the grilling time. Transfer the chops to a platter.

4. Using a cheese grater, shave the block of cold cheese over the chops. Sprinkle the dill on top and serve warm.

Catalan-Style Rack of Lamb

2 lamb racks, each 1½ to 1¾ pounds, fat cap removed, trimmed of excess fat, and frenched

1 teaspoon kosher salt

1 teaspoon ground black pepper

CATALAN MARINADE

4 large garlic cloves

1 cup packed fresh Italian parsley leaves and tender stems

1 cup packed fresh cilantro leaves and tender stems

1 teaspoon finely grated lemon zest

1 teaspoon smoked paprika

½ teaspoon ground cumin

½ teaspoon kosher salt

⅓ cup extra-virgin olive oil

SMOKY RED PEPPER SAUCE

2 large red bell peppers, each 8 to 9 ounces

2 plum tomatoes, each about 4 ounces, halved lengthwise and seeded

1 large garlic clove

2 tablespoons extra-virgin olive oil

1 tablespoon sherry vinegar

1 teaspoon smoked paprika

½ teaspoon crushed red pepper flakes

½ teaspoon kosher salt

¼ teaspoon ground black pepper

Chopped fresh mint

When grilling these lamb racks over direct heat, position the bare bones over indirect heat so they do not blacken. Also, be ready to move the racks away from flare-ups. In the end, the racks will probably spend about as much time over indirect heat as they do over direct heat.

SERVES **4-6**

PREP: **30 MIN**

MARINATE:
6-8 HOURS

GRILL: **30-40 MIN**

REST: **5 MIN**

1. Season the lamb with salt and pepper. Combine the marinade ingredients in a food processor and process to create a course puree. Spread the marinade evenly over the lamb. Cover with plastic wrap and refrigerate for 6 to 8 hours. Let stand at room temperature 30 minutes before grilling.

2. Prepare the grill for direct and indirect cooking over medium-high heat (400° to 450°F). Brush the cooking grates clean. Grill the bell peppers over **direct medium-high heat**, with the lid closed, until blackened all over, about 20 minutes, turning every 5 minutes. Halfway through cooking the peppers, oil the cut side of the tomato halves.

3. Grill the tomatoes cut side down over **direct medium-high heat**, with the lid closed, until softened and charred, 5 to 6 minutes. Remove the tomatoes and set aside to cool. Transfer the bell peppers to a bowl, cover with plastic wrap, and let steam for 10 to 15 minutes.

4. Pull off and discard the skins from the tomatoes. Cut away the stem and core from each pepper, then slit each pepper lengthwise and remove the seeds and membranes. Peel away and discard the charred skin. Put the tomatoes, peppers, and remaining sauce ingredients in the food processor and process until smooth.

5. Grill the lamb, meaty side down, over **direct medium-high heat** (the bones should fall over indirect heat), with the lid closed, until browned on both sides, about 8 minutes, turning once or twice. Finish the lamb over **indirect medium-high heat**, with the lid closed, to your desired doneness, 8 to 12 minutes for medium rare.

6. Check doneness with an instant-read thermometer inserted into the thickest part, without touching bone; it should register 125°F for medium-rare. Transfer to a cutting board, let rest for 5 minutes, then carve into chops. Divide the sauce among the serving plates, set the chops on the sauce, and garnish with the mint.

Family Picnic

St. Louis Ribs with Smoked Onion BBQ Sauce, recipe on page 192; **Grilled Onion and Sour Cream Dip**, recipe on page 70; **Pulled Pork with Carolina Sauce**, recipe on page 198; **Creamy Coleslaw**, recipe on page 341

PORK

Southwestern Sausage Sandwiches

2 large poblano or Anaheim chile peppers, seeded and cut crosswise into ⅓-inch-wide strips

1 medium yellow onion, halved lengthwise and cut crosswise into ⅓-inch-thick half-moons

1 tablespoon olive oil

½ teaspoon kosher salt

¼ teaspoon ground cumin

¼ teaspoon ground black pepper

6 fresh (uncooked) Mexican chorizo or hot Italian sausages, about 1½ pounds total

6 small sub or hoagie rolls (about 5 inches long), split

1½ to 2 cups coarsely grated cheddar cheese (6 to 8 ounces)

3 scallions, white and light green parts thinly sliced and dark green parts thinly sliced and reserved separately

⅓ cup coarsely chopped fresh cilantro leaves

Don't think you have to pack all of these items on the grate at once, especially if you have a small grill. You can cook the vegetables first, then the sausages, and then the buns. If you have a large grill, go ahead and use all of your real estate.

SERVES **6**

PREP: **10 MIN**

GRILL: **15–20 MIN**

SPECIAL EQUIPMENT:
**LARGE PERFORATED
GRILL PAN**

1. Prepare the grill for direct and indirect cooking over medium heat (350° to 450°F). Brush the cooking grates clean. Place a perforated grill pan over direct heat, close the lid, and preheat for 10 minutes. Combine the poblanos, onion, oil, salt, cumin, and black pepper and toss to coat.

2. Spread the vegetables on the pre-heated grill pan and cook over **direct medium heat**, with the lid closed, until softened and beginning to color, 6 to 8 minutes, stirring occasionally. Slide the pan to the cooler part of the grill and keep the vegetables warm while you finish grilling the sausages and buns.

3. Grill the sausages over **direct medium heat**, with the lid closed, until browned and fully cooked, 8 to 10 minutes, turning occasionally. During the last 4 minutes of grilling, toast the rolls cut side down, without separating the tops and bottoms, over **direct medium heat** until golden, 1 to 2 minutes.

4. Flip the rolls and move to indirect heat. Scatter the cheese over the cut sides of the rolls and sprinkle the white and light green scallions over the cheese. Grill over **indirect medium heat**, with the lid closed, until the cheese melts, about 2 minutes.

5. Remove the rolls from the grill and place on serving plates. Place a sausage on the bottom half of each roll and spoon the peppers and onion over the sausages. Garnish with the cilantro and remaining dark scallion greens and serve.

EVEN TENDERNESS

The heat from a charcoal fire is bound to be a little stronger in some spots and a little weaker in others. Move your ingredients accordingly. For example, if a couple of your sausages aren't browning as nicely as the others, move them over the stronger heat. Shouldn't they all get an equal opportunity to be delicious?

Beer-Braised Bratwurst with Sauerkraut

1 medium yellow onion, about 9 ounces

1 tablespoon olive oil

1½ cups (12-ounce bottle) beer, preferably German

3 tablespoons whole-grain mustard

1 tablespoon chopped fresh thyme leaves

2 teaspoons caraway seeds, crushed

8 fresh (uncooked) bratwursts, each 3 to 4 ounces

1 cup low-sodium beef broth

2 tablespoons unsalted butter

2½ cups drained jarred sauerkraut (one 25-ounce jar)

¼ teaspoon ground black pepper

2 tablespoons finely chopped fresh Italian parsley

No one wants their bratwursts to burst on the grill. To avoid that, we first simmer the sausages gently in beer and onions until almost fully cooked. Next we brown them on hot grates for a bit of char, and then we finish them in a pan of warm sauerkraut.

1. Prepare the grill for direct cooking over medium heat (as close to 400°F as possible). Cut the onion in half lengthwise (through the stem end), then cut each half crosswise into ¼-inch-thick half-moons.

2. Coat a 12-inch cast-iron skillet or griddle with the oil. Arrange the onion slices, overlapping them slightly, on the oiled pan. Brush the cooking grates clean. Set the skillet over **direct medium heat**.

3. Cook the onions until light golden brown and beginning to soften, 8 to 10 minutes, stirring occasionally. Slowly add the beer, then stir in the mustard, thyme, and caraway.

4. Set the bratwursts on top of the onion mixture in a single layer and cook over **direct medium heat**, with the lid closed, for 10 minutes, turning the bratwursts in the simmering liquid once halfway through for even cooking.

5. Transfer the bratwursts to the grill grates over **direct heat** and cook, with the lid closed, until well browned in spots, about 5 minutes, turning occasionally. At the same time, with the skillet still over direct heat, add the broth to the onions and simmer for 5 minutes to reduce slightly.

6. Add the butter and then the sauerkraut to the skillet. Return the bratwursts to the skillet and cook, with the lid closed, until the bratwursts are fully cooked (150°F on an instant-read thermometer) and the sauerkraut is warm, about 5 minutes. Season with the pepper. Garnish with the parsley and serve.

Fennel and Garlic Pork Chops
RECIPE ON PAGE 164

PORK CHOPS

Choose your chops wisely. The ones from the shoulder area—blade chops and country-style ribs—have quite a bit of fat and chewy sinew. The chops from the hip area—sirloin chops—are usually too lean for grilling. The pork chops you want, because of their inherently good taste and tenderness, are the center-cut rib chops and center-cut loin chops.

Top Tips for the Ultimate Pork Chops

1. Skinny pork chops love the grill. They cook fast, they react well to char and smoky flavor, and they're likely to be juicier than their thicker pork chop brethren. Really. That's because they're so thin that they need very little time on the fire—and less time over the flames means less time to dry out.

2. Give your chops some bling. Like many lean meats, chops love a little sparkle. A short soak in a flavorful marinade or a smear of spice rub will go a long way toward developing flavor. If you are marinating longer, pop them into the fridge for several hours and then remove them 15 minutes before grilling to allow them to come to room temperature. Got a glaze? Brush it on during the last minute of grilling and flip the chops once again to coat each side. Another flavor-building option is to grill your chops over a fragrant fire of briquettes and smoldering wood chips.

3. Don't walk away. Now is not the time for distractions. No refills. No shenanigans. Thin chops cook quickly, so stand near the grill and watch them closely.

4. Don't fret the warp. The grill is hot, the skinnies are cooking, and you're feeling good. Then you glance down and see them curling into a funky shape. Don't fret. We have a solution. Warping occurs when the band of fat around the exterior of the chop heats up and loses moisture faster than the rest of the meat. It shrinks, causing the meat to buckle. To prevent it—and enhance crispiness—make narrow crosswise incisions in the fat at 1-inch intervals, being careful not to pierce the meat.

5. Patience is the secret ingredient. To prevent chops from sticking or tearing, you need a little patience. The proteins found in meats that come in closest contact with the hot

grill grates are the first ones to "denature," or unwind, and start browning. As this unwinding occurs, the proteins let go of one another and grab onto the grill, hence the sticking. But if you wait just a little longer, the proteins will break down further and release from the grill.

Make sure the grill is piping hot before you add the chops. That way, the protein denaturing will happen quickly and efficiently. Second, oil the chops on both sides. Third, if the chops stick stubbornly, shove a metal spatula between the chops and the grate to release them.

6. Give the chops some beauty rest. Cutting into the meat too soon will release everything it's got. Allowing 3 to 5 minutes of rest will do the trick.

Fennel and Garlic Pork Chops

TOASTED FENNEL PASTE

1½ tablespoons fennel seeds

4 tablespoons extra-virgin olive oil, divided

2 garlic cloves, minced or pushed through a press

2 teaspoons dried oregano

1½ teaspoons kosher salt

1 teaspoon sweet paprika

¾ teaspoon crushed red pepper flakes

¾ teaspoon ground black pepper

8 thin bone-in center-cut pork chops, each about 4 ounces and ¼ inch thick

3 yellow onions, each 8 to 9 ounces, cut crosswise into ½-inch-thick slices

1 pound mini sweet peppers

Extra-virgin olive oil

Kosher salt and ground black pepper

Think of this as a new riff on the classic flavors of "sausage-n-peppahs." The results rely a lot on the assertive fennel paste on the pork. Then it is a matter of timing. Don't turn any of vegetables or the chops until their first sides are deeply browned with the flavors of the fire.

1. Prepare the grill for direct cooking over medium-high heat (about 450°F). Brush the cooking grates clean. Place a perforated grill pan over direct heat, close the lid, and preheat for 10 minutes. Toast the fennel seeds in a skillet over medium heat on the stove until fragrant, about 1 minute, stirring often.

2. Transfer the fennel seeds to a cutting board, drizzle with 1½ teaspoons of the oil, and chop finely. Transfer the fennel seeds to a small bowl, add all the remaining rub ingredients including the remaining 3½ tablespoons oil, and mix to form a paste.

5. Spread the onions and peppers on the preheated grill pan and grill over **direct medium-high heat**, with the lid closed, until the onions are tender and the peppers are charred in spots and slightly deflated, 10 to 12 minutes, turning occasionally. Remove each piece as it is done. Keep warm while grilling the chops.

6. Grill the pork chops on the grates over **direct medium-high heat**, with the lid closed, until well grill-marked on both sides but still juicy inside, 3 to 5 minutes, turning once. Transfer the chops to a platter and let rest for 3 to 5 minutes. Spoon the peppers and onions and any juices around the chops and serve warm.

				SPECIAL EQUIPMENT:
SERVES **4**	PREP: **25 MIN**	GRILL: **ABOUT 15 MIN**	REST: **3–5 MIN**	**LARGE PERFORATED GRILL PAN**

3. Coat both sides of each chop with the paste. Let the chops stand while you grill the peppers and onions.

4. Lightly coat the onion slices and sweet peppers with oil and season with ¾ teaspoon salt and ½ teaspoon black pepper.

FENNEL SEEDS

An essential spice in the Mediterranean pantry, fennel seeds have the distinctive flavor of anise and are a great addition to rubs.

To deepen their flavor, always toast the seeds before using them. Once they are toasted, grind, crush, or finely chop them. A mortar and pestle or a spice grinder is ideal for grinding them, or you can simply crush them with a heavy pot or the back of a chef's knife. To chop them, use a chef's knife on a cutting board. A drizzle of olive oil on the seed prevents them from jumping all over the cutting board.

FLAVOR BOMB *your* PORK CHOP

Think of these ideas as pork chop accessories. The chop is the culinary equivalent of the little black dress: nice on its own but better with something to lift it out of the ordinary. Here are some ideas for accessorizing your pork chops.

MUSHROOM STROGANOFF

In a large skillet, melt 2 tablespoons unsalted butter over medium-high heat on the stove. Add 12 ounces cremini mushrooms, cleaned, stem ends trimmed, and sliced, and sauté until browned and tender, about 8 minutes. Reduce the heat to medium. Add 1 garlic clove, minced; ½ teaspoon dried thyme; ½ teaspoon kosher salt; and ¼ teaspoon ground black pepper and sauté for 1 minute. Add 1½ cups heavy whipping cream and simmer until thickened and reduced by half, 6 to 8 minutes, stirring often. Keep warm while grilling the pork chops. Brush the chops with olive oil, season with 1½ teaspoons kosher salt and ½ teaspoon ground black pepper, and grill according to the recipe on page 164. Serve with the mushroom sauce.

ASIAN-STYLE SLAW

In a small bowl whisk together ¼ cup soy sauce, 2 tablespoons fresh lime juice, 2 tablespoons honey, 1½ tablespoons Sriracha sauce, 1 tablespoon toasted sesame oil, and 1 garlic clove, minced. Put the pork chops in a large resealable plastic bag, pour in the soy mixture, and seal closed. Turn to coat well, then refrigerate for at least 1 hour or up to 6 hours, turning occasionally. To make the slaw, in a medium bowl stir together 2 cups store-bought slaw mixture, 3 table-spoons chopped fresh cilantro leaves, 2 tablespoons seasoned rice vinegar, and 1 tablespoon toasted sesame oil. Cover and chill for 1 hour before serving. Remove the pork from the marinade and discard the marinade. Grill the chops according to the recipe on page 164. Serve with the Asian slaw.

TOMATILLO SALSA

In a small bowl stir together 3 tablespoons olive oil, 1½ teaspoons salt, 1 teaspoon ground cumin, 1 teaspoon ancho chile powder, ½ teaspoon ground black pepper, and 2 garlic cloves, minced to a paste. Coat the chops with this oil mixture according to the recipe and let stand while preparing the salsa: Grill 1 pound tomatillos, husked, and 1 large jalapeño chile pepper over direct medium heat, with the lid closed, until charred on all sides, about 10 minutes. Stem and seed the jalapeño. In a food processor combine the tomatillos, jalapeño, ½ cup chopped yellow onion, ½ cup packed fresh cilantro leaves, 2 tablespoons fresh lime juice, 1 large garlic clove, chopped, and ½ teaspoon kosher salt. Pulse until reduced to a chunky salsa consistency. Grill the chops according to the recipe on page 164. Serve with the salsa.

SWEET-AND-SOUR PINEAPPLE

In a small saucepan combine ½ cup balsamic vinegar; ¼ cup packed light brown sugar; 2 tablespoons fresh orange juice; 1 tablespoon soy sauce; 1 teaspoon finely grated orange zest; 1 garlic clove, minced; and ¼ teaspoon crushed red pepper flakes. Bring to a boil over medium-high heat on the stove and boil until syrupy and reduced to a scant ½ cup, about 5 minutes, stirring often. Brush the pork chops with olive oil, season with 1½ teaspoons kosher salt and ½ teaspoon ground black pepper, and grill according to the recipe on page 164. During the last minute of grilling, baste the chops on both sides with some of sauce to coat evenly and to brown. Remove from the grill and brush with more sauce. Garnish with chopped grilled pineapple slices (see Step 4, page 245) and chopped fresh cilantro leaves.

Brined Pork Chops with Romesco Sauce

BRINE

8 cups water

⅓ cup kosher salt

⅓ cup sugar

4 garlic cloves, smashed

1 tablespoon dried thyme

1 tablespoon ground
black pepper

6 bone-in pork chops, each
10 to 12 ounces and about
1 inch thick

ROMESCO SAUCE

2 large red bell peppers

¼ cup whole natural
almonds, toasted

1 garlic clove

½ cup loosely packed fresh
Italian parsley leaves and
tender stems

1 tablespoon sherry vinegar
or red wine vinegar

½ teaspoon kosher salt

¼ teaspoon ground
black pepper

¼ teaspoon dried thyme

¼ cup extra-virgin
olive oil

Extra-virgin olive oil for
brushing

Pork chops are not as fatty as they were in the past, so brining today's leaner chops and then grilling them over medium heat helps maximize their flavor and moisture. This heady sauce of roasted peppers, toasted almonds, and garlic takes these chops to a whole new level.

1. Combine all the brine ingredients in a large bowl or baking dish, whisking until the salt and sugar are dissolved. Submerge the pork chops in the brine. Cover and refrigerate for at least 3 hours and up to 24 hours.

2. Prepare the grill for direct cooking over high heat (450° to 550°F). Brush the cooking grates clean. Grill the bell peppers over **direct high heat**, with the lid closed as much as possible, until black and blistered all over, about 20 minutes, turning occasionally.

3. Place the peppers in a bowl and cover with plastic wrap; let steam 10 to 15 minutes. Cut away the stem and core from each pepper, then slit each pepper lengthwise, spread it open, and remove the seeds and membranes. Peel away and discard the charred skin. Roughly chop the peppers.

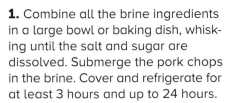

4. In a food processor combine the almonds and garlic and pulse to chop finely. Add the bell peppers, parsley, vinegar, salt, black pepper, and thyme and process to create a coarse paste. With the motor running, slowly add the oil and process to create a fairly smooth sauce. Taste and adjust the seasoning if needed.

5. Lower the heat for direct cooking over medium heat (350° to 450°F). Remove the chops from the brine, discard the brine, pat dry with paper towels, and brush lightly on both sides with the oil.

6. Grill the chops over **direct medium heat**, with the lid closed, until still barely pink in the center, 9 to 11 minutes (145°F), turning once. Serve the chops warm with the sauce.

Spicy Pork Tenderloin with Ginger Sauce
RECIPE ON PAGE 172

PORK TENDERLOIN

Have you compared the price per pound of pork tenderloin with beef tenderloin? Whoa and yay! Pork tenderloin is *much* easier on the wallet. Plus, it really does live up to its name, provided you don't overcook it. With that in mind, heed these important pointers.

Top Tips for the Ultimate Tenderloin

1. Say good-bye to silver skin. Take a look at your tenderloin. Does it have a white, sinewy layer over part of the meat? This is connective tissue, also known as silver skin, and you'll want to remove it before you season and cook the tenderloin. Silver skin becomes tough and chewy when cooked and may even cause your tenderloin to curl. It also makes slicing difficult. Get rid of it.

2. Maximize your surface area. This cylindrical cut of meat offers a large amount of exposed real estate for seasoning and browning. Take full advantage and season all of it, not just the surfaces that seem like the top and bottom. That's also true for browning. It's nice to develop some browned flavors on the top and bottom, but it's even better if you give the sides some time in direct contact with the hot grates. To do that when grilling two tenderloins, use tongs to hold them up and lean them against each other to prevent them from rolling.

3. Don't go over 145°F. The lack of fat in pork tenderloin means that the heat travels quickly from the surface to the center, so don't walk away. Have an instant-read thermometer ready. As soon as the temperature in the center reaches 145°F, pull the tenderloin off the grill. The heat bouncing around inside the meat will push the internal temperature to about 150°F, which is perfectly safe and juicy. Let the meat rest for a few minutes and then slice it to reveal moist rounds with a touch of pink. Perfect.

4. Think small, too. Grilling whole tenderloins may be the safest way to make them turn out moist, but it's not the only way. There are also advantages to cutting the meat into cubes first. You can create more surface area, and if evenly cut, the cubes cook more evenly, too. You can try a couple of fun techniques as well, such as grilling the cubes on skewers (see page 176) or stir-frying them (Yes, you can stir-fry on a grill. See details on pages 48 and 174).

5. Enjoy a quick smoke. Ribs and shoulders are not the only cuts of pork that benefit from the sweet fragrance of wood smoke. Enhance your pork tenderloins in just a few minutes by adding a few handfuls of soaked, drained wood chips to the charcoal fire or the smoker box of a gas grill.

Spicy Pork Tenderloin with Ginger Sauce

2 pork tenderloins, each 1 to 1¼ pounds

2 tablespoons extra-virgin olive oil

RED CHILI RUB

2 teaspoons prepared chili powder

1½ teaspoons kosher salt

1 teaspoon packed dark brown sugar

1 teaspoon granulated garlic

½ teaspoon ground black pepper

SPICY GINGER SAUCE

¼ cup soy sauce

2 tablespoons seasoned rice vinegar

1 tablespoon packed dark brown sugar

2 teaspoons chili-garlic sauce, such as Sriracha

½ teaspoon toasted sesame oil

⅓-inch piece fresh ginger, peeled

The objective here is to achieve tongue-tingling heat, courtesy of the now-ubiquitous (for good reason) condiment Sriracha. If your palate likes it cooler, halve the Sriracha. Steamed rice is a natural side, simultaneously soaking up the sauce and seasonings and mellowing some of the spiciness.

1. Using a sharp knife, trim the tenderloins of excess fat. Then, to trim each tenderloin of its silver skin, slide the tip of the knife under the skin and make a sawing motion while slightly angling the blade away from the meat.

2. Fold the thin flap end of each tenderloin over onto itself and tie with butcher's twine. This ensures the tenderloin is of even thickness and will help the tenderloin cook more evenly.

6. Brush the cooking grates clean. Grill the pork over **direct medium heat**, with the lid closed, until the exterior is evenly seared and an instant-read thermometer inserted into the center registers 145°F, 20 to 25 minutes, turning three times.

7. Transfer the tenderloins to a cutting board and let rest for 3 to 5 minutes. Cut into ½-inch-thick slices and arrange on a platter.

SERVES **4-6**

PREP: **15 MIN**

GRILL: **20-25 MIN**

REST: **3-5 MIN**

3. Drizzle the pork with the oil, then rub it evenly into the pork.

4. In a small bowl combine all the rub ingredients and mix well, then season the pork evenly all over with the rub. Let the pork stand at room temperature for 15 to 30 minutes while you prepare the grill.

5. Prepare the grill for direct cooking over medium heat (350° to 450°F). While the grill preheats, stir together all the sauce ingredients except the ginger in a small bowl. Using a fine-rasp grater, grate about ½ teaspoon ginger directly into the bowl. Stir and set aside.

8. Spoon the sauce over the meat and serve.

VARIATION

SWEET-AND-SOUR SAUCE

Omit the ginger sauce. In a small saucepan bring ½ cup balsamic vinegar, ½ cup fresh orange juice, and 2 tablespoons sugar to a boil over high heat. Lower the heat and simmer until the mixture is syrupy and thick enough to coat the back of a spoon lightly, about 20 minutes. Remove from the heat and swirl in 2 tablespoons cold unsalted butter. Drizzle the sauce over slices of the grilled meat.

Hoisin Pork and Vegetable Stir-Fry

1 pork tenderloin, about 1 pound

2 tablespoons soy sauce

3 tablespoons sake or mirin, divided

1 tablespoon toasted sesame oil

⅓ cup hoisin sauce

2 to 3 teaspoons chili-garlic sauce, such as Sriracha

2 tablespoons canola oil, divided

1 red bell pepper, seeded and cut into 1-inch dice

1 yellow onion, cut into 1-inch dice

1 tablespoon peeled, minced fresh ginger

3 large garlic cloves, minced

8 ounces asparagus, tough ends removed and cut into 1-inch pieces

8 ounces snow peas, stems trimmed and cut in half crosswise on the diagonal

4 scallions, white and light green parts cut into 1-inch pieces and dark green parts cut into 1-inch pieces and reserved separately, divided

¼ cup roasted cashews

4 cups steamed white rice

Don't blink—this recipe comes together in a flash. The most time-intensive part is cutting the ingredients uniformly so they are all done at the same time. Be sure to arrange everything you'll need on a tray beside the grill—and plan on staying put, because it's ready before you know it.

SERVES **4**

PREP: **40 MIN**

GRILL: **10–15 MIN**

SPECIAL EQUIPMENT:
**WEBER GBS
COOKING GRATE,
WEBER GBS WOK**

1. Trim the tenderloin as shown in Step 1 on page 172. Cut into 1-inch chunks: cut the narrow flap first, then the thicker piece in half lengthwise and then cross-wise. In a bowl toss the pork with the soy sauce, 1 tablespoon sake, and the sesame oil. In another bowl stir together the remaining sake, hoisin sauce, and chili-garlic sauce to taste and reserve.

2. Prepare the grill for direct cooking over high heat (450° to 550°F). Brush the cooking grates clean. Preheat a wok, with the lid closed, for 10 minutes. Heat 1 tablespoon oil in the wok. Use a slotted spoon to transfer the pork to the wok and cook over **direct high heat** for 30 seconds, stirring continuously. Discard the marinade.

3. Spread the pork in a single layer and cook, with the grill lid closed as much as possible, until lightly browned on all sides and cooked through, 2 to 3 minutes, stirring occasionally. Transfer the pork to a clean bowl.

4. Heat the remaining 1 tablespoon canola oil in the wok. Add the bell pepper, onion, ginger, and garlic and cook until fragrant, about 30 seconds, stirring constantly. Close the lid and continue cooking until the vegetables are slightly softened, 2 to 3 minutes, stirring occasionally.

5. Add the asparagus, snow peas, and white and light green scallion pieces. Cook for 30 seconds, stirring constantly, then close the grill lid and cook until bright green, 2 to 3 minutes.

6. Stir in the pork and any accumulated juices and the hoisin mixture and cook until heated through, about 1 minute, stirring constantly. Stir in the dark green scallion pieces and cashews. Wearing heavy insulated gloves, remove the wok from the grill and serve the stir-fry immediately over the rice.

Pork Souvlaki with Tzatziki

1½ pounds boneless
pork loin

MARINADE

¼ cup finely chopped
fresh mint

3 tablespoons extra-virgin
olive oil

2 tablespoons fresh lemon
juice (from 1 lemon)

1 tablespoon dried oregano

3 garlic cloves, minced

1 teaspoon kosher salt

½ teaspoon ground
black pepper

TZATZIKI

¾ cup coarsely grated
English cucumber

Kosher salt

1 cup plain whole-milk
Greek yogurt

2 tablespoons finely
chopped fresh mint leaves

1 tablespoon extra-virgin
olive oil

1 tablespoon fresh
lemon juice

1 clove garlic, minced or
pushed through a press

¼ teaspoon coarsely
ground black pepper

6 pita breads, each about
6 inches in diameter

Lemon wedges

Evenly cut cubes of pork marinated in iconic Greek flavors, then skewered and grilled, is like having Mykonos in your backyard. Leave a little room between the skewered pork pieces so the heat of the fire can reach all sides. Warm pita and a creamy yogurt sauce are the final *opa!*

| SERVES 4–6 | PREP: **30 MIN** | MARINATE: **2–4 HOURS** |  GRILL: **ABOUT 8 MIN** | SPECIAL EQUIPMENT: **6 LONG METAL OR BAMBOO SKEWERS (SOAK BAMBOO IN WATER 30 MIN)** |

1. Cut the pork loin into 1-inch-thick slices, then cut each slice into 1-inch cubes.

2. In a medium bowl whisk together all the marinade ingredients. Put the pork cubes in the bowl and stir to coat evenly. Cover and refrigerate for 2 to 4 hours.

3. In a fine-mesh sieve, toss the cucumber with ½ teaspoon salt, then press against the cucumber with the back of a spoon to force out excess moisture. In a bowl combine the cucumber and remaining tzatziki ingredients, stir to mix, and season with salt. Cover and refrigerate until serving.

4. Prepare the grill for direct cooking over high heat (450° to 550°F). Thread the pork onto 6 long metal or bamboo skewers, leaving a little space between the cubes.

5. Brush the cooking grates clean. Grill the skewers over **direct high heat**, with the lid closed as much as possible, until the pork is barely pink in the center, 5 to 7 minutes, turning once. Remove from the grill.

6. Grill the pita over **direct high heat** until streaked with light char marks, about 15 seconds on each side. To assemble, spoon some tzatziki down the middle of each pita and top with the meat. Wrap the bread around the meat and serve warm.

Tuscan Rotisserie Pork Roast

BRINE

1 cup dry white wine

½ cup cold water, plus 4 cups ice-cold water

½ cup kosher salt

¼ cup packed light brown sugar

2 fresh rosemary sprigs

2 fresh sage sprigs

1 boneless center-cut pork loin roast, about 3½ pounds

TUSCAN HERB PASTE

3 garlic cloves

2 tablespoons chopped fresh rosemary

2 tablespoons chopped fresh sage

1 tablespoon fresh lemon juice

½ teaspoon finely grated lemon zest

½ teaspoon kosher salt

¼ teaspoon ground black pepper

3 tablespoons extra-virgin olive oil

2 to 3 cups low-sodium chicken broth

4 to 5 ounces arugula

1 tablespoon extra-virgin olive oil

1 tablespoon fresh lemon juice

Finely grated zest of ½ lemon

Brining drives flavor and moisture into even the densest cuts of meat, including this lean pork loin roast. After its salty bath, the meat is smeared with a paste of garlic and herbs that also seasons the rich pan juices that are captured as the loin turns on the rotisserie.

SERVES 6-8

BRINE: **6 HOURS–OVERNIGHT**

MARINATE: **3-8 HOURS**

PREP: **35 MIN**

GRILL: **1 HOUR**

REST: **15 MIN**

SPECIAL EQUIPMENT: **ROTISSERIE, LARGE DISPOSABLE FOIL PAN**

1. In a saucepan combine the wine, cold water, salt, sugar, rosemary, and sage. Bring to a simmer over medium-high heat on the stove and simmer until the salt and sugar dissolve, stirring often. Remove from the heat and add the ice-cold water. Let the brine cool to room temperature.

2. Put the pork loin, fat side up, into a container deep and wide enough to contain it with room for the brine to cover it completely. Pour the brine over the pork. If the pork is not fully submerged, add enough cold water to cover, using a bowl or pot to weigh down the pork. Refrigerate, covered, for at least 6 hours or up to overnight.

3. Using a mortar and pestle (or a small food processor), grind together the garlic, rosemary, sage, lemon juice and zest, salt, and pepper until a relatively smooth paste forms. Blend in the oil.

4. Remove the pork from the brine and pat dry. Rub the herb paste all over the roast. Cover and refrigerate the roast for at least 3 hours and up to 8 hours. Remove from the refrigerator just prior to preparing the grill.

5. Prepare the grill for rotisserie cooking over indirect medium heat (350° to 400°F), removing the cooking grates. If using a charcoal grill, place a foil pan between the two piles of charcoal beneath the spit. If using a gas grill, place a foil pan on the grate under where the meat will be on the spit. Add 2 cups of the chicken broth to the pan.

6. To set up the spit, slide one pronged fork, with the tines facing inward, onto the spit about 10 inches from the end of the spit. Secure the fork but do not tighten it yet. Slide the spit through the roast as close to the center as possible and then gently push the meat onto the fork tines until they are deep inside. >

Tuscan Rotisserie Pork Roast

7. Add the other pronged fork to the spit with the tines facing inward and then push firmly into the meat. Secure the fork but don't tighten it yet. Wearing insulated mitts or gloves, place the spit into the rotisserie motor. If necessary, adjust the pork so it is centered over the drip pan. Tighten the forks and turn on the rotisserie.

8. Grill the pork loin over **indirect medium heat**, with the lid closed, until an instant-read thermometer inserted into the center registers 140° to 145°F, 50 minutes to 1 hour, turning off the motor before checking the temperature. Check the pan drippings after 40 minutes, and if they have evaporated, add another ½ cup to 1 cup broth.

9. Wearing insulated gloves, remove the spit from the grill and transfer the roast, on the spit, to a cutting board. Remove the drip pan from the grill. Let the meat rest for 15 minutes. Loosen the forks, slide the roast onto the board, and cut across the grain into ½-inch-thick slices. Add the juices from the board to the drip pan.

10. In a large bowl toss the arugula with the oil and lemon juice until lightly coated, then arrange on a large serving platter. (There's no need to salt the dressed arugula because the meat juices will be salty.) Place the pork slices, slightly overlapping, on the arugula. Drizzle some pan juices over the pork, then sprinkle the lemon zest over all. Serve immediately.

DINNER PARTY TIMELINE

The day before
- Buy the ingredients.
- Make the brine.
- Brine the pork overnight.

The morning of the dinner
- Make the herb paste.
- Discard the brine, rub the paste all over the pork.
- Marinate the pork in the refrigerator for 3 to 8 hours.

The evening of the dinner
- Preheat the grill.
- Start cooking at least 1¼ hours before you want to serve.

Just before serving
- Toss the arugula with dressing.
- Arrange the arugula on a platter.
- Slice the pork and arrange the slices on the platter.
- Drizzle pan juices on top and garnish with lemon zest.

Antipasti Party

ASSORTED
ITALIAN
CHEESES

MIXED
OLIVES

MARINATED
OR GRILLED
ARTICHOKE
HEARTS

ROASTED
RED PEPPERS

CRUSTY
BREAD

MARCONA ALMONDS
OR SALTED,
TOASTED NUTS

THINLY SLICED
PROSCIUTTO

BBQ GENIUS

Baby Back Ribs with Cola Barbecue Sauce
RECIPE ON PAGE 186

BABY BACK RIBS

Arcing 4 to 5 inches from each side of a hog's backbone (literally "high on the hog") are two top sections of a rib cage where we get racks of baby back ribs. The meat on each rack comes from the pork loin, a long cylinder of flesh that yields various pork chops. Baby back ribs are basically pork chop meat divided among several bones. If you season these ribs with a blend of spices and cook them gently with husky aromas of smoldering wood, the rewards are glorious. A thin layer of sauce on top moistens and sweetens the whole act.

everything ribs

Q: Should I make baby back ribs or spareribs?

A: Baby back ribs are smaller, potentially more tender, and also quite a bit more expensive. Spareribs are meatier, chewier, and less expensive. Usually spareribs take longer to cook than baby back ribs. For more details about these and other types of pork ribs, see page 195.

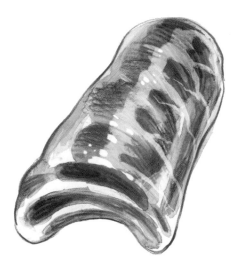

Q: What should I look for when choosing ribs?

A: It's the meat we eat, so look for a good ½ inch or so of meat riding on top of the bones. If you see any bare bones, that means a butcher has cut away too much meat and has created "shiners." Skip those ribs. The color of the meat on a good rack should be light pink (not too red) and evenly marbled with fat. Avoid racks with large sections of pure fat.

Q: Do I need to peel the membrane off of the ribs or not?

A: We recommend that you do peel the membrane from the bone side of your ribs. Some high-volume barbecue restaurants do not do this because it takes too much of their time, but we think it is worth doing at home. The membrane, which is a section of the pulmonary pleura that surrounds the lungs, acts like thin, tough layer of masking tape that just gets tougher and chewier as it cooks.

Q: What's the best method for cooking ribs?

A: For tender rib meat, use very low to low indirect heat (in the range of 225° to 275°F). Forget about any notion that boiling the ribs first will improve them. The hot water toughens the meat and pulls out all kinds of fat and flavor. A smoker designed to maintain low temperatures for hours is an ideal piece of equipment for this, but you can certainly use a kettle grill, too (see page 36). A gas grill will also work well (see page 40).

Q: What's the best kind of wood to use when smoking ribs?

A: A lot of hot air blows around the barbecue world regarding the "right" wood, yet even seasoned professionals are hard-pressed to identify accurately what kind of wood was used on a particular rack of ribs. Don't overthink this. Use whatever hardwood you like, such as hickory, oak, cherry, or apple.

The key is not to overdo the smoke. (Too much smoke is a much more common mistake than using the "wrong" type of hardwood.) Also, you don't need to smoke ribs every time. They can be quite good without smoke.

Q: I hear that pork ribs absorb smoke better when they are raw and/or wet. Is this because meat is more porous when raw, or that the smoke is water soluble?

A: The campers among us might be familiar with this principle. Ever pack up your tent and gear on a dewy morning after the campfire has been roaring all night? That smoky scent lingers . . . and lingers . . . and lingers. Smoke is nothing more than superfine particulate matter made up of nitrogen oxides and other by-products of burning fuel. As it wafts, those particulates will stick to clingy, moist surfaces like raw pork ribs—or a damp tent. As for the solubility factor, lots of these tasty compounds are actually fat soluble, so a layer of oil on the meat will be an additional help. Don't try that on tents, though.

Q: When should I sauce the ribs?

A: The sauce should go on early enough that it has time to cook into the meat but not so early that it might burn. A sweet barbecue sauce should go on during the final 20 to 30 minutes of cooking. Brush it on lightly; it should glaze the meat, not drown it.

Q: How will I know they are done?

A: When you lift a rack at one end with tongs, bone side up, and the rack bends so easily in the middle that the meat begins to tear open, the ribs are done. Also, when you twist the end of a bone with a pair of tongs, it should turn a bit. With each bite, the meat should pull clean off the bone, but it should not be mushy.

GRILL SCIENCE

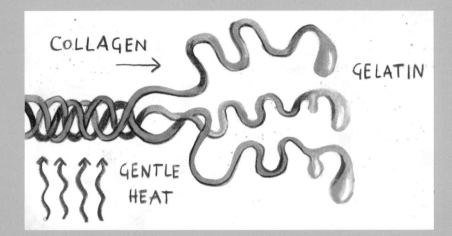

Why do ribs take so long to cook? Why is the "low and slow" approach better than cooking "hot and fast"?

First, don't think of that extra cooking time as a burden. Look on it as an opportunity to tackle such grill-adjacent chores as pulling weeds, cleaning out the car, or drinking a beer. But the reason we can't blast ribs with a few minutes of heat and call it a day is the sinewy connective tissue that gives them their tough texture.

Ribs need both the right temperature (225° to 300°F) and plenty of time (could be hours, depending on the kind of ribs) to break down the collagen in the connective tissue—and lots of tissue means lots of work to be done. As those collagen molecules slowly unravel in the heat, they loosen their kung fu grip on one another and become gelatin, which imparts a velvety, toothsome quality to ribs cooked low and slow. Additionally, the collagen binds with water and helps that moisture to stay put.

Baby Back Ribs with Cola Barbecue Sauce

RIB RUB

1 tablespoon kosher salt

1 tablespoon smoked paprika

1 tablespoon granulated onion

1 tablespoon prepared chili powder

2 teaspoons ground cumin

1 teaspoon celery seeds

1 teaspoon ground black pepper

2 racks meaty baby back ribs, each about 3 pounds

2 tablespoons yellow mustard

BASTING MIXTURE

6 tablespoons (¾ stick) unsalted butter

2 tablespoons cider vinegar

COLA BARBECUE SAUCE

1 cup ketchup

1 cup cola

3 tablespoons cider vinegar

2 tablespoons molasses

2 tablespoons yellow mustard

1 tablespoon Worcestershire sauce

1 teaspoon prepared chili powder

Here, a crunchy, flavor-packed corona of spice, fat, and char dutifully shields the supple meat within. Achieving this outcome depends on maintaining a steady low temperature (no higher than 300°F) and periodically basting any dry-looking areas with a butter-vinegar mixture.

1. In a small bowl mix together all the rub ingredients. Set aside 2 teaspoons for the basting mixture.

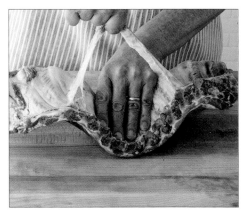

2. Trim any excess fat from the ribs. Using a dull knife, slide the tip under the membrane covering the back of each rib rack. Lift and loosen the membrane until you can pry it up, then grab a corner of it with a paper towel or your fingers and pull it off.

6. Meanwhile, combine the sauce ingredients in a saucepan and bring to a gentle boil over medium-high heat on the stove, stirring often. Reduce the heat to low and simmer until the mixture thickens to a consistency that coats the back of a spoon, 15 to 20 minutes, stirring occasionally. You should have about 1½ cups sauce.

7. When the ribs have cooked for 1½ hours, swap the positions of the racks for even cooking. Lightly baste both sides of the ribs with the butter mixture. Continue cooking, bone side down, over **indirect very low heat,** with the lid closed, for 1½ hours longer.

3. Lightly coat the ribs evenly with the mustard and then season them all over with the rub. The mustard will help the seasoning to stick to the meat. Let the ribs stand at room temperature for 30 minutes to 1 hour before cooking.

4. Meanwhile, prepare a grill or smoker for indirect cooking over very low heat (250° to 300°F). Melt the butter with the vinegar in a small saucepan or skillet over low heat on the stove and stir in the reserved 2 teaspoons rub. Set aside off the heat for basting.

5. Brush the cooking grates clean. Add the wood chunks to the coals (or drain and add wood chips to the grill) and close the lid. When smoke appears, grill the ribs flat, bone side down, over **indirect very low heat**, with the lid closed, for 1½ hours. During that time, maintain the temperature between 250° and 300°F.

8. After 3 hours of cooking, work quickly to brush the ribs on both sides with some of the sauce. Close the lid quickly to maintain the temperature. Continue to cook the ribs, bone side down, over **indirect very low heat** for about 15 minutes.

9. Check for doneness. The meat should have shrunk back from the ends of most of the bones by ¼ inch or more. If it has not, continue cooking until nearly done, about 15 minutes. Lightly brush each rack again on both sides with more sauce.

10. The ribs are done if when you pick up a rack at one end with tongs and bend it, the meat near the middle begins to tear. Remove from the grill, lightly brush with more sauce, and cut between the bones into individual ribs. Serve warm with the remaining sauce on the side.

Honey-Teriyaki Glazed Baby Back Ribs

FIVE-SPICE RUB

3 tablespoons packed dark brown sugar

1½ tablespoons kosher salt

2 teaspoons Chinese five spice

3 racks meaty baby back ribs, each 2½ to 3 pounds

HONEY-TERIYAKI GLAZE

1 tablespoon toasted sesame oil

3 tablespoons peeled, finely chopped fresh ginger

3 garlic cloves, minced

1 tablespoon sesame seeds

⅔ cup honey

⅓ cup reduced-sodium soy sauce

2 tablespoons seasoned rice vinegar

1 tablespoon chili-garlic sauce, such as Sriracha

1 tablespoon cornstarch, dissolved in 3 tablespoons cold water

This recipe is for all you gas grillers with smoker boxes. Smoking in a charcoal grill is always an option (follow the instructions on page 38), but we like the ease of setting a grill to cook and smoke at a steady 275°F for a few hours without any fire tending necessary.

1. In a small bowl mix together all the rub ingredients. To remove the membrane from the racks, see Step 2 on page 186. Season the racks with the rub, being sure to put more of it on the meaty side of each rack and less on the bone side.

2. For the glaze, heat the oil in a skillet over medium heat on the stove. Add the ginger, garlic, and sesame seeds and cook, stirring often, until fragrant and slightly softened, 2 to 3 minutes. Add the honey, soy sauce, vinegar, and chili-garlic sauce, bring to a simmer, and cook for 2 minutes, stirring occasionally.

3. Increase the heat to medium-high and bring the mixture to a boil. Stir the cornstarch mixture briefly to recombine, then gradually add it to the pan while whisking constantly and boil until thickened, about 1 minute. Remove from the heat and reserve.

4. Before lighting the grill, drain the wood chips and add them to the smoker box. If you don't have a built-in smoker box, set the box you are using under the cooking grate directly over a burner to one side of the grill. If it will not fit, place it on top of the cooking grate to one side over the burner.

5. Prepare the grill for indirect cooking over high heat (450° to 550°F). Brush the cooking grates clean. When smoke appears, lower the temperature to low heat (275° to 300°F). Lay the rib racks, bone side down, on the cooking grates over **indirect low heat**. Close the lid and cook for 1½ hours, keeping the temperature at 275° to 300°F. >

REGULATING HEAT

You shouldn't let any parts of these ribs cook over direct heat, even just a little. The flames below could blacken the ribs. If your grill is wide enough, light one burner on the far right and one on the far left, leaving plenty of room in the middle for the ribs to cook over indirect heat. If your grill is not that wide, light just one burner on one side. After each hour of cooking, swap the positions of the racks so they cook evenly.

6. Brush the racks lightly on both sides with the glaze. Turn them bone side up and continue cooking over **indirect low heat**, with the lid closed, for 30 minutes. Continue to brush the racks with the glaze on both sides and to turn them every 30 minutes, rotating the position of the racks occasionally, until fully cooked. The total cooking time will be 2½ to 3½ hours.

7. The ribs are done if when you pick up a rack at one end with tongs and bend it, the meat near the middle begins to tear.

8. Remove the racks from the grill. With the bone side facing up so you can see the ribs clearly, cut between the bones into individual ribs to serve. Serve warm.

The Snake Method on a Charcoal Grill

This method with a daunting name is a clever way to keep a fire burning low and slow for hours without needing to replenish it. You arrange the briquettes in a snake-like curve around the perimeter of a charcoal grill, and the fire burns slowly from one end to the other (like a bomb's fuse in an old cartoon), getting neither too hot nor requiring a lot of babysitting. Here's how to do it.

First, make sure the bottom of the grill is swept clean of ashes and the bottom vents are wide open so the fire will get plenty of air. Then form two rows of briquettes, neatly packed and touching, around the perimeter of about half of the charcoal grate. The longer the snake, the longer the fire will last. Stack two more rows on top of the first two rows, to create a charcoal configuration that is two briquettes wide and two briquettes high. Arrange four or five wood chunks in a row over one end of the snake. This is where you will start the fire.

In a chimney starter, light 10 to 12 briquettes. Meanwhile, place a disposable foil pan on the charcoal grate next to the snake and fill the pan about three-fourths full with warm water. When the briquettes are covered with white ash, use tongs to pile them carefully over the "head" of the snake, near the wood chunks.

Set the cooking grate in place, close the grill lid, and adjust the damper on the lid so the vent is about halfway open. Preheat the grill until the temperature falls between 250° and 300°F. Brush the cooking grate clean, then place your food in the center of the grate so no part is directly above the snake. Use the damper on the lid to control the airflow and temperature of the fire. Sit back and listen to that grill hiss.

St. Louis Ribs with Smoked Onion BBQ Sauce

RUB

2 tablespoons kosher salt

2 tablespoons coarsely ground black pepper

2 tablespoons packed dark brown sugar

2 tablespoons granulated garlic

3 racks St. Louis–style spareribs, each 2½ to 3 pounds

APPLE CIDER MOP

⅔ cup apple juice

¼ cup cider vinegar

3 tablespoons packed dark brown sugar

1 tablespoon hot sauce, such as Frank's RedHot®

SMOKED ONION BBQ SAUCE

1 medium Vidalia or other sweet onion (10 to 12 ounces), unpeeled, halved lengthwise

2 tablespoons extra-virgin olive oil

2 large garlic cloves, minced

1¼ cups ketchup

¼ cup cider vinegar

¼ cup packed dark brown sugar

1 tablespoon Worcestershire sauce

2½ teaspoons prepared chili powder

2 teaspoons smoked paprika

Move quickly when basting and repositioning these ribs so the lid goes back on the smoker before too much heat is lost. When the ribs are done, a toothpick should slide through the meat as smoothly as poking a ripe banana through the peel: a little resistance at first, then an easy slide.

1. Following the directions on pages 38 and 39, prepare a water smoker for indirect cooking over very low heat (225° to 275°F). In a small bowl stir together all the rub ingredients.

2. Place the rib racks, bone side up, on a cutting board. If the ribs still have the membrane attached, remove it: Using a dull knife, slide the tip under the membrane covering the back of each rib rack. Lift and loosen the membrane until you can pry it up, then grab a corner of it with a paper towel and pull it off.

3. Season the racks on both sides with the rub, rubbing more of the mixture into the meaty side of each rack. In a medium bowl whisk together all the mop ingredients until the sugar dissolves.

4. Add four hardwood chunks to the charcoal. Place the onion halves on the lower rack over indirect heat. Place the ribs, meaty side up, on the top rack over indirect heat. Smoke the onion and ribs over **indirect very low heat**, with the lid closed, for 1½ hours.

5. Using long tongs, transfer the onion halves to a cutting board. Check the ribs at this point, and if the surface is starting to look dry, transfer them to a baking sheet (this ensures the smoker remains at the ideal heat) to brush with the apple cider mop.

6. After brushing both sides of each rib rack with the mop, add the remaining two wood chunks to the charcoal. Cook the ribs for 1½ to 3 hours longer. After each hour, brush each rack quickly with the mop, then rotate the position of each rack so they cook evenly. Add charcoal as needed to maintain the temperature. >

St. Louis Ribs with Smoked Onion BBQ Sauce

7. While the ribs are cooking, peel and mince the smoked onion (about 1 cup). Heat the oil in a medium saucepan over medium heat on the stove. Add the onion and cook, stirring occasionally, until very soft and golden brown, 5 to 10 minutes. Add the garlic and cook for 30 seconds, stirring frequently.

8. Stir in the ketchup, vinegar, sugar, Worcestershire sauce, chili powder, and paprika. Reduce the heat to low and simmer, stirring frequently, until the sauce is thickened and reduced to about 2 cups, about 5 minutes.

9. The ribs are done when the meat has shrunk back from the bones by at least ½ inch and you can easily slide a skewer through the meat between the bones. Another good test is to lift a rack by picking up one end with tongs. If the rack bends in the middle and the meat tears easily, the ribs are ready. Discard any remaining mop.

10. When the ribs are ready, brush both sides of each rack generously with the onion sauce. Close the lid and continue to cook over **indirect very low heat** for 10 to 20 minutes.

11. Transfer the racks to a cutting board. Let rest for 5 to 10 minutes. Cut between the bones into individual ribs. Serve warm with the remaining sauce on the side.

All About Ribs

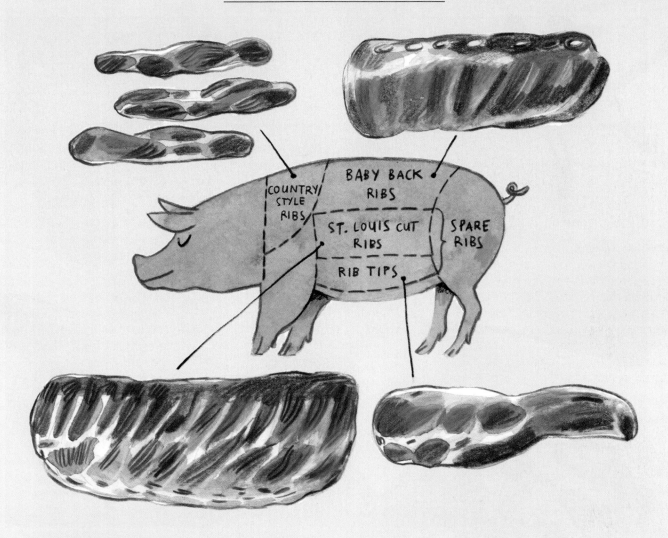

BABY BACK RIBS Let's consider "the highs and lows" of a hog's rib section. Way up high, near the backbone, is a section 4 to 5 inches tall where we get racks of baby back ribs. A full rack of these ribs will usually have 12 bones spaced tightly together, with less than an inch of meat between them. Most of the meat sits on top of the bones, and the total weight of the rack is 2 to 2½ pounds.

SPARERIBS The area just below the baby back ribs is where a full rack of spareribs (or "spares") begins The bones spread apart a bit as they get closer to the belly, so there is more meat between them. A full rack, weighing 3 to 4 pounds, still has the sternum attached. If you cut off the sternum, which a lot of butchers do because it has so much cartilage and connective tissue, the spareribs start to look more like baby back ribs. If you

cut off the triangular tip on one end, you get a rectangular shape called the St. Louis cut. St. Louis ribs lie flat, while the bones of baby back ribs are curved.

RIB TIPS Rib tips are the chewy bands of cartilage, bone, and scant meat that are cut from the lower (belly) end of spareribs. In some parts of the world, chewing on them is considered a primal pleasure. In other parts, gnawing on them is considered more work than they are worth, even though they are usually cheap.

COUNTRY-STYLE RIBS Country-style ribs don't come from a rib cage; they come from a shoulder. Yes, they are a part of the shoulder near the baby back ribs, but they are still not really ribs. Meaty and gristly, they are more like pork chops and sold individually, so they are usually cooked with direct (not indirect) heat.

Pulled Pork with Carolina Sauce
RECIPE ON PAGE 198

PULLED PORK

The shoulder of a pig bears a good deal of weight and gets a fair amount of exercise, so the muscle gets quite firm and tight. One of the best ways to tenderize that muscle is to cook it slowly to break down the fibers and connective tissue. Here are some pointers on how to do that properly, so you can pull the meat into delectable shreds.

Top Tips for the Ultimate Pulled Pork

1. Choose the preferred part. A whole shoulder consists of two parts: the upper and the lower part. The upper part is the "Boston butt," the section closest to the neck. It has more connective tissue and less bone than the lower part, so it has the potential to be more tender. The lower part is the "picnic" or "picnic ham," which tends to have larger sections of fat and a lot more bone. We prefer to use Boston butt or simply "pork butt" for making pulled pork.

2. Bone in or boneless? A bone-in or boneless pork butt will work on a grill or smoker, but for the ultimate version, bone-in pork butt is a better choice. A solid piece of meat made up of a few different muscles held together by bone and connective tissue will always cook more evenly than a hunk of meat that has been divided into uneven sections. Yes, a boneless pork butt will cook faster, but here, more time means better results.

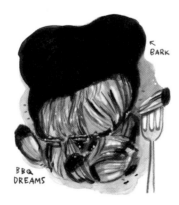

3. Focus on temperature. A pork butt is a forgiving cut of meat, which means you can overcook it a bit or cook it a little too hot and fast and it will still be good. But for ultimate results, you will want your grill or smoker to be holding a steady 250°F. That's the temperature that will give you both moist results and a nice, crusty "bark," that highly-seasoned layer of fat, smoke, and spices that is the goal of every barbecue fanatic. Another important number is 203°F, which is the internal temperature you want the meat to reach before you take it off the heat. At that point, the abundant connective tissue will have melted into luscious gelatin—the stuff of barbecue dreams.

4. Buy extra, especially for a party. Plan to buy about 1 pound pork shoulder per person. More than one-fourth of that weight will be lost during cooking. If you have leftovers, toss them with barbecue sauce and freeze them. Reheat by microwaving the frozen meat. The texture will lose some of its succulence, but the meat will still make mighty fine eating the second time around.

5. Wrap the meat. Just like with brisket, the internal temperature of pork will climb and climb and then suddenly plateau in the cooking process. At that point, there will be so much evaporation occurring on the surface of the meat that it will cool the meat, and the internal temperature will temporarily stall at about 150° to 160°F. When that happens, wrap the meat in butcher paper to slow the rate of evaporation and speed up the cooking.

Pulled Pork with Carolina Sauce

1 bone-in pork shoulder roast (Boston butt), about 6 pounds

RUB

1 tablespoon packed dark brown sugar

1 tablespoon sweet paprika

1 tablespoon kosher salt

1½ teaspoons garlic powder

1 teaspoon onion powder

1 teaspoon ground black pepper

½ teaspoon dry mustard

1 tablespoon olive oil

About ½ cup cider vinegar

CAROLINA SAUCE

¾ cup cider vinegar

¼ cup water

4 teaspoons packed dark brown sugar

1½ teaspoons sweet paprika

1½ teaspoons hot sauce, such as Tabasco®

1 teaspoon crushed red pepper flakes

¾ teaspoon dry mustard

¾ teaspoon garlic powder

¾ teaspoon kosher salt

10 to 12 burger buns, split

Creamy Coleslaw (page 341) or your favorite coleslaw (optional)

This classic, straight from the canon of American barbecue, is best when the meat pulls apart effortlessly. That happens when the pork is cooked gently for a long time so the collagen in its proteins melts into soft gelatin. Though the meat is "overcooked," the rendered fat and gelatin keep it moist.

1. Using a sharp knife, trim the fat on the roast down to a thickness of ¼ inch. This will allow the remaining fat to melt more easily while in the smoker. Flip the roast over, slide the knife under any visible fibrous silver skin, and use a sawing motion to remove it.

2. In a bowl stir together the rub ingredients. Rub the roast all over with the oil, then season it all over with the rub. Allow the roast to stand at room temperature for 30 minutes. Following the directions on page 38, prepare a water smoker for indirect cooking over very low heat (225° to 250°F). Brush the grates clean.

6. After 4 hours of cooking, use an instant-read thermometer to check the internal temperature of the roast. If it has not reached 160°F, continue cooking it until it does, as much as 1 hour longer.

7. Once the roast has reached 160°F, it will have developed a nice exterior "bark," (see page 145) and the bark will have split so the fat is visible.

3. Add half of the wood chunks to the charcoal and close the lid. When smoke appears, place the roast, fat side up, over **very low indirect heat** and cook, with the lid closed, adjusting the bottom vents and adding additional charcoal as needed to maintain the temperature of the smoker at 225° to 250°F.

4. After 2 hours of cooking, add the remaining wood chunks. Put the vinegar in a spray bottle and lightly spray the roast with the vinegar. Repeat to spray the roast every 2 hours.

5. Meanwhile, make the sauce: In a medium bowl whisk together all the sauce ingredients until the sugar and salt dissolve.

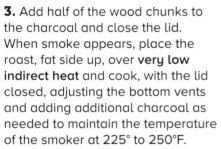

8. Stack two large sheets of butcher paper or heavy-duty aluminum foil. Wearing insulated gloves, transfer the roast to the stacked sheets. Spray the meat again with vinegar, wrap the meat in the paper or foil, and set in a large, heavy-duty aluminum roasting pan.

9. Return the roast to the smoker and cook over **indirect very low heat**, with the lid closed, until the internal temperature registers 200° to 205°F, 2 to 3 hours longer. At that point, the blade bone should look moist but separate easily from the meat. Remove the pan from the smoker and let the roast rest, wrapped, for 1 hour.

10. Unwrap the roast. When it is just cool enough to handle (it will still be quite hot, so gloves are a good idea), use two forks or "bear claws" to pull the meat apart into shreds. Discard any large pieces of fat and sinew. Transfer to a bowl and moisten the meat with the sauce. Serve at once on buns, with coleslaw if you like.

Carnitas with All the Fixings
RECIPE ON PAGE 202

CARNITAS

When planning your next party, look to *carnitas* tacos. A single pork shoulder produces enough meat to feed a crowd, and an assemble-it-yourself taco topping bar makes life easier for the hosts. The amount of slaw here is just enough for the tacos, but you may want to double the recipe and serve it as a side salad, too. It's that good!

Carnitas with All the Fixings

RUB

1 tablespoon kosher salt

1 tablespoon ground cumin

1 tablespoon prepared chili powder or chipotle chile powder

1 teaspoon ground black pepper

1 boneless pork shoulder roast (Boston butt), 3 to 4 pounds

2 tablespoons packed light brown sugar

2 teaspoons dried oregano

1 large yellow onion, cut into eighths

5 garlic cloves, smashed

¼ cup finely chopped chipotle chile peppers in adobo sauce

2 bay leaves

1 orange, cut into eighths

¼ cup olive oil

RED CABBAGE SLAW

⅓ cup fresh lime juice

3 tablespoons vegetable oil

2 teaspoons kosher salt

½ teaspoon ground cumin

½ teaspoon ground black pepper

1 head red cabbage, shredded

2 carrots, peeled and coarsely grated

Corn or flour tortillas, warmed

Pico de Gallo (page 340)

Guacamole (page 340)

Queso fresco

Fresh cilantro sprigs

2 limes, quartered

Velvety, moist *carnitas* may look like pulled pork, but they are actually more like pork confit, or pork cooked in its own fat. The fat acts as a heat buffer, keeping the muscle fibers from cooking too fast and squeezing out all their moisture before the collagen has had time to melt into rich gelatin.

1. Prepare the grill for direct cooking over medium heat (350° to 450°F). In a small bowl stir together all the rub ingredients. Evenly coat the pork with the rub. Brush the cooking grates clean.

2. Grill the pork over **direct medium heat**, with the lid closed, until browned on all sides, 8 to 10 minutes, turning as needed. Transfer the pork to a cutting board. Adjust the heat for indirect cooking over low heat (325°F).

6. While the pork is cooking, make the slaw. In a large bowl whisk together the lime juice, vegetable oil, sugar, salt, cumin, and pepper. Add the cabbage and carrot and toss to coat well. Let stand for 30 minutes, stirring occasionally (or refrigerate if not using right away).

7. When the pork is ready, adjust the grill for direct cooking over medium-high heat (about 450°F). Place a cast-iron griddle over direct heat, close the lid, and preheat until very hot. Using tongs, transfer the pork to a cutting board. Pour the cooking liquid through a fine-mesh sieve into a bowl (discard the solids). Allow the fat to rise to the surface.

3. Cut the pork into roughly 2-inch chunks and add to a 12-inch cast-iron skillet or 8-quart Dutch oven. Sprinkle with the brown sugar and oregano and toss to coat.

4. Evenly distribute the onion, garlic, chipotle chiles, and bay leaves among the meat. Squeeze the orange pieces over all the ingredients, then tuck the spent rinds into the meat. Pour the olive oil evenly over all. Cover with aluminum foil or a lid.

5. Cook the pork over **indirect low heat**, with the grill lid closed, until fork-tender, about 3 hours. (The meat should easily pull apart when gently tugged with a fork.)

8. Using your fingers or two forks, shred the pork into bite-size chunks.

9. Skim the fat off the top of the cooking liquid and transfer to a bowl. Drizzle 2 to 3 tablespoons of the fat over the pork to moisten. Grease the hot griddle with another tablespoon of the fat, then add half of the pork.

10. Fry the pork until the edges are crisp and caramelized, about 5 minutes, stirring occasionally. Transfer to a serving bowl. Repeat with the remaining pork, adding more fat if needed. Season the pork with salt if desired. Serve family-style with the tortillas, slaw, pico de gallo, guacamole, queso fresco, cilantro, and limes.

Dinner with Friends

Asparagus with Lemon Vinaigrette, recipe on page 288; **Spatchcocked Chicken with Chimichurri,** recipe on page 230; **Grilled Peach Salad with Goat Cheese,** recipe on page 74; **Roasted Red Potatoes with Herbs,** recipe on page 316

POULTRY

BBQ
GENIUS

Chicken Breasts with
Green Herb Salsa
RECIPE ON PAGE 210

CHICKEN BREASTS

Boneless, skinless chicken breasts can seem like the romantic comedies of the food world: light and easy to consume. But what makes them approachable is also what leaves them lacking in depth or complexity. Although the health benefits might be formidable, the bland flavors are often forgettable. It's time we give these birds some help. When seasoned and grilled correctly, white chicken meat can be juicy, succulent, and flavorful. Consider what follows your winning script for blockbuster chicken.

Q&A

everything chicken breasts

Q: Okay, I'm at the meat counter. What should I be looking for?

A: Bigger does not necessarily mean better. Larger chicken breasts take longer to cook, which can lead to judgment errors in determining done-ness and thus overcooking. For the best results, choose chicken breast halves that weigh 6 to 8 ounces.

Consider shape, too. Boneless chicken breasts are naturally plump in the middle and tapered at the ends, meaning the ends cook long before the center. Most prepackaged chicken breasts are uniform in thick-ness. If the breasts you buy are uneven, either lightly pound them to an even ¾ inch thick or butterfly the thicker part of each breast.

Q: What kind of chicken should I buy: organic, free-range, or conventional?

A: It's up to your taste, wallet, and consumer philosophy. Keep in mind that conventional chicken is sometimes plumped with a saline solution, which can affect cooking time and sodium content. Check the label before purchasing.

Q: What are some easy ways to add flavor?

A: The seasoning does not need to be fancy. A liberal sprinkling of kosher salt and ground black pepper along with a drizzle of olive oil to prevent sticking is simple yet tasty. But ratcheting up the flavors with a robust spice rub or a tangy marinade (see pages 212 and 213)—even if it is just a store-bought vinaigrette or teriyaki sauce—is encouraged, too.

Scoring the chicken is an optional step that will help any marinade or other seasoning flavor the meat more fully. Using a sharp knife, lightly score on the diagonal on the smooth (skin) side of the breasts, cutting about ¼ inch deep into the meat.

Q: Any good ground rules for seasoning or marinating?

A: If using oil and spices, coat the meat with oil first so the spices will stick better. For a liquid marinade, put the chicken in a resealable plastic bag, add the marinade, and seal closed. Turn the bag to distribute the marinade evenly, then refrigerate, turning the bag occasionally. When ready to grill, lift out the chicken, letting any excess liquid drip back into the bag. If the chicken is drip-ping wet, it will steam, rather than brown, on the grill.

Q: How long should the chicken marinate?

A: The minimum is 30 minutes, which will add decent flavor and gives you time to prepare the grill and set the table, and the maximum is 24 hours. Keep in mind the longer the chicken marinates, the deeper the flavor. Of course, if your marinade contains an acidic ingredient, like vinegar or lemon juice, you'll want to be sure to pull the chicken from the marinade by that 24-hour mark, or the acid will start breaking down the proteins in the meat too much.

Q: What's the best way to prepare the grill for chicken breasts?

A: Set up the grill for direct cooking over medium heat. It should be as close to 400°F as possible, which is the midpoint of the medium-heat range. To prevent sticking, be sure to clean the grill grates well before placing the chicken on them. If the chicken is well browned before it's cooked through, slide it to a cooler area of the grill to finish.

Q: Cool. Grill is prepared. So what's the best way to grill the chicken?

A: Arrange the chicken breasts at an angle to the grill grates and resist the temptation to move them. Let them cook on the first side, with the lid closed, for 4 to 6 minutes—sufficient time to develop flavorful grill marks—before flipping.

If the breasts don't release easily, leave them a little longer. Cook on the second side until well grill-marked and cooked through, 4 to 6 minutes longer. The total cooking time will vary depending on the thickness of the breasts. Let rest for a few minutes before serving.

Q: Do I have to watch the chicken while it grills?

A: Yes. It's worth 10 minutes of your time, especially if the marinade or seasoning contains sugar, which can burn on the grill. If the chicken begins to scorch, move it to a cooler area to finish cooking.

Q: When do I apply a glaze?

A: Glazes, such as a barbecue sauce or a reduced marinade, are often rich in sugar and should only be applied in the last few minutes of grilling or they can burn.

Q: When is a chicken breast done?

A: Some chefs and experienced grillers can tell if the chicken is done by the texture of the meat. It's soft when raw. It's still a little jiggly when undercooked. And when it is fully cooked, it feels firm, like a peeled soft-boiled egg, but not hard. The surest way to know is with a good thermometer. Insert the probe into the thickest part of the breast. When the internal temperature registers 165°F, the chicken is done.

GRILL SCIENCE

What must a marinade include to make chicken taste better?

Do you have a sweet tooth? Do you like tangy flavors? Do you err on the side of salt? Knowing what you and your dining partners enjoy will inform your choices. But first, the caveats: The sugars in sweet ingredients could quickly and easily burn, turning your marinade to a bitter-tasting mess if you're not careful. Opt for sweeter sauces, like barbecue sauces, on the side instead.

On the other hand, salt should be part of any marinade. Beyond the flavor aspect, salt throws its little molecular elbows around the meat proteins, clearing the way for—and clinging to—moisture. Soy sauce, fish sauce, and jalapeño pickling liquid will add the necessary NaCl (salt) and a unique flavor profile.

Plus, add some oil. Use a type with a high smoke (read: burning) point, like corn, canola, or safflower oil. The oil will prevent sticking and will help keep the outermost layer of flavorings on the meat, rather than on the grill grates.

Chicken Breasts with Green Herb Salsa

GREEN HERB SALSA

1 cup packed fresh
Italian parsley leaves
and tender stems

½ cup packed fresh
cilantro sprigs

½ cup packed fresh
mint leaves

2 large garlic cloves

1 small jalapeño or serrano
chile pepper, stemmed
and quartered

1 tablespoon red
wine vinegar

1 tablespoon fresh
lemon juice

1 teaspoon finely grated
lemon zest

¾ teaspoon kosher salt

½ cup extra-virgin
olive oil

4 boneless, skinless
chicken breast halves,
tenders removed, each
6 to 8 ounces

Lemon wedges, for serving
(optional)

Chicken breasts are easy to overcook. Two simple adjustments will keep them juicy and flavorful. First, remove the tenders and cook them separately. Then make a few shallow cuts into the smooth side of each breast. Now the meat will cook more quickly, meaning less time to dry out.

1. In a food processor combine all the salsa ingredients except the oil. Pulse to chop coarsely.

2. With the motor running, add the oil through the feed tube in a steady stream, processing until a pesto-like consistency forms (the herbs will be finely chopped).

6. Prepare the grill for direct cooking over medium heat (about 400°F). Brush the cooking grates clean. Remove the chicken from the marinade, allowing any excess marinade to drip back into the bowl to avoid flare-ups. Place the chicken, smooth (skin) side down, on an angle to the grate bars over **direct medium heat.** (Discard the marinade.)

7. Grill on the first side, with the lid closed, until the chicken breasts are well grill-marked and release easily from the grates, 4 to 6 minutes. Flip the chicken and repeat on the other side, until firm to the touch and opaque all the way to the center, 4 to 6 minutes longer.

SERVES **4**

PREP: **15 MIN**

MARINATE:
30 MIN–24 HOURS

GRILL: **8–12 MIN**

REST: **3 MIN**

3. Transfer ⅓ cup of the herb mixture to a shallow medium bowl and reserve the remaining salsa for serving. (The flavors of the salsa will develop as it stands while you marinate the chicken.)

4. Lightly score the chicken breasts on the diagonal, on the smooth (skin) side, making 3 or 4 evenly spaced slashes each about ¼ inch deep.

5. Put the chicken in the bowl with the herb mixture and turn the chicken to coat evenly with the marinade. Cover with plastic wrap and refrigerate for at least 30 minutes and up to 24 hours, turning the chicken occasionally.

8. Remove from the grill and let rest for a few minutes. Serve with the reserved salsa and the lemon wedges, if using.

FLAVOR BOMB *your* CHICKEN BREAST

You'll appreciate what a difference you can make when you marinate chicken breasts in something wonderful for at least half an hour. After being expertly grilled, it makes perfect sense to top them off with flavors that play well with what was in the marinade.

TOMATO BRUSCHETTA

Marinate the chicken in 1 cup Balsamic Vinaigrette (page 340) for at least 30 minutes and up to overnight. To make the topping, stir together 2 cups finely chopped seeded tomatoes, 2 tablespoons finely chopped fresh basil leaves, 2 teaspoons extra-virgin olive oil, ½ teaspoon kosher salt, ¼ teaspoon ground black pepper, and 1 large garlic clove, minced. Season the chicken with salt and pepper. Grill the chicken according to the recipe on page 210. Spoon the topping over the chicken. Serve with grilled bread.

HONEY SRIRACHA LIME

In a small bowl whisk together ¼ cup fresh lime juice, ¼ cup honey, 2 tablespoons soy sauce, 2 tablespoons Dijon mustard, 2 tablespoons vegetable oil, 1½ tablespoons Sriracha sauce, and 2 garlic cloves, minced. Use half to marinate the chicken according to the recipe on page 210. In a saucepan, boil the remaining sauce on the stove until thickened to a glaze. Grill the chicken according to the recipe. Brush the glaze over the grilled chicken. Garnish with chopped scallions or fresh cilantro and slices of lime.

HAWAIIAN

Marinate the chicken in ¾ cup store-bought teriyaki sauce for at least 30 minutes and up to overnight. To make the salsa, stir together 1 cup finely diced pineapple, ½ cup finely diced red bell pepper, ¼ cup finely diced red onion, 2 tablespoons finely chopped fresh cilantro leaves, 1 tablespoon fresh lime juice, ¼ teaspoon kosher salt, ⅛ teaspoon ground black pepper, and 1 small jalapeño chile pepper, seeded and minced. Grill the chicken according to the recipe on page 210. Serve with the salsa.

ASIAGO BREAD CRUMBS

Marinate the chicken in 1 cup Italian Vinaigrette (page 341) for at least 30 minutes and up to overnight. Combine ¼ cup freshly grated Asiago cheese, 1 tablespoon finely chopped fresh Italian parsley leaves, ¼ teaspoon kosher salt, ⅛ teaspoon ground black pepper, and ¼ cup panko (Japanese bread crumbs), toasted, and mix well. Season the chicken with ¾ teaspoon kosher salt and ½ teaspoon ground black pepper, then grill the chicken according to the recipe on page 210. During the last 3 to 4 minutes of cooking, spread the seasoned bread crumbs evenly over the tops of the chicken breasts. Serve with lemon wedges.

Chicken Breasts with Red Wine–Onion Jam

RED WINE–ONION JAM

1 large red onion, finely chopped

1½ cups fruity red wine, such as Zinfandel

2 tablespoons cassis

1 tablespoon red wine vinegar

1 large fresh rosemary sprig

½ teaspoon kosher salt

¼ teaspoon ground black pepper

1 tablespoon extra-virgin olive oil

2 teaspoons maple syrup or packed light brown sugar

1 teaspoon finely grated orange zest

4 boneless, skinless chicken breast halves, each 6 to 8 ounces

3 tablespoons extra-virgin olive oil

2 tablespoons white wine vinegar

1 teaspoon finely chopped fresh oregano leaves, or ½ teaspoon dried oregano, crushed between your fingertips

1 teaspoon kosher salt

½ teaspoon ground black pepper

For quick, consistent grilling, use a flat meat pounder or the bottom of a small, heavy skillet to pound chicken breasts gently and evenly to about ½ inch thick. Grill the first side long enough to create deep grill marks for flavor and presentation. The second side will need less time.

1. In a skillet or saucepan combine the onion, wine, cassis, vinegar, rosemary, salt, and pepper. Place over low heat on the stove and bring to a gentle simmer. Cover partially and simmer for 10 minutes. Uncover and continue to simmer gently until only a thin layer of the wine remains in the pan, 20 to 25 minutes.

2. Stir in the oil and continue cooking over low heat until jammy, glossy, and very thick, 8 to 10 minutes more, stirring frequently. Remove from the heat and discard the rosemary sprig. Let cool for 10 minutes, then stir in the maple syrup and orange zest. You should have about 1 cup.

3. While the jam is cooking, place each chicken breast between two sheets of plastic wrap, opening out the fillets, or "tenders," if still attached. Working from the center outward, pound firmly with a flat meat pounder or small, heavy skillet to an even overall thickness of about ½ inch.

4. In a 13-by-9-inch baking dish combine the oil, vinegar, oregano, salt, and pepper and mix well. Add the chicken breasts, one at a time, brushing both sides with the olive oil mixture. Marinate in the refrigerator for 30 minutes (no need to cover).

5. Prepare the grill for direct cooking over medium-high heat (about 450°F). Brush the cooking grates clean. Grill the breasts over **direct medium-high heat**, with the lid closed as much as possible, until firm to the touch and opaque all the way to the center, about 5 minutes on the first side and 2 to 3 minutes on the second side. Serve topped with the jam.

Tuesday Night Marinated Chicken Thighs

LEMON-HERB MARINADE

½ cup packed fresh
Italian parsley leaves
and tender stems

¼ cup extra-virgin olive oil

5 or 6 garlic cloves

Finely grated zest of
1 lemon

1 tablespoon fresh
lemon juice

1 tablespoon dried
oregano leaves

1 teaspoon kosher salt

½ teaspoon ground
black pepper

6 boneless, skinless
chicken thighs (about
1½ pounds total)

This is the essence of speedy weeknight cooking. Coat boneless chicken thighs in herbs, garlic, and lemon and throw them on the grill for less than 10 minutes. Try to expose as much of the meat's surface area as possible to the hot grates, which amps up the flavors and charred textures.

1. Combine all the marinade ingredients in a food processor and process until a coarse paste forms.

2. Place the chicken thighs in a medium bowl and add the marinade. Mix well to coat the chicken evenly. Cover and refrigerate for 1 to 4 hours, turning the chicken occasionally in the marinade.

3. Prepare the grill for direct cooking over medium-high heat (400° to 450°F). Brush the cooking grates clean. Using tongs, remove the thighs from the marinade, letting any excess marinade fall back into the bowl.

4. Grill the chicken thighs over **direct medium-high heat**, with the lid closed, until the meat is firm and the juices run clear, 8 to 10 minutes, turning once or twice. Remove from the grill and serve warm.

VARIATION

SMOKED PAPRIKA AND LEMON MARINADE

Omit the marinade ingredients. Instead combine ¼ cup extra-virgin olive oil, finely grated zest of 1 lemon, 2 tablespoons fresh lemon juice, 1½ teaspoons smoked paprika, 1 teaspoon kosher salt, 1 teaspoon granulated garlic, and ¼ teaspoon ground black pepper in a food processor and process until well combined. Continue with the recipe from Step 2.

Thai Chicken Skewers with Peanut Sauce

1½ to 2 pounds boneless, skinless chicken thighs

MARINADE

¼ cup vegetable oil

2 tablespoons fresh lime juice

2 teaspoons Thai red curry paste

2 garlic cloves, minced

1 teaspoon kosher salt

¼ teaspoon ground black pepper

PEANUT SAUCE

½ cup unsweetened coconut milk, stirred

¼ cup smooth peanut butter

1 tablespoon fresh lime juice

1 tablespoon soy sauce

2 to 3 teaspoons Thai red curry paste

2 thin scallions, white and light green parts only, thinly sliced on the diagonal

Chicken thighs, not breasts, are your best bet for these skewers, as they are less prone to drying out. The chicken pieces should be touching, but not crammed, on the skewers, so the meat stays moist. Grill the first side a little longer than the second to get a flavorful crust.

SERVES **4**

PREP: **20 MIN**

MARINATE:
1–24 HOURS

GRILL:
8–10 MIN

SPECIAL EQUIPMENT:
**4 LONG METAL OR
BAMBOO SKEWERS
(SOAK BAMBOO
IN WATER 30 MIN)**

1. Cut the chicken thighs into 1½-inch uniform pieces. In a medium bowl whisk together all the marinade ingredients. Add the chicken to the bowl and mix well. Cover and refrigerate for at least 1 hour and up to 24 hours.

2. In a small skillet or saucepan combine all the sauce ingredients. Place over medium heat on the stove and bring to a gentle simmer, whisking until smooth. Remove from the heat and set aside to cool.

3. Prepare the grill for direct cooking over medium-high heat (400° to 450°F). Thread the chicken pieces onto 4 metal or bamboo skewers, dividing them evenly. The pieces should be touching but not smashed together.

4. Brush the cooking grates clean. Grill the chicken skewers over **direct medium-high heat**, with the lid closed, until the meat is firm to the touch and opaque all the way to the center, 8 to 10 minutes, turning once or twice. Arrange the skewers on a platter and garnish with the scallions. Serve with the dipping sauce.

Barbecued Chicken Adobo

ADOBO MARINADE

6 large garlic cloves, smashed

2-by-1-inch piece fresh ginger, peeled and coarsely chopped

2 teaspoons black peppercorns

1 cup distilled white vinegar

½ cup soy sauce

2 tablespoons vegetable oil

8 bone-in, skin-on chicken thighs, each about 6 ounces, trimmed of excess fat and skin

2 tablespoons packed light brown sugar

4 bay leaves

When removing the chicken from the marinade, let the marinade drip off the meat for a few seconds; raw chicken that is too wet will steam rather than grill over the fire. Boil the leftover marinade (for food safety) and use it to baste and to sauce this winning Filipino-inspired dish.

1. In a food processor combine the garlic, ginger, and peppercorns and pulse until finely ground, about 3 minutes, scraping down the sides of the bowl occasionally. Add the vinegar, soy sauce, and oil and process until pureed, about 30 seconds.

2. Put the chicken in a large resealable plastic bag and pour in the marinade. Press the air out of the bag and seal closed. Turn the bag to distribute the marinade. Place the bag in a bowl and refrigerate for at least 2 hours and up to 4 hours.

3. Prepare the grill for direct and indirect cooking over medium heat (350° to 375°F). Meanwhile, remove the chicken from the marinade, letting the excess drip back into the bag and reserving the marinade.

4. Transfer the marinade to a small skillet or saucepan and stir in the sugar and bay leaves. Bring to a boil over high heat on the stove. Reduce the heat to medium-high and continue to boil until reduced to ¾ cup glaze, about 8 minutes, whisking occasionally (lower the heat to prevent burning). Remove the bay leaves and set aside off the heat.

5. Brush the cooking grates clean. Grill the chicken, skin side down first, over **direct medium heat**, with the lid closed as much as possible, until golden brown, about 10 minutes total, turning once. Move the chicken pieces, skin side up, over **indirect medium heat**, and brush with some of the glaze.

6. Grill, with the lid closed, until an instant-read thermometer inserted into the thickest part (not touching the bone) registers 165°F, 15 to 20 minutes. Turn and brush with more glaze halfway through cooking. Remove from the grill. Bring the remaining glaze to a boil on the stove. Serve the chicken with the glaze.

Golden Roasted Chicken
with Buttery Broth
RECIPE ON PAGE 224

WHOLE CHICKEN

A simple roast chicken is a thing of beauty and, potentially, a source of savory, juicy meat. Much depends on the chicken and you. Chickens raised on factory farms tend to be pretty bland. Better-tasting chickens come from old-fashioned breeds that are raised in free-range environments. Buy a good bird, then follow these pointers for the best results.

Top Tips for the Ultimate Roast Chicken

1. Salt the skin well ahead. If a golden crispy skin is on your list of must-haves for chicken, shower the skin with kosher salt (about 1 teaspoon per pound) at least an hour (and as much as 24 hours) before cooking. Leave the salted chicken uncovered in the refrigerator, allowing the skin to dry out a bit. That's what will make it crispy. For more flavor, season the skin with pepper and stuff the cavity with a mixture of fresh herbs, onion slices, and citrus wedges.

2. Marinate or brine the bird. If you want to go the extra culinary mile, give your chicken deeper flavors by letting it soak in a marinade or brine. We like the citrus marinade on page 228, but you have many other options. Using some acid, like vinegar or even buttermilk, will help tenderize the meat. Avoid supersweet marinades, as the sugars tend to burn. We like to "dry-brine" our whole chicken (see Tip 1) but if you prefer to wet brine your chicken, dissolve ½ cup kosher salt in 4 cups hot water and then add about 4 cups ice cubes to cool the brine to room temperature.

3. Open it up like a book. Spatchcocking is an English term for butterflying a piece of poultry so it lies relatively flat on grill grates or other cooking surfaces. One advantage is that the flatter shape shortens the grilling time. Another is that more skin is in direct contact with the grates, meaning the skin will develop a drier, crispier texture. Check out the recipe on page 230.

4. Truss it up. If you are roasting a whole chicken on the grill or rotisserie, it's a good idea to pull out the butcher's twine and truss the chicken. It might seems like a chore, but we'll walk you through it on pages 224 and 225. Trussing helps the bird keeps its shape and protects the breast meat from drying out during cooking, resulting in a juicier chicken.

5. Put the feet to the fire. One of the challenges when roasting a whole chicken is to have both the leg meat and breast meat reach their ideal internal temperatures at the same time. The leg meat, which has almost twice as much fat as the breast meat, usually takes longer. To work around this, position the legs closer to the fire, if possible. The higher heat on the legs will speed up their cooking.

Golden Roasted Chicken with Buttery Broth

DIJON-HERB PASTE

1 tablespoon Dijon mustard

2 teaspoons Worcestershire sauce

2 teaspoons dried thyme or dried Italian seasoning blend

2 large garlic cloves

¾ teaspoon kosher salt

½ teaspoon ground black pepper

1 whole chicken, 4 to 5 pounds, neck, giblets, and excess fat removed

1 tablespoon extra-virgin olive oil

¾ teaspoon kosher salt

¼ teaspoon ground black pepper

BUTTERY BROTH

1 cup unsalted or low-sodium chicken broth

2 tablespoons cold unsalted butter

Kosher salt and ground black pepper

Chicken begs to be seasoned, and this simple paste of pantry ingredients under the skin is enough to give the meat the flavor it deserves. Chicken also needs the right type of even heat. Keep the lid closed as much as possible and rotate the bird halfway through cooking.

1. In a small bowl whisk together the mustard, Worcestershire sauce, and thyme. On a cutting board smash the garlic cloves with the side of a knife and then mince. Sprinkle with the salt and then use the side of the knife to mash the garlic and salt together to make a paste. Stir into the mustard mixture, along with the pepper.

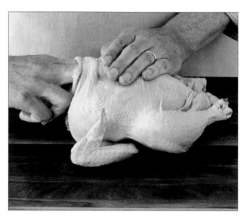

2. Remove the neck, giblets, and any excess fat from the chicken. Place the chicken on a baking sheet and pat the skin dry with paper towels. Starting at the neck end, gently slide your fingers under the skin over the breast and thighs to loosen it, being very careful to avoid tearing the skin.

6. Pull the twine tightly along the chicken toward the neck cavity, making sure to capture the wings.

7. Tie the twine tightly at the neck end of the chicken. Trim any excess twine. If time allows, transfer the chicken to a plate or baking sheet and let it rest in the refrigerator, uncovered, for up to 4 hours. If not, roast the chicken right away.

3. Using your fingers, spread about one-half of the paste under the skin of the breast and thigh areas, smearing it as evenly over the meat as possible. Using your hands, rub the remaining paste over the outside of the chicken.

4. To truss the chicken, cut a long piece of butcher's twine (about 3 feet should be plenty). With the chicken breast side up, center the twine underneath the legs and tailbone and bring it up and over the legs, crossing the twine and pulling it tight.

5. Wrap the twine back underneath the legs, cross again, and pull it tight to bring the legs together.

8. Prepare the grill for indirect cooking over medium heat (350° to 375°F). Coat the chicken with the oil and sprinkle evenly with the salt and pepper.

9. Cook the chicken over **indirect medium heat**, with the lid closed, for 30 minutes. Then, for even cooking, rotate the chicken 180 degrees, working quickly so as little heat as possible escapes. If the chicken is getting dark too quickly, tent it with a sheet of aluminum foil. Cook, with the lid closed, for an additional 30 minutes.

10. Take the internal temperature of the chicken after the initial 60 minutes of cooking. You want the meat in the thickest part of the thighs (not touching the bone) to register 165°F; it may take 15 to 30 minutes longer. Watch carefully so the chicken skin does not burn. (The skin is most delicious when it is very dark brown.) >

Golden Roasted Chicken with Buttery Broth

11. When the chicken is cooked, transfer to a cutting board and let rest for 10 to 15 minutes.

12. While the chicken is resting, make the sauce. In a small saucepan boil the broth over high heat on the stove until reduced to ¼ cup, 5 to 10 minutes. Remove from the heat and whisk in the cold butter, 1 tablespoon at a time, until smooth. Season with salt and pepper (about a generous pinch of each).

13. To carve the chicken into serving pieces, first cut off and discard the twine. Remove the leg and thigh by running the knife blade along the chicken and then through the joint while pulling the thigh gently away from and off the chicken. Repeat with the second leg and thigh.

14. With the chicken facing breast side up, position the knife underneath the breastbone and cut away the backbone.

15. Cut the breast in half, then arrange on a rimmed platter with the legs. Pour the sauce over the chicken. Serve warm.

Weber's Ultimate Green Salad

THE ULTIMATE VINAIGRETTE

In a small glass or stainless-steel bowl whisk together ¼ cup red wine, champagne, sherry, or balsamic vinegar; 1½ tablespoons minced shallot; 2 teaspoons fresh lemon juice (omit if using balsamic vinegar); 1 tablespoon Dijon mustard; and 1 teaspoon finely chopped fresh thyme. Slowly whisk in ¾ cup extra-virgin olive oil until the mixture is emulsified. Season to taste with kosher salt and ground black pepper. Makes about 1¼ cups.

CHOOSE YOUR LETTUCES

Butter lettuce

Red or green leaf lettuce

Chopped romaine

Arugula

Mixed greens

CHOOSE YOUR ADD-INS

Chopped ripe tomatoes or halved cherry tomatoes

Diced avocado

Sliced cucumber

Thinly sliced radishes

Thinly sliced red onion or scallions

Shaved fennel

Sliced olives

Dried cranberries

Crumbled feta, blue, or goat cheese

Shaved Parmesan cheese

Crumbled cooked bacon

Chopped hard-boiled eggs

Toasted almonds or walnuts

Croutons

Rotisserie Chicken with Citrus Marinade

CITRUS MARINADE

Finely grated zest and juice of 1 large lemon

Finely grated zest and juice of 1 large lime

½ cup fresh orange juice

⅓ cup extra-virgin olive oil

1½ teaspoons kosher salt

1 teaspoon ground cumin

1 teaspoon dried oregano

1 teaspoon granulated garlic

½ teaspoon ground black pepper

1 whole chicken, 4 to 5 pounds, neck, giblets, and excess fat removed

Use a large resealable plastic bag to ensure the chicken is completely enveloped in this zippy citrus marinade. Pro-tip: To ensure maximum flavor, position the breast meat facedown in the bottom of the bag where a lot of the marinade pools.

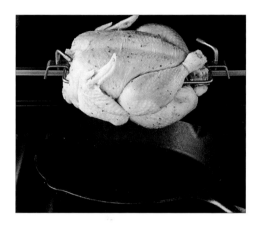

1. In a large bowl whisk together the lemon zest and juice, lime zest and juice, orange juice, oil, salt, cumin, oregano, garlic, and pepper. Transfer ⅓ cup of the marinade to a separate small bowl and set aside to serve later as a sauce.

2. Put the chicken in a large resealable plastic bag, set the bag in a bowl, and pour in the marinade. Press the air out of the bag and seal closed. Turn the bag to distribute the marinade. Refrigerate for at least 4 hours and up to overnight.

3. Let the chicken stand at room temperature while you prepare the grill. Prepare the grill for rotisserie cooking over indirect medium heat (about 400°F), removing the cooking grates. To catch the drippings, place a cast-iron or aluminum foil pan underneath the cooking grates below the chicken.

4. Truss the chicken with butcher's twine (see pages 224 to 225), then place the chicken on the rotisserie (see pages 139 and 140). Roast the chicken over **indirect medium heat**, with the lid closed, until an instant-read thermometer inserted into the thickest part of the thigh (not touching bone) registers 165°F, 1 to 1½ hours.

5. Remove the chicken from the rotisserie and let rest for 10 minutes. Cut the chicken into serving pieces (see page 226), transfer to a platter, and drizzle with the reserved sauce. Serve warm or at room temperature.

CHICKEN FAT POTATOES

Take advantage of the dripping juices by roasting about one pound of small, whole Yukon gold potatoes in the cast-iron skillet that sits below the chicken.

They take about one hour to roast, so after the chicken has been cooking for 15 minutes, toss the potatoes in kosher salt and olive oil, then add them to the hot pan. Just before serving, if you like the potatoes browned even more, set the pan over direct heat for a few minutes.

Spatchcocked Chicken with Chimichurri

1 whole chicken, 4 to 5 pounds, neck, giblets, and excess fat removed

1½ teaspoons kosher salt

CHIMICHURRI SAUCE

3 garlic cloves

2 cups loosely packed fresh Italian parsley leaves

½ cup loosely packed fresh cilantro leaves

¼ cup loosely packed fresh oregano leaves

¾ to 1 cup extra-virgin olive oil

2 tablespoons red wine vinegar

1 teaspoon kosher salt

¼ teaspoon crushed red pepper flakes

¼ teaspoon ground black pepper

The benefits of removing a chicken's backbone and flattening the bird on the grill include fast and even cooking of both the light and dark meat and some beautifully crisped skin. Add the garlicky herb flavors of chimichurri and you have a double winner.

1. To spatchcock the chicken, place the chicken, breast side down, on a work surface. Holding on to the tail end of the backbone with one hand and using sharp kitchen shears with the other, cut along one side of the backbone from the tail to the neck end.

2. Rotate the chicken 180 degrees and, starting at the neck end, cut along the other side of the backbone. Discard the backbone (or save for stock).

3. Flip the chicken over and, using the heel of your hand, press firmly on the breastbone to flatten the bird slightly. Pat the chicken dry with paper towels.

4. Put the garlic in a food processor and process until it sticks to the bowl. Scrape down the bowl, then add the herbs and pulse until coarsely chopped. Add ¾ cup oil, the vinegar, salt, red pepper flakes, and black pepper and process just until blended. Loosen with more oil if needed. Set aside half the sauce for serving.

5. Starting at the tail end, slide your fingers under the skin over the breast to loosen it. Rub the breast meat and the creases between the breast and thighs with about half of the remaining sauce, then smooth the skin to distribute the sauce. Rub the remaining sauce all over the outside of the chicken. Season with salt. Let stand at room temperature for 30 minutes.

6. Prepare the grill for direct cooking over medium heat (350° to 450°F). Brush the cooking grates clean. Grill the chicken, skin side down, over **direct medium heat**, with the lid closed but watching for flare-ups, until the skin releases easily from the grates and is golden, 5 to 10 minutes. >

Spatchcocked Chicken with Chimichurri

7. Using tongs and a large spatula, turn the chicken over and continue to grill with the lid closed until an instant-read thermometer inserted into the thickest part of the breast (not touching bone) registers 165°F, 25 to 35 minutes more. Transfer to a cutting board and let rest for 10 minutes. The internal temperature will rise during this time.

8. Using a sharp knife, cut the chicken into serving pieces (see page 226) and serve with the reserved sauce.

CHIMICHURRI: WONDER SAUCE

If there was a Hall of Fame for grilling sauces, chimichurri would have been inducted decades ago. This easy and versatile sauce is a must-have accompaniment in Argentina and Uruguay for steak, chicken, and almost anything else coming off the grill.

Chimichurri varies a little from region to region—sometimes family to family—but the green (and most popular) version is almost always made with parsley, oregano, garlic, olive oil, and vinegar. In the red version, tomatoes and red bell peppers are added.

While this uncooked sauce is primarily for grilled meats, it also works wonders as a marinade. You can use different herbs, such as cilantro in place of parsley, and add dried spices like cumin and coriander, to create a fantastic marinade for shrimp and other seafood. You wouldn't find an Argentine gaucho using chimichurri sauce like that, but we think it just happens to make almost everything taste better.

Weeknight Side Dishes for Chicken

COUSCOUS WITH LEMON AND MINT

Cook 1 cup instant or regular couscous according to package directions. Lightly drizzle the couscous with extra-virgin olive oil, then fluff it with a fork. Transfer to a bowl. Add 3 scallions, white and light green parts only, thinly sliced; 1 garlic clove, minced; ½ cup chopped fresh Italian parsley leaves; ¼ cup chopped fresh mint leaves; 1 teaspoon finely grated lemon zest; 1 tablespoon extra-virgin olive oil, and ½ teaspoon kosher salt and stir to combine. Taste and adjust the seasoning with salt and pepper if needed.

CAPRESE SALAD

Slice 2 pounds tomatoes, preferably a mixture of varieties and/or colors, and 8 ounces fresh mozzarella cheese. Arrange the tomato and mozzarella slices attractively on a serving platter. Sprinkle with kosher salt and ground black pepper. Drizzle with extra-virgin olive oil and balsamic vinegar and finish with fresh basil leaves, pesto, or chimichurri sauce.

APPLE-CASHEW SLAW

In a small bowl whisk together ½ cup plain whole-milk Greek yogurt, ¼ cup mayonnaise, 2 tablespoons rice or champagne vinegar, and ¼ teaspoon ground black pepper to make a dressing. In a large bowl toss together 1 bag (12 to 16 ounces) precut cabbage slaw or broccoli slaw; ½ cup shredded carrots; 1 small apple, cored and shredded; ¼ cup chopped roasted cashews; and 3 scallions, white and light green parts only, sliced. Drizzle the slaw mix with as much dressing as you like, then season with kosher salt and ground black pepper. Cover and refrigerate for 30 minutes to soften the vegetables slightly; toss well before serving.

Duck Breasts with Hot Pepper Pan Sauce

FIVE-SPICE RUB

1½ teaspoons kosher salt

1½ teaspoons Chinese five spice

1 teaspoon smoked paprika

1 teaspoon dry mustard

½ teaspoon ground black pepper

4 boneless, skin-on duck breast halves (preferably Pekin), each 8 to 10 ounces

HOT PEPPER SAUCE

⅓ cup minced shallots

⅓ cup hot pepper jelly

⅓ cup low-sodium chicken broth

Duck skin is fatty and can cause flare-ups, so we like to sear the breasts in a cast-iron skillet first, while they are still cold from the refrigerator. The chill slows interior cooking and means the skin can get crisp and smoky in just a few minutes directly over the fire.

1. Prepare the grill for direct and indirect cooking over medium heat (350° to 450°F). Brush the cooking grates clean. Place a large cast-iron skillet over direct heat, close the lid, and preheat for 10 minutes. In a bowl mix together the salt, five spice, smoked paprika, dry mustard, and pepper.

2. Trim any excess fat from the edges of the duck breasts. With a very sharp knife, score the skin of the breasts on the diagonal in a crisscross pattern, making the cuts about ½ inch apart. (Do not cut through to the meat.) This will help to prevent the skin from shrinking during cooking.

3. Season the duck breasts on both sides with the rub.

4. Place the duck breasts, skin side down, in the preheated skillet. Cook over **direct medium heat**, with the lid closed, until the fat renders and the skin is golden brown, 7 to 8 minutes, checking on the progress every few minutes.

5. Turn the breasts in the skillet to coat them all over with the rendered fat.

6. Remove the breasts from the skillet, place flesh side down on the grill over **direct medium heat**, and cook, with the lid closed, to your desired degree of doneness, 2 to 4 minutes for medium rare (130°F to 135°F on an instant-read thermometer). If flare-ups occur, move the breasts temporarily over indirect heat. >

Duck Breasts with Hot Pepper Pan Sauce

7. Turn the breasts skin side down and cook for about 1 minute to crisp the skin.

8. Remove the breasts from the grill and let rest for about 5 minutes.

9. Meanwhile, drain off all but 1 tablespoon of the duck fat from the skillet (reserve for another use, like roasting potatoes). Set the skillet over **direct medium heat**, add the shallots, and cook, scraping up the browned bits from the pan bottom, until tender, 2 to 3 minutes.

10. Stir in the jelly and broth, breaking up the pieces of jelly to help them dissolve. Simmer until reduced to a thin sauce consistency, 1 to 2 minutes.

11. To serve, cut the breasts crosswise into ½-inch-thick slices and drizzle with the pan sauce.

Simple Sauces for Duck

SPICY HERB CHUTNEY

In a food processor or blender combine 2 cups loosely packed fresh cilantro leaves; 2 small serrano chile peppers, seeded and roughly chopped; 3 tablespoons fresh lemon juice; 2 garlic cloves, roughly chopped; 1 tablespoon peeled, roughly chopped fresh ginger; 1 tablespoon sugar; and 1½ teaspoons kosher salt and process until fairly smooth. With the motor running, slowly add 2 tablespoons extra-virgin olive oil until a smooth sauce forms.

DIJON-SOY DIPPING SAUCE

In a small bowl whisk together ¼ cup Dijon mustard, 2 tablespoons soy sauce, 1 tablespoon honey, and ¼ teaspoon hot chili oil. Drizzle with a little more chili oil before serving, if desired.

ORANGE HOISIN SAUCE

In a small saucepan over low heat, gently cook 1 tablespoon peeled, minced fresh ginger and 1 teaspoon minced garlic in 2 teaspoons vegetable oil until just fragrant, about 2 minutes. Whisk in 1 tablespoon finely grated orange zest, ⅓ cup fresh orange juice, and ¼ cup hoisin sauce and simmer until slightly thickened, about 5 minutes.

SPICED CHERRY COMPOTE

In a small saucepan over medium heat, combine 1 cup cherry jam (about one 13-ounce jar), 1 tablespoon red wine vinegar, ¼ teaspoon ground cinnamon, ¼ teaspoon ground ginger, ⅛ teaspoon ground cloves, and a pinch of kosher salt. Simmer, stirring often, until the mixture is bubbling, fragrant, and coats the back of a spoon, about 8 minutes.

Grill-Roasted Whole Turkey with Gravy
RECIPE ON PAGE 240

ROAST TURKEY

Millions of Americans are known to panic every November trying to crack the code of how to turn out a moist, flavorful turkey from a frozen lump of dry, lean protein. We have tried our share of turkey hacks, some of them successfully, but the version on the following pages has become our go-to recipe. Just keep in mind, roasting a turkey is not hard. You can do this.

Top Tips for the Ultimate Roast Turkey

FRIDGE
THAWING
TIME:

8-12 lb =
1-2 DAYS

12-14 lb =
3-4 DAYS

15-20 lb =
4-5 DAYS

1. Plan ahead. Turkeys are big and quite often come frozen, which means they need to be defrosted, and it's going to take some time. If your turkey is frozen, thaw it in the refrigerator, allowing 24 hours for every 4 pounds of its weight, or 3 to 4 days for the 12- to 14-pound turkey called for here.

2. To brine or not to brine. If we dissolve salt or sugar in a solution of water (aka brine) and let meat soak in it, the salt or sugar slowly penetrates the meat. Then, as the meat cooks and the proteins unfold, the salt or sugar exerts force on the water to hold it in the meat, keeping it juicier. To wet-brine a turkey, you need 1 cup kosher salt per 4 quarts of water. A 10- to 12-pound turkey will need 8 quarts of water. That's a lot

of salt, which is one reason we prefer dry-brining instead, a technique that uses much less salt with equally good results.

3. Get in the zone. Consistent heat somewhere in the range of 350° to 400°F is important. The heat should penetrate the bird in a slow, steady way—not slowly for 1 hour and aggressively the next hour. A gas grill can handle this steadiness easily. A charcoal grill will require more of your attention. Before you invite the whole family over for turkey roasted over hot coals, take a couple of practice rounds and get a feel for how much charcoal to add to the fire and when.

4. Use a thermometer you trust. There will come that moment when the bird appears

brown and glorious on the grill. It will look done on the outside, but you won't be sure about the inside. You will need to turn to a thermometer for an accurate test of doneness. But can you trust your thermometer? Not all thermometers are equal. The one banging around in a kitchen drawer is probably not reliable. Put your trust in a new instant-read thermometer or in one that you have stored in a safe place. To test its accuracy, take the temperature of boiling water. If it doesn't read 212°F, it's time for a new thermometer.

5. Expect carryover cooking. After a big, plump bird has absorbed heat for more than a couple of hours, that heat doesn't just go away in an instant. As the bird sits on the counter at room temperature, the heat will continue to work on the meat. You should expect the internal temperature to rise 5 to 10 degrees over the course of 30 minutes. That's one reason why it's wise to take the turkey off the grill when the thickest part of the thigh registers 165°F. By the time you eat, it will be closer to 175°F.

Grill-Roasted Whole Turkey with Gravy

1 whole turkey, 12 to 14 pounds, thawed if frozen (see Tip 1, page 239)

1 tablespoon kosher salt

1 teaspoon ground black pepper

1 medium yellow onion, cut into wedges

½ cup (1 stick) unsalted butter

Traditional Turkey Gravy (page 243; optional)

Covering a turkey breast with butter-soaked cheesecloth is a key to moist and tender meat. Elevating the turkey on a rack in the roasting pan so the legs are exposed to plenty of heat is another key. Otherwise, the legs will take too long to cook and the breast will dry out.

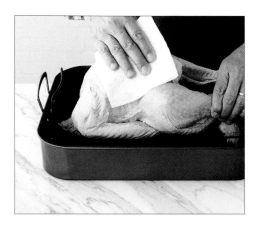

1. Two hours before grilling the turkey, remove it from the refrigerator. Place a V-shaped rack (or other rack) in a large roasting pan (or two nested foil pans). Set aside the neck, heart, and gizzard for gravy, if making. Place the turkey, breast side up, in the pan and pat dry with paper towels.

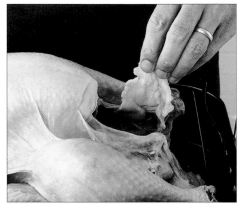

2. Gently pull off the large lump of fat from each side of the inside tail area and place the lumps in the pan beside the rack. If the bird has a plastic pop-up timer in the breast and/or a plastic cage holding its legs in place from inside the tail end, remove and discard them.

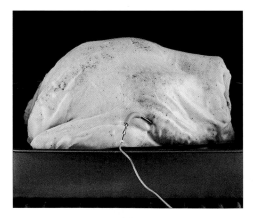

6. Prepare the grill for indirect cooking over medium-low heat (about 350°F). Brush the cooking grates clean. Place the pan with the turkey on the grates and grill over **indirect medium-low heat**, with the lid closed and keeping the grill temperature as close to 350°F as possible.

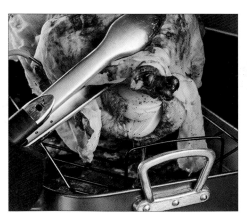

7. After 1½ hours, begin checking the temperature in each thigh. If one side is cooking faster, rotate the pan 180 degrees. Move quickly so as not to lose too much heat. Occasionally during grilling, tilt the pan so the juices run out of the turkey cavity into the pan. They will add color and rich flavor to your gravy.

SERVES **8–12**

PREP: **30 MIN, PLUS
2 HOURS WAITING TIME**

GRILL:
2½–3 HOURS

REST:
30–60 MIN

SPECIAL EQUIPMENT:
**V-SHAPED RACK; 2 LARGE
DISPOSABLE FOIL PANS OR
1 LARGE ROASTING PAN;
CHEESECLOTH**

3. Sprinkle the salt and pepper evenly all over the inside and outside of the turkey. Put the onion wedges in the main cavity of the turkey. Tuck the wings so the tips sit under the turkey. Tie the drumsticks together with butcher's twine. Refrigerate the turkey for 1 hour.

4. Remove the turkey from the refrigerator. In a skillet melt the butter over medium-low heat on the stove. Place a double thickness of cheesecloth the length of the turkey in the skillet and use the back of a spoon to press against the cloth, saturating it with butter.

5. Drape the cheesecloth over the turkey, stretching it to cover the top and sides. If any butter is left in the pan, scrape it onto the top of the cheesecloth. Let the prepped turkey stand at room temperature for 1 hour before grilling.

8. The turkey is ready when an instant-read thermometer inserted into the thickest part of the thigh (not touching the bone) registers 165°F and the breast registers 155°F, 2½ to 3 hours.

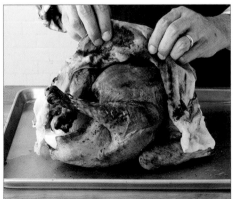

9. Transfer the turkey to a baking sheet and then gently peel off and discard the cheesecloth. Tent the turkey loosely with extra-wide aluminum foil and let it rest for 30 minutes to 1 hour (the internal temperature will rise 5 to 10 degrees during this time). If preparing gravy, reserve the drippings in the pan for making it.

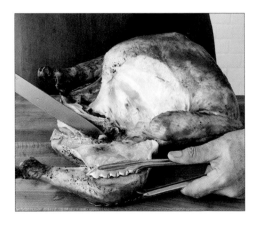

10. Before carving the turkey, cut off and discard the twine holding the legs together. Carve one side of the turkey before turning to the second side. To start, cut off the leg by running the blade of the knife along the carcass and then through the joint while pulling the thigh gently away from and off the carcass. **>**

POULTRY **241**

11. Cut the drumstick apart from the thigh at the joint and place the thigh and drumstick on a serving platter.

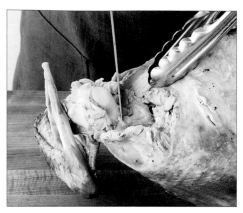

12. Tip the turkey on its side, cut off the entire wing at the joint where it meets the breast, and add it to the platter.

13. Remove the breast from the same side of the turkey. First, make a series of slits to the side of the breastbone, severing the meat from the carcass. Then use your free hand to separate the meat from the carcass while continuing to make small cuts, carving the breast meat off the carcass in a single large piece.

14. Place the boneless breast on the cutting board and cut it crosswise into slices. Slide the knife blade under the sliced breast and use the blade as a spatula to transfer the breast to the platter, fanning out the slices.

15. Repeat to carve the second side of the turkey and arrange it on the platter. Garnish the platter as you wish and serve warm. Accompany with the gravy, if using.

CHARCOAL GRILLING

Prepare a charcoal grill for indirect cooking over medium-low heat (350°F) with a drip pan centered between two charcoal baskets (see page 17). Position the cooking grate with the hinged openings over the charcoal so you can add more coals during grilling. Position the grill lid with the thermostat over the turkey, not the coals. After every hour of grilling, add about five unlit briquettes to the coals on each side.

Traditional Turkey Gravy

If you're grilling a whole turkey (page 240), plan to make a turkey stock the day before, to use as the base of your gravy. To make the stock, use only the neck, heart, and gizzard, as the liver can add an off flavor. When the turkey is done, tip the bird onto its legs to allow the juices to spill out into the pan, so you can use the rich pan juices to fortify your gravy.

Raw neck, heart, and gizzard from a whole turkey

1 pound chicken wings

2 tablespoons extra-virgin olive oil

1 small yellow onion (6 to 7 ounces), chopped (about 1⅓ cups)

1 tablespoon dried thyme

8 cups low-sodium chicken or turkey broth, plus more if needed to thin

½ cup fat drippings skimmed from the turkey pan juices and supplemented, if necessary, with melted butter to equal ½ cup, or ½ cup (1 stick) unsalted butter

½ cup all-purpose flour

¼ cup dry white wine or dry sherry

2 teaspoons finely chopped fresh sage leaves

2 teaspoons chopped fresh thyme leaves

Kosher salt and ground black pepper

MAKES ABOUT 4 CUPS

1. Using a heavy knife or cleaver, chop the neck into 2-inch chunks. Cut each of the wings at the joints into 3 pieces. Heat the oil in a Dutch oven over medium-high heat on the stove. Add the poultry pieces to the pot and cook until very deeply browned, 12 to 15 minutes, turning occasionally.

2. Add the onion and dried thyme and cook, stirring occasionally, until the onion softens, 3 to 5 minutes. Add the broth and bring the mixture to a boil, scraping up the browned bits on the bottom of the pot with a wooden spoon. Reduce the heat to low, cover partially, and simmer for at least 1 hour and up to 2 hours.

3. Strain the stock through a fine-mesh sieve set over a bowl. Discard the solids. Measure the stock. If you have more than 4 cups, return the stock to the pot and simmer until reduced to 4 cups. If you are making the gravy without using pan juices from a grilled turkey, proceed to Step 6.

4. When the turkey is cooked (before resting), lift the turkey and tilt it in its pan, allowing the juices from inside the bird to flow into the pan. Strain the juices from the pan through a fine-mesh sieve placed over a fat separator. Discard the onion pieces.

5. Let the juices stand for a few minutes to allow the fat to rise to the top of the separator. Pour off the fat into a 1-cup liquid measuring pitcher. You will need ½ cup fat. If necessary, supplement with enough melted butter to equal ½ cup. Reserve the defatted pan juices. (If you have more than 1 cup pan juices, add an additional 1 tablespoon flour in the following step.)

6. In a large saucepan heat the fat (or butter if not using pan juices from the turkey) over medium heat until it begins to sizzle. Whisk in the flour all at once and let it bubble for 1 minute, whisking constantly. Gradually whisk in the 4 cups stock, slowly at first, letting the flour mixture absorb the liquid before adding more.

7. Whisk in the wine and bring the gravy to a simmer, whisking continuously. Reduce the heat to low, add the sage and fresh thyme, and simmer for about 10 minutes, whisking occasionally.

8. At this point, add the reserved defatted pan juices, if using. If the gravy is too thin, raise the heat and boil until reduced to the desired consistency. If the gravy is thicker than you like, add more stock, 2 tablespoons at a time. Taste the gravy and adjust the seasoning with salt and pepper to taste. Serve warm.

Dry-Brined Turkey Breast with Tropical Salsa

DRY BRINE

2 teaspoons kosher salt

2 teaspoons chipotle chile powder

1 teaspoon ground cumin

1 teaspoon packed light brown sugar

1 boneless, skin-on turkey breast half, 1½ to 2 pounds

2 teaspoons unsalted butter, melted

TROPICAL SALSA

½ pineapple, peeled and cut crosswise into ½-inch-thick slices

½ cup diced red bell pepper, in ¼-inch dice

1 tablespoon finely chopped jalapeño chile pepper (with or without seeds)

2 tablespoons chopped fresh cilantro leaves and tender stems

1 tablespoon fresh lime juice

¼ teaspoon kosher salt

Turkeys don't like to be rushed, this recipe included. For the piquant spices of this dry brine to penetrate a boneless turkey breast properly, allow it to sit for at least 6 hours. For the salsa, select a pineapple with a sweet scent at the base and golden hue on the skin, indicators of peak ripeness.

| SERVES 4–6 | PREP: 35 MIN | BRINE: 6–24 HOURS | GRILL: 45–60 MIN | SPECIAL EQUIPMENT: **LARGE DISPOSABLE FOIL PAN; 4 LARGE HICKORY WOOD CHUNKS (IF USING CHARCOAL); 2 HANDFULS HICKORY WOOD CHIPS, SOAKED IN WATER 30 MIN AND SMOKER BOX (IF USING GAS)** |

1. In a bowl stir together all the brine ingredients, breaking up any clumps. Pat the turkey breast dry with paper towels. Set the turkey on a wire rack on a baking sheet. Rub the turkey on all sides with the brine mixture, then refrigerate, uncovered, for at least 6 hours and up to 24 hours.

2. Let the turkey stand at room temperature for 1 hour. Brush the top and sides of the turkey with the melted butter. Prepare the grill for direct and indirect cooking over medium heat (350° to 400°F). Brush the cooking grates clean. For gas grilling, have ready a smoker box.

3. For charcoal grilling, add hot coals to two charcoal baskets, placing a foil pan between the baskets (see page 17). Position the cooking grate with the hinged openings directly over the charcoal for adding wood chunks later.

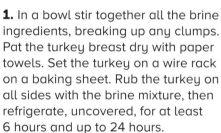

4. Grill the pineapple slices over **direct medium heat**, with the lid closed as much as possible, until lightly charred and tender, 10 to 12 minutes, turning every 2 minutes and swapping places to ensure even cooking. Transfer the pineapple to a cutting board and let rest.

5. If using a gas grill, add the soaked wood chips to the smoker box. When smoke appears, reduce the heat of the grill for indirect cooking over medium-low heat (325°F). If using a charcoal grill, adjust the vents on the grill to reduce the heat for indirect cooking over medium-low (325°F). Add one wood chunk to each charcoal basket.

6. Place the turkey breast, skin side up, on the grate(s) over indirect heat. Grill the turkey breast over **indirect medium-low heat**, with the lid closed as much as possible. For the charcoal grill, add the two remaining wood chunks when the temperature starts to drop below 325°F. >

Dry-Brined Turkey Breast with Tropical Salsa

7. Cook until the skin is dark brown and an instant-read thermometer inserted into the thickest part of the breast registers 150° to 155°F, 45 to 60 minutes. Start checking the internal temperature after the first 30 minutes of cooking, rotating the turkey breast if one side is cooking faster than the other.

8. Transfer the turkey to a cutting board and let rest for 10 minutes. Meanwhile, cut away the core from each pineapple slice, then cut the pineapple into ½-inch dice and transfer to a medium bowl. Add all the remaining salsa ingredients and toss to combine.

9. Cut the turkey crosswise into ¼- to ½-inch-thick slices. Transfer the slices to a platter and drizzle with any juices from the cutting board. Serve warm or at room temperature with the salsa.

VARIATION

PEACH BARBECUE SAUCE

Omit the tropical salsa. In a large saucepan combine 2 cups canned crushed tomatoes, with their juices; 1 cup peach jam; ⅓ cup white wine vinegar; 2 tablespoons unsulfured molasses (not blackstrap); 1 teaspoon mustard powder; ½ teaspoon *each* onion powder, ground allspice, and kosher salt; and ¼ teaspoon *each* crushed red pepper flakes, garlic powder, and ground mace. Bring to a low boil over medium-high heat, stirring often. Reduce the heat to low and simmer, uncovered, until reduced to about 2 cups, about 1 hour, stirring often.

The Ultimate Turkey Sandwich

Frankly, if the turkey is good, we would be happy with a sandwich of just turkey, sliced bread, mayonnaise, and crisp lettuce. However, if you are setting your sights on the ultimate version, let's consider the best options.

THE BREAD
white, whole wheat, multigrain, ciabatta, baguette, sourdough, rye, hoagie roll, bagel, large flour tortilla (for a wrap)

THE SPREAD
mayonnaise, mustard, cranberry sauce, honey mustard, aioli, cream cheese, pesto, fruit chutney, barbecue sauce, softened butter, hummus, mashed avocado

THE TURKEY ITSELF
thin or thick, light or dark

THE GREENS
iceberg lettuce, romaine lettuce, mixed greens, arugula, watercress

THE SUPPORTING ACTORS
tomato, bacon, roasted peppers, leftover stuffing, grilled onions, fresh spinach, shredded cabbage, sun-dried tomatoes, pickles, cucumber, thinly sliced apple or pear

THE CHEESE
cheddar, Swiss, provolone, Gruyère, Brie, goat

Backyard Fiesta

Tequila-Smoked Salmon with Radish Salsa, recipe on page 258; **Fish Tacos with Southwestern Slaw,** recipe on page 262; **Corn on the Cob with Chile Oil and Lime,** recipe on page 292; **Guacamole,** recipe on page 340

SEAFOOD

Planked Salmon with Gremolata
RECIPE ON PAGE 252

SALMON FILLETS

You know how a grill can bring heft and depth to the glorious characteristics of salmon. But you may be wary of that beautiful coral flesh sticking to the grate. That's understandable but also solvable. Salmon is one of our favorite fish to grill, and we'll show you how to do it three different ways: on the grate, on a cast-iron griddle, and on a cedar plank. A plank infuses salmon with a subtle wood-smoked flavor and will enable you to grill a whole side of salmon or individual fillets without the fish ever having the chance to stick to the grates. Plus, it's a built-in serving dish!

Planked Salmon with Gremolata

GREMOLATA SAUCE

¼ cup extra-virgin olive oil

Finely grated zest of
1 orange (about
1 tablespoon)

2 tablespoons fresh
orange juice

¼ cup chopped
fresh cilantro

1 tablespoon capers,
rinsed and drained

½ teaspoon kosher salt

¼ teaspoon ground
black pepper

SPICE RUB

½ teaspoon kosher salt

½ teaspoon smoked
paprika

½ teaspoon dried thyme,
crushed between your
fingertips

¼ teaspoon ground cumin

¼ teaspoon ground
black pepper

1 skin-on center-cut
salmon fillet, 1½ to
2 pounds and ¾ to 1 inch
thick, pin bones removed

2 teaspoons extra-virgin
olive oil

Consider this your plank primer. To score perfectly with your fish à la plank, toast the well-soaked cedar plank until you hear popping sounds and start to see smoke. Putting the salmon directly on the toasted wood allows it to absorb even more sweet smokiness. Bonus: It won't stick to the grate!

1. Submerge the cedar plank in water and let soak for at least 1 hour and up to 1 day. This step is important, as it prevents the wood from catching on fire. Use a medium bowl filled with water or a couple of cans of beer to weight the plank down.

2. For the sauce, whisk together the oil, orange zest, and orange juice in a small bowl. Stir in the cilantro, capers, salt, and pepper. Set aside.

5. Grill over **direct medium-high heat**, with the lid closed, until the salmon is cooked to your desired doneness, 15 to 30 minutes (depending on the thickness) for medium rare (125° to 130°F on an instant-read thermometer). To serve, transfer the fillet on the plank to a heatproof surface. Cut crosswise into four portions and serve with the sauce.

				SPECIAL EQUIPMENT:
SERVES **4**	PREP: **30 MIN**	SOAK: **AT LEAST 1 HOUR (PLANK)**	GRILL: **15–30 MIN**	**UNTREATED CEDAR PLANK, ABOUT 15 INCHES LONG AND 5½ INCHES WIDE**

3. In a small bowl combine all the rub ingredients and mix well. Place the salmon, skin side down, on a work surface. Coat the salmon flesh with the oil and season evenly with the rub.

4. Prepare the grill for direct cooking over medium-high heat (400° to 450°F). Brush the cooking grates clean. Drain the cedar plank. Place it over direct heat and close the lid. When the plank begins to smoke and toast, after 3 to 10 minutes, use long-handled tongs to turn it over. Slide the salmon, skin side down, onto the toasted side of the plank.

WELL-CUT FILLETS

It's nearly impossible to cut picture-perfect, individual servings of salmon from a large fillet that has already been cooked. The edges would be rough and ragged. For much tidier servings, cut the large fillet while it is still raw. Cut right down to the skin but not through it. After the fish is cooked, use a spatula to scoop your well-trimmed servings off the skin.

KEEP THE PLANK!

Planks can be reused. Wash and scrub off any foodstuffs using a brush and some kosher salt as your scrubbing agent. Let the board dry completely. If a plank is soaked long enough, it retards the charring, hence it can be reused at least once more.

FLAVOR BOMB
your
SALMON

Grilling salmon on a wood plank is as much about function as it is about that smoky, sweet-charred flavor the wood imparts. The result depends on the type of wood you use—cedar, alder, or fruitwood—and the sauce, marinade, or rub you choose.

LIME-SOY BUTTER SAUCE

Omit the sauce and rub. In a small saucepan melt 4 tablespoons (½ stick) unsalted butter over medium heat. Add 1 teaspoon minced garlic and ½ teaspoon crushed red pepper flakes and stir until fragrant, about 1 minute. Add ¼ cup packed light brown sugar, ¼ cup soy sauce, and 3 tablespoons fresh lime juice. Bring to a simmer, stirring frequently until the sugar is fully dissolved, 1 to 2 minutes. In a small dish stir together 1 teaspoon cornstarch and 1 teaspoon water. Add to the sauce mixture and simmer, stirring, until thickened, about 1 minute. Set aside. Brush the salmon with olive oil and sprinkle lightly with salt and pepper. Grill on the soaked cedar plank as directed in the recipe on page 252. Rewarm the sauce over medium-low heat. Serve the grilled salmon with the sauce spooned over the top. Garnish with lime wedges.

HERB YOGURT SAUCE

Omit the sauce and rub. In a food processor combine 1 garlic clove; finely grated zest of ½ large lemon (about 1 teaspoon); ½ teaspoon *each* kosher salt, ground black pepper, ground coriander, and ground cumin; and ¼ teaspoon crushed red pepper flakes. Process until the garlic is minced. Add 1 cup loosely packed fresh Italian parsley leaves, ½ cup loosely packed torn fresh basil leaves, and 2 tablespoons extra-virgin olive oil. Process until the herbs are finely chopped. Add ¾ cup plain whole-milk Greek yogurt and 2 tablespoons fresh lemon juice and process until combined. Set aside. Brush the salmon with olive oil and sprinkle lightly with salt and pepper. Grill on the soaked cedar plank as directed in the recipe on page 252. Serve the grilled salmon with the sauce spooned over the top. Garnish with chopped parsley or basil leaves.

TOMATO-CAPER SAUCE

Omit the sauce. In a skillet over medium-high heat, combine 2 tablespoons extra-virgin olive oil; 2 tablespoons capers, rinsed and drained; 1 small shallot, minced (about 2 tablespoons); 1 tablespoon red wine vinegar; and ¼ teaspoon *each* kosher salt, ground black pepper, and crushed red pepper flakes. Cook for 2 to 3 minutes, stirring occasionally. Add 1 can (14½ ounces) crushed tomatoes, mix well, and simmer for 2 to 3 minutes longer. Taste and adjust the seasoning if needed. Add 2 tablespoons finely chopped fresh basil and remove from the heat. Brush the salmon with olive oil and season evenly with the rub. Grill on the soaked cedar plank as directed in the recipe on page 252. Serve the grilled salmon with the sauce spooned over the top. Garnish with small fresh basil leaves.

CREAMY LEMON-DILL SAUCE

Omit the sauce and rub. In a small saucepan melt 2 tablespoons unsalted butter over medium-high heat and cook until the milk solids turn golden and smell nutty, about 3 minutes. Add 1 shallot, minced (about ¼ cup), and cook until tender, about 3 minutes, stirring often. Add ¾ cup heavy whipping cream (do not substitute), ¼ cup low-sodium chicken broth or fish stock, finely grated zest of 1 lemon, and 2 tablespoons fresh lemon juice. Season with ½ teaspoon kosher salt and ¼ teaspoon ground black pepper. Simmer the sauce until thickened and reduced to ¾ cup, about 5 minutes. Stir in 3 tablespoons chopped fresh dill. Keep warm off the heat. Brush the salmon with olive oil and sprinkle lightly with salt and pepper. Grill on the soaked cedar plank as directed in the recipe on page 252. Serve the grilled salmon with the sauce spooned over the top. Garnish with fresh dill and lemon slices.

Plancha Salmon Rice Bowl

SOY-GINGER MARINADE

¼ cup soy sauce

2 tablespoons mirin

2 tablespoons sake or Shaoxing wine (Chinese rice wine)

2 tablespoons packed light brown sugar

1 tablespoon peeled, finely grated ginger

4 skin-on salmon fillets, each about 6 ounces, pin bones removed

1 tablespoon vegetable oil

3 cups hot steamed jasmine rice

4 scallions, white and light green parts only, thinly sliced on the diagonal

1 large carrot, peeled and cut into matchsticks

1 large red or green jalapeño chile pepper, halved, seeded, and thinly sliced crosswise

¼ cup fresh cilantro leaves, coarsely chopped

2 tablespoons sesame seeds, toasted

1 lime or lemon, cut into 4 wedges

Spare yourself some fish-grilling anxiety by using a well-seasoned cast-iron griddle placed directly on the cooking grate. Just sear the skin side of the fillets until crispy and then finish them with the flesh side down. Use this sensible technique with any meaty fish and marinade.

1. Whisk together all the marinade ingredients in a glass baking dish large enough to accommodate the salmon in a single layer. Arrange the salmon in the same dish and turn the pieces to coat all sides with the marinade. Let marinate at room temperature for 30 to 60 minutes.

2. Prepare the grill for direct cooking over medium heat (350° to 450°F). Brush the cooking grates clean. Place a cast-iron griddle or skillet over direct heat, close the lid, and preheat for 10 minutes. Meanwhile, remove the salmon from the dish, reserving the marinade, and pat dry with paper towels.

3. Transfer the marinade to a small saucepan. Bring to a boil over medium-high heat on the stove, then reduce the heat to medium-low and simmer for 2 minutes. You should have about 6 tablespoons. Remove from the heat.

4. Add the oil to the preheated griddle or skillet, place the salmon fillets, skin side down, on the pan, and cook over **direct medium heat**, with the lid closed, until the skin is crisp and lifts without resistance with a spatula, about 5 minutes.

5. Using two flat spatulas, flip the fillets and continue to cook, with the lid closed, until the salmon is golden brown and cooked to your desired doneness, about 3 more minutes for medium rare. Transfer to a plate and brush each fillet with some of the reduced marinade, reserving the remaining marinade.

6. Spoon the rice into individual bowls. Remove and discard the salmon skin. Arrange a salmon fillet over the rice, breaking it into pieces, then divide the scallions, carrot, and jalapeño evenly among the bowls. Drizzle each bowl with the marinade, sprinkle with the cilantro and sesame seeds, and garnish with a lime wedge.

Tequila-Smoked Salmon with Radish Salsa

½ cup packed light brown sugar

¼ cup kosher salt

¼ cup plus 1 tablespoon tequila, divided

¼ cup chopped fresh cilantro leaves and tender stems

1 jalapeño chile pepper, finely chopped (about 1 tablespoon)

1 tablespoon finely grated lime zest

1 tablespoon finely grated lemon zest

1 teaspoon ancho chile powder

1 skin-on center-cut salmon fillet, 2 to 2¼ pounds and 1¼ to 1½ inches thick, pin bones removed

1 tablespoon olive oil

SALSA

1 bunch radishes (12 to 16), trimmed and cut into very fine matchstick strips (about 1¾ cups)

½ cucumber, peeled, seeded, and cut into ⅛-inch dice (about ½ cup)

¼ cup finely chopped red onion

2 tablespoons chopped fresh cilantro leaves

½ to 1 jalapeño chile pepper, seeded and finely chopped (2 to 3 teaspoons)

5 teaspoons fresh lime juice

½ teaspoon granulated sugar

¼ teaspoon kosher salt

Tortilla chips

This multistage process is worthwhile for turning out salmon with a silky-tender texture. Tequila and smoke give the fish fabulous flavors that work great with the slightly spicy, slightly bitter radish salsa in this stand-out appetizer. The smoked fish also makes a terrific main dish on its own.

1. In a small bowl mix together the brown sugar, salt, ¼ cup tequila, cilantro, jalapeño, lime zest, lemon zest, and chile powder. Place the salmon, skin side down, in a glass or ceramic baking dish just large enough to hold it.

2. Remove any pin bones using a small piece of paper towel to help you grasp one end of the bone while you pull it out. Spread the sugar mixture over the salmon, covering it entirely. Cover with plastic wrap and refrigerate for 7 to 8 hours.

3. Rinse the salmon well under cold running water to remove the sugar mixture. Pat it dry with paper towels, then place, flesh side up, on a baking sheet. Brush the flesh with the oil and the remaining 1 tablespoon tequila. Refrigerate uncovered until the salmon looks lightly glazed, about 45 minutes.

4. Prepare the grill for indirect cooking over very low heat (200° to 250°F). Brush the cooking grates clean. Drain half of the wood chips, scatter over the coals or add to the smoker box of a gas grill, and close the lid.

5. When smoke appears, grill the salmon over **indirect very low heat**, with the lid closed, until it is firm to the touch and has a golden patina, 55 minutes to 1¼ hours. After about 30 minutes of cooking, add the remaining wood chips. Remove the salmon from the grill and let cool for 20 minutes.

6. In a medium bowl, combine all the salsa ingredients and mix well. Slice or flake the cooled salmon into bite-size pieces and serve on tortilla chips topped with the salsa.

Fish Tacos with
Southwestern Slaw
RECIPE ON PAGE 262

FISH FILLETS

Grilling was likely the first way that humans cooked fish. And we believe it is still the best and most flavorful way to do it. The porous nature of most fish allows the flavors of the fire to work their way inside within just a few minutes. To achieve that requires some skill and vigilance, which is exactly what we cover here.

Top Tips for the Ultimate Fish Fillets

1. Choose your fish. There are all kinds of fish out there, but some types are just better suited to the grill. We generally avoid delicate flaky fish like tilapia or sole (unless we are using the appropriate accessories) and opt instead for firm, meaty fish. Beyond salmon, our favorites include halibut, mahimahi, swordfish, and tuna steaks. Purchase fish from a reputable fishmonger for the best quality and to ensure that it comes from a sustainable source.

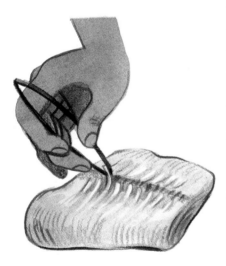

2. Remove tiny bones. Many finfish have tiny, soft bones called pin bones. The best tools for removing them are either a pair of needle-nosed pliers, purchased at a hardware store or kitchen shop, or a small square of paper towel. The pin bones run lengthwise, with the grain of the flesh, so the bones all point in the same direction. Run your hand along the flesh to feel the exposed ends, then use the pliers or a small piece of paper towel to extract the bones one at a time, pulling parallel to the direction of the bone. Pin bones are easier to remove if the fish is cold, as warmer flesh tears more easily.

3. Wait your turn. People tend to turn fish while it is still sticking to the grates. When you put fish on a hot grill, the grates sear it, which both firms the flesh and causes it to develop a crust. It's the crust that will allow you to turn the fish without it sticking. The crust can take just a couple of minutes or as long as 7 or 8 minutes to develop. You have to wait your turn. You may also find that the first side needs to grill longer than the second side. Fortunately, the second side tends to stick less.

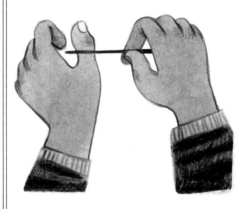

4. Don't overcook your fillets. When the flesh turns from translucent to opaque all the way to the center and just begins to flake around the edges, the fish is done. This typically happens when the internal temperature reaches 125° to 130°F. If you don't have an instant-read thermometer, insert a metal skewer into the thickest part of the fish for a few seconds and then touch the skewer on a sensitive part of your skin. If the skewer feels cold to an area like the base of your thumb, the fish is underdone. If the skewer feels warm, the fish is cooked. If the skewer feels hot, the fish is overcooked.

Fish Tacos with Southwestern Slaw

SOUTHWESTERN SLAW

2 cups thinly sliced red cabbage (about ¼ head)

2 tablespoons coarsely grated yellow onion

2 tablespoons fresh lime juice

2 tablespoons fresh orange juice

1 teaspoon sugar

¾ teaspoon kosher salt

¾ teaspoon ground cumin

⅛ teaspoon cayenne

AVOCADO CREMA

1 garlic clove

1 large avocado, halved, pitted, and peeled

½ cup sour cream

2 tablespoons fresh lime juice

½ teaspoon kosher salt

¼ teaspoon chipotle chile powder

¼ teaspoon Mexican hot sauce, such as Cholula®

RUB

2 tablespoons extra-virgin olive oil

1½ teaspoons kosher salt

1 teaspoon garlic powder

½ teaspoon sweet paprika

½ teaspoon ground cumin

¼ teaspoon ground coriander

¼ teaspoon ground black pepper

2 pounds skinless mahimahi, halibut, or cod fillets, pin bones removed (see page 261) and cut into 1-inch pieces

8 (8-inch) flour or corn tortillas

Lime wedges

Fresh cilantro leaves

1 jalapeño chile pepper, thinly sliced

These hearty tacos have the ideal balance of creamy and crunchy. Use a meaty white fish, such as mahimahi, halibut, or cod, and cut the fillets into same-size cubes to ensure even doneness. Refrigerate the slaw for at least 1 hour to allow the flavors to develop and the cabbage to soften.

1. In a medium bowl mix together all the slaw ingredients. Cover and refrigerate for at least 1 hour and up to 6 hours to allow the flavors to develop.

2. In a food processor pulse the garlic to mince finely. Add all the remaining crema ingredients and process until smooth, scraping down the sides of the bowl once or twice. You should have about 1½ cups. Transfer to a small bowl, cover, and refrigerate for up to 6 hours.

6. Warm the tortillas over **direct medium-high heat** until lightly toasted on each side, 30 to 60 seconds total. Transfer to a plate. Drain the slaw.

7. Spoon 1 tablespoon of the crema onto each warm tortilla. Slide the fish from a skewer onto each tortilla, and add a squeeze of lime juice. Top with the slaw, dividing it equally. Garnish with the cilantro, jalapeño, and a drizzle of crema. Serve right away, with lime wedges on the side.

 MAKES **8 TACOS**; SERVES **4–6**	PREP: **35 MIN**	MARINATE: **30 MIN**	GRILL: **8–10 MIN**	SPECIAL EQUIPMENT: **8 METAL OR BAMBOO SKEWERS (SOAK BAMBOO IN WATER 30 MIN)**

3. Thirty minutes before grilling, mix together all the rub ingredients in a medium bowl. Add the fish pieces and turn to coat on all sides. Let stand at room temperature while you prepare the grill.

4. Prepare a grill for direct cooking over medium-high heat (400° to 450°F). Thread the fish pieces onto 8 bamboo skewers, leaving a little space between the pieces and filling each skewer with pieces of uniform size so they cook evenly.

5. Brush the cooking grates clean. Grill the fish skewers over **direct medium-high heat**, with the lid closed, until the fish pieces are golden and beginning to turn opaque in the center but are still moist, 7 to 9 minutes, turning a few times. Transfer to a platter.

VARIATIONS

AS YOU LIKE IT

This recipe is just a starting point. Any other firm, meaty fish would work well, including tuna and salmon. You could also use shrimp or scallops with great results.

The other taco components are replaceable as well. Instead of the cabbage slaw, just use 2 cups shredded green cabbage. Instead of the avocado crema, use 1 cup store-bought salsa. You might also want to add some guacamole or sour cream (or both).

Mahimahi with Green Goddess Dressing

GREEN GODDESS DRESSING

⅔ cup mayonnaise

½ cup buttermilk

½ cup chopped fresh Italian parsley leaves

⅓ cup chopped fresh chives

2½ tablespoons chopped fresh tarragon leaves

1 garlic clove, chopped

1 teaspoon white wine vinegar

¼ teaspoon kosher salt

¼ teaspoon ground black pepper

4 skinless mahimahi or halibut fillets, each about 6 ounces and 1 inch thick

3 tablespoons extra-virgin olive oil, divided

2 teaspoons ground cumin or smoked paprika

1 teaspoon kosher salt

1 teaspoon ground black pepper

2 hearts romaine lettuce, halved lengthwise

2 firm but ripe tomatoes, halved crosswise

Brushing fish with a mayonnaise dressing before it goes on the grill? Believe it. This dressing brings major flavor and keeps the fish from sticking. For added insurance, cook the fish a little longer on the first side, which makes it easier to turn the fillets without difficulty.

1. In a food processor combine all the dressing ingredients and process until the herbs are minced and the dressing is a uniform light green, 2 to 3 minutes. Transfer about ⅓ cup to a small liquid measuring pitcher. Cover and refrigerate the rest for serving. (The dressing can be made up to 1 day ahead.)

2. Prepare the grill for direct cooking over high heat (450° to 550°F) and medium heat (350° to 450°F). Brush the fish fillets on both sides with 1 tablespoon of the oil, then season all over with the cumin, salt, and pepper. Brush evenly on both sides with the reserved ⅓ cup dressing. Place on a baking sheet.

3. Drizzle the lettuce and tomato halves with the remaining 2 table-spoons oil. Place on the baking sheet with the fish. Brush the cooking grates clean.

4. Grill the fish fillets, skin side up, over **direct high heat**, with the lid closed as much as possible, until grill marks appear and the fish releases easily from the grates, 5 to 6 minutes. Turn the fish over and grill until the flesh is opaque in the center but still moist, 2 to 3 minutes more. Remove the fish from the grill; cover to keep warm.

5. Grill the lettuce and tomato halves, starting cut side down and turning once or twice, over **direct medium heat**, with the lid open. They are ready when the lettuce is lightly charred around the edges but still bright green, and light brown grill marks appear on the tomato halves, 30 to 60 seconds for the lettuce and 1 to 2 minutes for the tomato halves.

6. Transfer 1 fish fillet to each of four plates. Arrange a lettuce half and a tomato half alongside the fish on each plate. Spoon some of the remaining dressing generously over the fish, lettuce, and tomatoes. Pass any remaining dressing alongside. Serve warm.

Swordfish with Blistered Tomatoes

MARINADE

3 tablespoons olive oil

Finely grated zest of
1 lemon

2 tablespoons fresh
lemon juice

3 garlic cloves, finely
grated or pushed through
a press

4 swordfish steaks, each
6 to 8 ounces and about
1 inch thick

1 teaspoon kosher salt

½ teaspoon ground
black pepper

BLISTERED TOMATOES

1 pound cherry or grape
tomatoes

1 tablespoon capers,
rinsed, drained, and
roughly chopped

½ teaspoon kosher salt

¼ to ½ teaspoon crushed
red pepper flakes

2 tablespoons chopped
fresh dill

Lemon wedges

Prep and measure all the sauce ingredients before you begin so you can pay undivided attention to cooking the swordfish. It should still be a little undercooked when you add it to the griddle with the sauce, which allows it to finish in a sweet, briny bath.

SERVES **4**

PREP: **15 MIN**

MARINATE:
15–30 MIN

GRILL: **ABOUT
20 MIN**

SPECIAL
EQUIPMENT:
**12-INCH CAST-
IRON SKILLET
OR GRIDDLE**

1. In a baking dish combine the marinade ingredients and mix well. Add the swordfish steaks and turn to coat. Let marinate at room temperature for 15 to 30 minutes. Prepare the grill for direct and indirect cooking over medium-high heat (400° to 450°F). Brush the cooking grates clean.

2. Place a griddle or 12-inch cast-iron skillet over indirect heat, close the lid, and preheat for 10 minutes. Meanwhile, remove the swordfish from the baking dish, reserving the marinade, and place on a baking sheet. Season the steaks on both sides with the salt and pepper, pressing the pepper gently so it adheres to the fish.

3. Add the tomatoes and marinade to the griddle, stir quickly to combine, and cook over **indirect medium heat**, with the lid closed, until the tomatoes just begin to shrivel and burst, 10 to 15 minutes, stirring occasionally.

4. Add the capers, salt, and pepper flakes and cook, with the lid closed, until the tomatoes have released most of their juices, about 5 minutes longer, stirring once or twice. Some tomatoes will shrivel but remain whole. Add the dill, smash the tomatoes slightly, and cook, with the lid closed, for a couple of minutes. Remove from the heat.

5. While the tomatoes are cooking, place the swordfish on the cooking grates and grill over **direct medium heat**, with the lid closed, until the flesh is just opaque in the center but still moist, 8 to 10 minutes, turning once. It is okay to cut into a fillet to check. Swordfish is lean and can dry out quickly, so take care not to overcook it.

6. Transfer the steaks to the griddle and spoon the tomato mixture over and around the fish. Serve immediately with lemon wedges.

Grilled Whole Fish with Hazelnut Butter
RECIPE ON PAGE 270

WHOLE FISH

With a deft hand and a moderate fire, you can grill almost any whole fish. Fish that weigh 3 pounds or less do well over direct heat. Larger ones do better when roasted over indirect heat. Either way, their natural flavors improve with lemon, herbs, nuts, and, of course, butter.

Grilled Whole Fish with Hazelnut Butter

½ cup (1 stick) unsalted butter

½ cup toasted, peeled, and coarsely chopped hazelnuts (see box, opposite)

1 whole fish, such as branzino or red snapper, 2 to 3 pounds, gutted and scaled, very cold

½ lemon, thinly sliced

2 garlic cloves, thinly sliced

2 fresh thyme sprigs

2 fresh Italian parsley sprigs

Extra-virgin olive oil

Kosher salt and ground black pepper

Small handful of chopped fresh herbs, such as dill, Italian parsley, basil, and/or chives

A fish basket will keep fish from sticking to the grate, but as a precaution, always brush the fish and basket with oil. An easy way to test for doneness: Insert a metal skewer near the backbone for a few seconds, then immediately hold the tip against your lower lip. If it's warm, the fish is done.

1. Prepare the grill for direct cooking over medium-high heat (400° to 450°F). Brush the cooking grates clean. Melt the butter with the hazelnuts in a small skillet over medium heat on the stove, swirling until the butter begins to turn nut brown, then set aside off the heat.

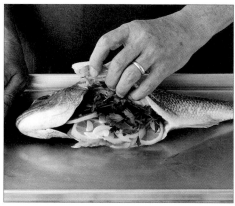

2. Just before you are ready to grill, stuff the fish cavity with the lemon slices, garlic, and thyme and parsley sprigs.

5. Using tongs, turn the basket and continue grilling, with the lid closed, until done through to the center, 4 to 6 minutes more. Carefully remove the fish from the basket and transfer the fish to a large platter.

6. Bring the hazelnut butter quickly up to the sizzling point, then pour the bubbling mixture over the fish. Scatter the chopped herbs over the top and serve at once.

3. Brush both sides of the fish with oil, then season the fish lightly on both sides with salt and pepper. Brush the inside wires of the fish basket with oil, where the fish will touch the basket.

4. Secure the fish in the fish basket. Grill over **direct medium-high heat**, with the lid closed, for 4 to 6 minutes (timing depends on the thickness).

HAZELNUTS

Toasting hazelnuts in a skillet raises the volume on their flavor and makes them crispier. To toast the nuts: Spread the nuts in a single layer in a heavy, dry skillet. Heat them over medium high-heat, stirring frequently, and cook until the nuts are browned in spots and fragrant. They will not be evenly browned, but that's okay.

To skin the toasted nuts: Wrap the nuts in a kitchen towel, let them steam for about a minute, and then vigorously rub them inside the towel. Most of the skins will flake off, though some tiny bits of skin will cling to the nuts. That's okay. Those toasted bits of skin will be welcome in the sauce. Be sure to coarsely chop the nuts before adding them to the butter.

Garlic Shrimp with Lemon-Dill Sauce
RECIPE ON PAGE 274

SHRIMP

Seared over direct medium heat for just a few minutes on each side, shrimp become an infinitely versatile kitchen staple. Add them to tacos or salads, serve them over rice or polenta, toss them with pasta and a squeeze of lemon, or skewer them to appreciate on their own. Here are some pointers to guide you at the grill.

Top Tips for the Ultimate Shrimp

1. Be specific about size. Terms like small, medium, and large mean different things to different people. The best way to know what you are buying is by knowing the number of shrimp per pound. A label that says "16/20" means there will be 16 to 20 shrimp in a pound. Those are pretty "large" shrimp. Shrimp labeled "21/30" or "31/35" will be smaller. Generally speaking, 16/20 and 21/30 shrimp are the best for grilling because they are easy to peel and they don't dry out as quickly on the grill.

2. Remove the shells. You can grill shrimp in their shells, and some people claim the meat will be juicier that way. But then your guests will need to peel them at the table and will be discarding some seasonings and char with the shells. We like to peel the shrimp prior to grilling, but leave the tails on if you are serving them on their own or skewered.

3. Remove the vein. Use a small, sharp knife to cut down the back of each peeled shrimp. Cut no more than ¼ inch deep or so, just enough to expose the black vein. Lift out the vein with the tip of your knife and discard it.

4. Pat them dry. Most shrimp sold at fish counters are thawed from frozen, so always pat the shrimp very dry before grilling to prevent them from sticking to the grates.

5. Skewer them tightly. Arranging shrimp back to back on skewers, with no space between them, slows down the rate of cooking, which means they won't dry out as easily.

6. Use a pan for the small ones. Any shrimp smaller than 31/40 will tend to overcook quickly. Use a perforated grill pan to cook this size. Get the pan nice and hot, then quickly spread the shrimp in a single layer. Give the pan a shake halfway through the cooking to flip the shrimp over.

Garlic Shrimp with Lemon-Dill Sauce

⅔ cup mayonnaise

2 tablespoons finely chopped fresh dill leaves

Finely grated zest of 1 lemon

1 tablespoon fresh lemon juice

½ teaspoon Worcestershire sauce

4 to 8 drops Tabasco® sauce (to taste)

1 garlic clove, minced or pushed through a press (about 1 teaspoon)

1½ pounds large shrimp in the shell (16/20 count)

1 tablespoon extra-virgin olive oil

1 tablespoon finely chopped fresh dill leaves

1 to 2 garlic cloves, chopped

½ teaspoon kosher salt

¼ teaspoon cayenne or ground black pepper

Shrimp can be a little type A—they benefit from order. Arrange them on the grate from left to right. That way, you'll remember which shrimp went on the grill first. The ones on the left should be the first ones off. With or without the sauce, these garlicky shrimp make a tasty, and quick, meal.

1. In a small bowl combine all the ingredients for the sauce and whisk until smooth. Cover and refrigerate until serving time (the sauce can be made up to 4 hours ahead).

2. To peel each shrimp, grab the shell just above the tail and break it loose. Peel away most of the shell, pulling off the little legs and leaving the tail shell intact.

5. Prepare the grill for direct cooking over medium-high heat (400° to 450°F). Brush the cooking grates clean. Arrange the shrimp on the grill in an orderly way, such as left to right, so you can easily remember which shrimp started cooking first.

6. Grill over **direct medium-high heat,** with the lid closed as much as possible, until firm to the touch and just turning opaque at the center, 4 to 5 minutes, turning once. Serve at once, with the sauce on the side.

SERVES **4**

PREP: **20 MIN**

GRILL: **4–5 MIN**

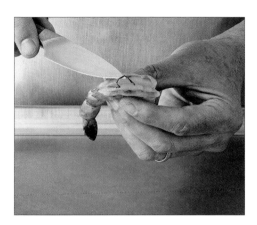

3. To devein each shrimp, using a sharp paring knife, make a shallow slit along the back of the shrimp. Lift the black vein out of the slit and discard it. In a medium bowl combine the shrimp, oil, and dill.

4. On a cutting board mash together the garlic and salt, using the sharp blade and the side of the knife to create a paste. Add the paste to the shrimp along with the pepper. Toss to coat evenly. Set aside while you prepare the grill.

VARIATION

AVOCADO-CLEMENTINE SALSA

For a fresh take, omit the lemon-dill sauce and replace it with this citrus and avocado salsa.

To make the salsa, cut away all the peel and white pith from 1 pound clementines or seedless tangerines (3 or 4 fruits). Halve, pit, and peel 1 large, firm but ripe avocado. Cut the clementines and avocado into ½-inch pieces and put them in a medium bowl. Add ¼ cup minced red onion, 2 tablespoons finely chopped fresh cilantro, 1 tablespoon fresh lime juice, ¼ teaspoon kosher salt, and ¼ teaspoon ground black pepper and stir. Serve alongside the grilled shrimp or over grilled fish.

Grilled Oysters with
Spiced Butter
RECIPE ON PAGE 278

SHELLFISH

Compared to red meat or pork, shellfish have a much higher water content, a much lower fat content, and much softer strands of connective tissue. These sea creatures also deteriorate much faster than meat. For all those reasons, it's important to buy them fresh and to grill them hot and fast. Oysters, clams, and mussels should still be alive when you purchase them. Keep them that way by setting them on a bed of ice for a day (or two, max).

Top Tips for the Ultimate Shellfish

Oysters

We love grilling freshly shucked oysters until their briny liquor bubbles and their flesh absorbs a bit of smokiness. It works best when the oysters are big enough to stay juicy throughout the grilling, so look for shells that are 3 to 4 inches long (but no bigger). Things get even better with a bit of your favorite sauce. Maybe a classic mignonette, a barbecue sauce, or garlic butter?

Scallops

Grilled scallops generally fall into one of two categories. They are either nicely seared and translucent in the center or overcooked and rubbery. To avoid the latter, pat scallops dry before grilling and let your grill preheat thoroughly before setting each scallop, widest side down, over the fire. The bigger the scallops, the better your opportunity for a nice sear.

Clams

When clams are placed over heat, their natural liquid boils, and the steam released puts pressure on the inside of the shells, causing them to open. This process works well on a grill, especially when the clams are in a vessel, like a cast-iron pan or a wok made for your grill, as it keeps their meats surrounded by liquid. Cover the pan (or close the grill lid) as they cook. (To clean clams, rinse and scrub them under cold water, then soak in cold salted water for 1 hour so they purge any sand and grit.)

Mussels

Mussels, like clams (see above), are well suited to grilling, as long as they're not overcooked. If some mussels remain closed when the cooking time has finished, discard the closed ones, as cooking them longer will only dry them out. Like clams, mussels should be cooked in a vessel, such as a cast-iron pan or a wok made for your grill. (To debeard a mussel, grasp the beard with your thumb and forefinger and pull sharply, perpendicular to the mussel.)

Crab

Crab can be cooked on the grill in at least two ways: the raw legs can be laid directly on the grates, or the legs can be broken into pieces and sautéed in a heavy pan set directly on the grates or in a wok made for your grill.

Grilled Oysters with Spiced Butter

SPICED BUTTER

¼ cup (½ stick) unsalted butter

1 tablespoon minced shallot

½ teaspoon finely grated lemon zest

2 teaspoons fresh lemon juice

1 teaspoon Worcestershire sauce

¼ teaspoon prepared chili powder

¼ teaspoon smoked paprika

¼ teaspoon kosher salt

12 large oysters in the shell, well scrubbed under running water

Crusty Italian or French bread slices

Large oysters with deeply cupped shells are the best for grilling. Small oysters cook too quickly, flat ones don't provide enough shell space for the topping, and lopsided ones will spill their liquor when opened. To keep large oysters from spilling, prop the shells against each other for balance.

1. In a small saucepan melt the butter over medium-low heat on the stove. Add the shallot and cook until translucent, about 3 minutes, stirring occasionally with a whisk. Remove from the heat and whisk in the lemon zest and juice, Worcestershire sauce, chili powder, smoked paprika, and salt. Set aside.

2. On a work surface, fold a kitchen towel in half (as if closing a book). Fold it again the same way, and then once or twice more to create a sturdy roll. Place an oyster, flat side up, with the hinge (pointed end) near one end of the towel.

6. Using insulated gloves or long tongs, place the oysters on the cooking grate. Grill over **direct high heat**, with the lid closed as much as possible, until the liquid in the oysters begins to bubble and the edges of the oysters curl, 3 to 5 minutes. Transfer back to the platter, being careful not to spill the liquid.

7. If necessary, rewarm the butter mixture until melted. Spoon the butter mixture into the oysters. Serve warm with bread.

SERVES **2-4**
AS AN APPETIZER

PREP: **15 MIN**

GRILL: **3-5 MIN**

SPECIAL EQUIPMENT:
**OYSTER KNIFE
FOR SHUCKING,
ROCK SALT, HEAVY
INSULATED GLOVES
OR LONG TONGS**

3. Fold the towel over on top of the oyster so the tip of the oyster is facing out toward your dominant hand and your other hand firmly holds the oyster down. Look for the hinge, which is your point of entry. Wiggle the tip of an oyster knife into the hinge until it goes in completely, then rotate the blade to pry open the shell.

4. Wipe the knife to remove any grit and continue around the edge of the shell to open fully. Scrape the knife along the top shell to release the muscle. Lift off and discard the top shell.

5. Slide the knife under the oyster to release it from the bottom shell, leaving it resting in the shell and taking care not to lose the liquor. Nestle the oyster on a platter of rock salt to help keep it upright. Repeat with the remaining oysters. Prepare the grill for direct cooking over high heat (450° to 550°F).

Super-Simple Smoked Clams

24 littleneck or other medium hard-shell clams, about 2 pounds total, rinsed and scrubbed

Kosher salt

4 tablespoons (½ stick) unsalted butter, cut into chunks

3 garlic cloves, very thinly sliced

This is the essence of a seaside summer meal: fresh clams, garlic butter, and the delightful, irresistible scent of smoke. Use an aluminum foil roasting pan to trap the smoke around the clams as they open.

SERVES **2**

PREP: **10 MIN**

SOAK:
1–2 HOURS

GRILL:
5–7 MIN

SPECIAL EQUIPMENT:
LARGE DISPOSABLE FOIL ROASTING PAN, 3 LARGE HANDFULS ALDER OR OAK CHIPS (DRY)

1. Put the clams in a bowl and add enough salted ice water (1 teaspoon salt per cup of water, stirred until the salt has dissolved) to cover by about 1 inch. Let sit for 1 to 2 hours so the clams will expel any sand trapped in their shells. Keep the water well chilled, adding more ice or refrigerating the bowl if needed.

2. Prepare the grill for indirect cooking over medium-high heat (400° to 450°F). Melt the butter in a small skillet over medium-low heat on the stove. Add the garlic slices and cook until tender and the edges are golden, 4 to 6 minutes. Set aside off the heat.

3. Drain the clams in a colander and quickly rinse under cold running water. Add the wood chips directly to the charcoal or to the smoker box of a gas grill and close the lid.

4. When the chips begin to smoke heavily, place the clams on the cooking grates over **indirect medium-high heat**.

5. Cover the clams with a large foil pan and then close the lid.

6. Grill the clams until they open, 5 to 7 minutes. They are cooked as long as they open even slightly. Discard any clams that fail to open. Using tongs, transfer the clams to a serving bowl, being careful not to lose the juice in the shells. Rewarm the butter, divide between two small bowls, and serve alongside for dipping.

Beer-Steamed Mussels with Garlic Crostini

GARLIC CROSTINI

1 baguette, about 15 inches long, cut on a sharp diagonal into 12 slices

2 tablespoons extra-virgin olive oil

1 large garlic clove

MUSSELS

3 tablespoons unsalted butter

1 tablespoon extra-virgin olive oil

½ cup chopped shallots (about 2 medium)

4 garlic cloves, minced

¼ teaspoon crushed red pepper flakes

¼ teaspoon kosher salt

1 bottle (12 ounces) lager or wheat beer

8 fresh Italian parsley sprigs

6 fresh thyme sprigs

4 pounds mussels, scrubbed and debearded (see page 277)

6 to 8 fresh basil leaves

White wine is the usual liquid suspect when steaming mussels, but beer enhances the sweet-briny character of these bivalves and makes a great broth for dipping garlic crostini. The beer must be hot enough to generate sufficient steam to open the mussels, so medium-high heat is the way to go.

SERVES **4**

PREP: **20 MIN**

GRILL: **13–16 MIN**

SPECIAL EQUIPMENT:
**LARGE GRILL-PROOF
POT WITH LID (AT LEAST
12 INCHES WIDE AND
5 INCHES DEEP)**

1. Prepare the grill for direct cooking over medium heat (350° to 450°F). Brush the cooking grates clean. Brush the bread slices lightly on both sides with the oil. Grill over **direct medium heat**, with the lid closed, until golden brown, 1 to 1½ minutes, turning once.

2. Remove the bread from the grill and rub one side of each slice with the garlic clove; set the crostini aside. Place a large grill-proof pot over **direct medium heat**, close the grill lid, and preheat for 5 minutes.

3. Add the butter and oil to the pot and stir until the butter melts. Stir in the shallots, garlic, red pepper flakes, and salt. Close the grill lid and cook until the shallots soften, 3 to 4 minutes, stirring occasionally. Add the beer, parsley, and thyme and bring to a boil. Close the grill lid and cook for 3 minutes.

4. Add the mussels to the pot and cover the pot with its lid. Close the grill lid and cook until the mussels open, 6 to 10 minutes.

5. Remove the pot from the grill and discard any unopened mussels and the herb sprigs (squeeze unopened mussels with tongs; if they still don't open, discard).

6. Divide the mussels among four bowls and ladle in the broth. Cut the basil into thin strips and garnish the bowls with the strips. Serve with the garlic crostini.

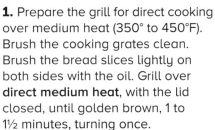

Summer Harvest

Ember-Roasted Corn with Fresh Dill Butter, recipe on page 294; **Globe Eggplant with Mediterranean Relish,** recipe on page 299; **Summertime Bruschetta,** recipe on page 69; **Flank Steak with Cherry Tomatoes and Arugula,** recipe on page 103

VEGETABLES
& SIDES

Asparagus with Lemon Vinaigrette
RECIPE ON PAGE 288

BBQ
GENIUS

ASPARAGUS

Asparagus spears are truly transformed when cooked on a grill—the color brightens; the spears intensify in flavor, developing a smoky sweetness; and the exterior crisps while the interior softens. A brush of olive oil and a sprinkle of good salt are all that are needed to grill asparagus, as the searing and caramelizing that happen over the fire add plenty of flavor. That said, a boldly seasoned sauce spooned on top turns grilled asparagus into a spectacular side dish.

Top Tips for the Ultimate Asparagus

1. Buy thick asparagus. Look for thick, meaty spears that stand firm and tall and have healthy, fresh-looking tips. Pencil-thin spears, while delicious in other recipes, can easily slip through the bars of the cooking grate, and because they lack meatiness, they can overcook and char in an instant.

2. Snap to trim. The base of each asparagus spear is woody and fibrous and not very nice to eat, so you should get rid of it before you cook the asparagus. The easiest way to do this is to snap it off. Grasp the bottom end of each spear and bend it gently at its natural point of tenderness, usually about two-thirds of the way down the stalk. Discard the tough ends. If you like, use a paring knife to trim the snapped end of each spear to create a clean edge.

3. Oil the asparagus, not the cooking grate. Rinse the asparagus under cold running water and blot dry with paper towels; this will help the oil adhere to the vegetable better. Place the spears in a shallow bowl or on a baking sheet and toss or brush with olive oil to coat lightly.

4. Clean your cooking grates. Always be sure to brush your cooking grates clean before adding anything to them. Even small bits of charred food left on the grates will stick to the raw spears, either tearing the flesh when you try to move them or imparting an off flavor. The easiest way to do this is to preheat the grates for 10 minutes prior to brushing them.

5. Use the right tools. For easy maneuverability and better control, use tongs, rather than a two-pronged fork, to move or turn the asparagus. Thick spears aren't likely to fall through the bars of the grates when arranged perpendicular to them. If the spears are thinner, cook them in a perforated grill pan on the cooking grates.

Asparagus with Lemon Vinaigrette

LEMON VINAIGRETTE

¼ cup extra-virgin olive oil

1 teaspoon finely grated lemon zest

2 tablespoons fresh lemon juice

1 garlic clove, minced or pushed through a press

¾ teaspoon kosher salt

½ teaspoon Dijon mustard

½ teaspoon sugar

¼ teaspoon ground black pepper

¼ cup pine nuts

28 thick spears asparagus, about 1½ pounds

Extra-virgin olive oil

Kosher salt and ground black pepper

Finely grated lemon zest

Grilled asparagus makes a terrific foundation for all kinds of sauces and toppings, like this bright, lemony version with pine nuts. The thick spears taste best when their texture is somewhere between crisp and tender, so get them off the grill before they turn limp.

1. In a small bowl whisk together all the vinaigrette ingredients. Set aside until ready to serve.

2. Heat a small skillet over medium-low heat on the stove. When hot but not smoking, add the pine nuts and toast them, stirring constantly, until lightly browned, 3 to 4 minutes (they will burn easily so watch closely). Pour onto a small plate and set aside.

5. Brush the cooking grates clean. Arrange the asparagus perpendicular to the grate bars. Grill over **direct medium heat**, with the lid closed, until well grill-marked and crisp-tender, 6 to 10 minutes, rolling the spears once or twice to sear all sides. Remove from the grill.

6. Arrange the asparagus on a warmed platter. Scatter the pine nuts over the asparagus. Whisk the vinaigrette to recombine, then drizzle some over the asparagus. Garnish with a little lemon zest. Serve warm with the remaining vinaigrette.

SERVES **6**   PREP: **20 MIN**   GRILL: **6–10 MIN**

VARIATIONS

The lemon vinaigrette here is endlessly customizable. Here are some examples:

- Substitute 2 tablespoons red wine vinegar for the lemon zest and juice.
- Substitute ¼ cup hazelnut or macadamia nut oil for the olive oil.
- Substitute chopped almonds or cashews for the pine nuts.
- Add some milder herbs such as 2 teaspoons of finely chopped parsley, basil, or dill.
- Add 2 teaspoons poppy seeds, as they have a strong affinity with lemon.

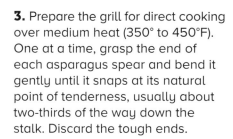

3. Prepare the grill for direct cooking over medium heat (350° to 450°F). One at a time, grasp the end of each asparagus spear and bend it gently until it snaps at its natural point of tenderness, usually about two-thirds of the way down the stalk. Discard the tough ends.

4. Place the asparagus spears on a baking sheet and toss with olive oil to coat lightly. Season lightly with salt and pepper.

FLAVOR BOMB *your* ASPARAGUS

The char of the grill and assertive, grassy flavors of thick asparagus spears welcome other flavors. Obvious (and excellent) choices include a vinaigrette, as in the recipe on page 288, or aioli. We thought you might want to try something less obvious. Hint: The sweet chili glaze is awesome.

ORANGE-TARRAGON AIOLI

In a mini food processor combine 1 small garlic clove, finely grated zest of 1 small orange, ½ teaspoon kosher salt, and a few grinds of black pepper. Pulse to mince the garlic. Add 1 teaspoon Dijon mustard, 2 tablespoons fresh orange juice, 2 tablespoons extra-virgin olive oil, and ½ cup mayonnaise and process until smooth and emulsified. Transfer to a small bowl and stir in 1 tablespoon minced fresh tarragon leaves. Spoon the sauce over grilled asparagus and serve.

SWEET CHILI GLAZE

In a square baking dish mix together ¼ cup Thai sweet chili sauce, 2 tablespoons mayonnaise, 1 tablespoon fresh lime juice, 2 teaspoons fish sauce, and 1 teaspoon peeled, finely grated fresh ginger until smooth. Add the asparagus, turn to coat, and marinate for 15 to 30 minutes. Grill the asparagus as directed in the recipe on page 288, then return the asparagus to the baking dish, turn to coat evenly in the marinade, and serve.

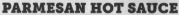

PARMESAN HOT SAUCE

In a small bowl whisk together 3 tablespoons extra-virgin olive oil, 1 tablespoon hot sauce (we recommend Tapatío®, Frank's RedHot®, or Sriracha), and ¼ cup freshly grated Parmesan cheese. Spoon the sauce over grilled asparagus and serve.

SIEVED EGG AND CAPER SAUCE

Separate the yolk and white of 1 hard-boiled egg. Using the back of a spoon, press the yolk through a small fine-mesh sieve set over a medium bowl. Finely chop the egg white and set aside. Add ¼ teaspoon kosher salt, ½ teaspoon ground black pepper, ½ teaspoon Dijon mustard, and ¼ cup extra-virgin olive oil to the yolk. Whisk to combine. Add 2 tablespoons rinsed and drained small capers, 2 tablespoons finely chopped fresh dill leaves, finely grated zest of 1 small lemon, 1 tablespoon fresh lemon juice, and the chopped egg white. Stir to combine. Spoon the sauce over grilled asparagus and serve.

Corn on the Cob with Chile Oil and Lime

CHILE-SPIKED OIL

¼ cup extra-virgin olive oil

1 teaspoon kosher salt

½ teaspoon ground cumin

½ teaspoon ancho chile powder or prepared chili powder

¼ teaspoon sweet or hot paprika

4 ears corn, husked

1 lime, cut into 4 wedges

Chopped fresh cilantro (optional)

Maldon salt (optional)

You want the cooking grates to be popping hot here so that they sear and caramelize the corn kernels to the point that they develop dark brown spots. The squeeze of lime at the end ties all the flavors together.

SERVES **4**

 PREP: **10 MIN**

 GRILL: **10–15 MIN**

1. Prepare the grill for direct cooking over medium-high heat (400° to 450°F). In a small bowl whisk together the oil ingredients. Brush the corn evenly with about two-thirds of the seasoned oil.

2. Grill the ears of corn over **direct medium-high heat**, with the lid closed, until browned in spots and tender, 10 to 15 minutes, turning occasionally.

3. During the last 1 to 2 minutes of grilling, lightly baste the corn with the remaining seasoned oil. Remove from the grill and squeeze a lime wedge over each ear. Garnish with cilantro and Maldon salt, if using, and serve.

VARIATION

MEXICAN STYLE

Husk the corn and rub the ears very lightly with oil. Grill the corn as directed. While warm, spread mayonnaise over each ear of corn, about 1 tablespoon for each. Sprinkle the corn ears with ⅓ cup finely grated Cotija cheese, 2 teaspoons prepared chili powder, and 1 tablespoon chopped fresh cilantro.

Ember-Roasted Corn with Fresh Dill Butter

4 ears corn with husks, freshly picked if possible

DILL BUTTER

4 tablespoons (½ stick) unsalted butter, softened

1 tablespoon finely chopped fresh dill leaves

2 teaspoons finely grated lemon zest

½ teaspoon kosher salt

⅛ teaspoon ground black pepper

1 slice white bread (optional)

Kosher salt

Corn is tailor-made for this sort of cooking because it comes with its own protective covering. The husks provide a buffer to the extreme heat of the embers while the kernels gently steam within. A slathering of softened butter and a sprinkling of fresh dill are all the adornment necessary.

1. Peel back the husks on each corn ear just to the base, leaving them attached. Clean away the silk, then fold the husks back in place as evenly as possible, covering the kernels completely. Put the corn in a large bowl or pan, add water to cover, and let soak for about 30 minutes.

2. Prepare a charcoal grill for direct cooking over medium heat (350° to 450°F). Arrange the coals in an even layer in the center of the grill grate. You won't need the cooking grate for this recipe.

3. In a small bowl combine all the ingredients for the dill butter and mash together with a fork to mix well. Set aside.

4. Lift the corn from the bowl and shake off the excess water. Carefully arrange the ears on top of the coals. Close the lid and roast until the husks are well charred on one side, 6 to 8 minutes.

5. Use tongs to rotate each ear a one-third turn, close the lid, and cook until this second side is nicely charred, 3 to 4 minutes. Rotate the ears the same way one last time and cook until evenly charred all over, 3 to 4 minutes longer. Transfer the corn to a work surface and let cool for a few minutes.

6. Remove the husks from the corn and place the ears on a serving platter. Using the bread slice or a small knife, spread the flavored butter all over the corn. Sprinkle with some salt, if desired, and serve warm.

Marinated Asian Eggplant with Tahini

TAHINI DRESSING

2 tablespoons tahini

1 tablespoon fresh lemon juice

1 tablespoon extra-virgin olive oil

1 garlic clove, minced or pushed through a press

1 teaspoon toasted sesame oil

4 Chinese or Japanese eggplants, each about 6 ounces

ASIAN SOY MARINADE

¼ cup soy sauce

¼ cup mirin or dry sherry

1 tablespoon toasted sesame oil

2 teaspoons peeled, finely grated fresh ginger

2 teaspoons minced or grated garlic

2 teaspoons packed light brown sugar

1 teaspoon chili-garlic sauce, such as Sriracha

Vegetable oil

2 tablespoons finely chopped fresh cilantro leaves

1 teaspoon sesame seeds, toasted (optional)

Slender, lavender-to-purple Asian eggplant has a subtler flavor and more porous texture than the globe varieties, which means it takes well to short marinating. The sugar in the marinade could cause sticking on the grates, but if you oil the eggplant just before grilling, you should have no trouble.

SERVES 4–6	PREP: **20 MIN**	MARINATE: **1 HOUR**	GRILL: **8–10 MIN**

1. In a small bowl whisk together all the dressing ingredients and set aside. Trim off the stem end of each eggplant, then cut in half lengthwise.

2. In a glass or ceramic baking dish long enough to hold the eggplant halves flat, whisk together all the marinade ingredients. Add the eggplant, flesh side down, turning to coat evenly in the marinade, and let stand at room temperature for about 1 hour.

3. Remove the eggplant from the marinade, shaking off the excess, and place on a baking sheet. Reserve the marinade. Brush each eggplant half on all sides with oil. Add just enough of the marinade (about ¼ cup) to the dressing to give it a pourable, but not thin, consistency.

4. Prepare the grill for direct cooking over medium-high heat (400° to 450°F). Brush the cooking grates clean. Grill the eggplant, flesh side down first, over **direct medium-high heat**, with the lid closed, until well grill-marked and tender, 8 to 10 minutes, turning once or twice.

5. Arrange the eggplant on a serving platter and drizzle the dressing on top. Sprinkle with the cilantro and sesame seeds (if using). Serve warm or at room temperature.

WHAT IS TAHINI?

Tahini, the main ingredient in the dressing here, is an oily paste made from soaked, crushed sesame seeds that are toasted and then ground. Tahini is rich and nutty and a key ingredient in recipes like hummus and baba ghanoush. There are basically two kinds of tahini: good and bad. The good stuff has great flavor, a light ivory color, and a smooth, creamy consistency. The bad stuff? Well, it's bitter, dark, and mealy.

Globe Eggplant with Mediterranean Relish

MEDITERRANEAN RELISH

1 cup finely diced roasted red bell peppers (2 to 3 peppers)

1 cup grape tomatoes, halved (or quartered if large), or 1 cup diced salad tomatoes

½ cup pitted black or green olives, halved or quartered lengthwise

⅓ cup roughly chopped fresh Italian parsley leaves

3 tablespoons extra-virgin olive oil

1 tablespoon balsamic or red wine vinegar

½ teaspoon kosher salt

½ teaspoon dried thyme or oregano

¼ teaspoon crushed red pepper flakes (optional)

⅛ teaspoon ground black pepper

2 globe eggplants, each about 1 pound

½ to 1 cup extra-virgin olive oil

1 teaspoon kosher salt

½ teaspoon ground black pepper

The hardest part of this recipe is making sure the eggplant slices are uniformly ½ inch thick. Any parts thinner than ½ inch can overcook easily, turning limp and mushy. The goal here is eggplant slices that are tender but still have a bit of bite.

SERVES **6**

PREP: **15 MIN**

GRILL: **7–9 MIN**

1. Prepare the grill for direct cooking over medium-high heat (400° to 450°F). In a medium bowl, mix together all the relish ingredients and set aside.

2. Cut about ½ inch off both ends of each eggplant. Cut the eggplants crosswise into ½-inch-thick slices.

3. Lightly brush both sides of each eggplant slice with the oil and then season evenly with the salt and pepper.

4. Brush the cooking grates clean. Grill the eggplant slices over **direct medium-high heat**, with the lid closed, until well grill-marked and tender, 7 to 9 minutes, turning once.

5. Arrange the eggplant slices in a single layer on a serving platter and spoon the relish on top. Serve warm.

GLOBE EGGPLANTS

Look for globe eggplants that are cylindrical rather than bulbous or tapered. The latter are likely to have a lot of seeds, which are potentially bitter.

Portabello Mushrooms
with Chard and Feta
RECIPE ON PAGE 302

PORTABELLO MUSHROOMS

Dark and thick, firm and flavorful, mushrooms are the meat of the vegetable kingdom. But they are ultralean meat, which means they can dry out on the grill if your technique is off. Solutions include marinating them, basting them on the grill, or stuffing them with something cheesy and spectacular.

Portabello Mushrooms with Chard and Feta

4 large portabello mushrooms, each 3 to 4 ounces

Extra-virgin olive oil for brushing, plus 1 tablespoon

1 very large bunch Swiss chard, 12 to 14 ounces

½ cup crumbled feta cheese (about 2½ ounces)

½ cup coarsely grated whole-milk mozzarella cheese (about 2 ounces)

¼ cup plus ⅓ cup freshly grated Parmigiano-Reggiano® cheese, divided

2 tablespoons mayonnaise

2 small scallions, white and light green parts only, finely chopped (about 3 tablespoons)

1 garlic clove, minced

⅛ teaspoon ground nutmeg, or several fresh grindings whole nutmeg

⅓ cup panko (Japanese bread crumbs)

Ground black pepper

Grilling sturdy greens is easy when you have a perforated pan to keep them from falling between the grate bars. Rinse them well and use the water clinging to the leaves to wilt them. If you can't find large mushrooms, buy 6 smaller mushrooms and reduce the cooking time.

1. Prepare the grill for direct cooking over high heat (450° to 550°F). Using a damp paper towel, wipe the outside of each mushroom cap to clean. Using a small knife, cut out the stems.

2. Holding 1 mushroom in your palm and using a small spoon, gently scrape out all the black gills, being careful not to tear the delicate cap. (It's important to remove the gills, as they will discolor the filling during grilling.) Repeat with the remaining mushrooms.

6. In a medium bowl mix together the chopped greens, feta, mozzarella, ¼ cup Parmigiano Reggiano®, the mayonnaise, scallions, garlic, and nutmeg.

7. In a small bowl mix together the panko, the remaining ⅓ cup Parmigiano Reggiano®, and the remaining 1 tablespoon oil. Stir 1 tablespoon of the panko mixture into the greens filling. Season the filling to taste with pepper (about ¼ teaspoon).

SERVES **4**

PREP: **30 MIN**

GRILL: **13–18 MIN**

SPECIAL EQUIPMENT:
**LARGE PERFORATED
GRILL PAN**

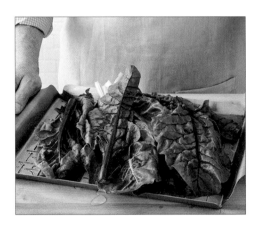

3. Brush a large perforated grill pan with oil. Rinse the chard under cold running water. Stack the wet leaves in the prepared pan.

4. Grill the chard over **direct high heat**, with the lid closed, until the greens begin to wilt, 5 to 6 minutes, turning once or twice with tongs. Remove from the grill.

5. Cut off the stem at the base of each leaf and discard. Fold the leaves in half lengthwise and twist to wring out the excess moisture. Using a heavy, large knife, coarsely chop the greens. You should have a generous 1 cup.

8. Divide the greens filling evenly among the mushrooms, then pat gently with your hand to fill to the edges.

9. Sprinkle the remaining panko mixture evenly over the filling.

10. Place the mushrooms on the same grill pan. Grill over **direct high heat**, with the lid closed, until the cheese melts and the topping is deep brown, 8 to 12 minutes. Using a metal spatula and tongs, transfer the mushrooms to plates and serve.

Roasted Mushrooms with Umami Glaze

¼ cup balsamic vinegar

2 tablespoons soy sauce

3 tablespoons unsalted butter

2 teaspoons minced garlic

1½ teaspoons minced fresh rosemary leaves, divided

1 pound cremini mushrooms (about 30), each 1½ inches in diameter, cleaned and stem ends trimmed

Kosher salt and ground pepper (optional)

Umami is that taste you know you love but have trouble describing. Often billed as meaty or brothy, it's abundant in soy sauce and balsamic vinegar. This recipe uses an umami bomb in its own right, mushrooms, to aggregate all the bold flavors.

SERVES 4–6

PREP: **15 MIN**

GRILL: **15–20 MIN**

SPECIAL EQUIPMENT:
**LARGE PERFORATED
GRILL PAN**

1. Prepare the grill for indirect cooking over medium-high heat (400° to 450°F). Combine the vinegar, soy sauce, butter, garlic, and ½ teaspoon of the rosemary in a small skillet over medium heat on the stove and whisk until the butter melts. Simmer until reduced to ⅓ cup, 2 to 3 minutes.

2. Pour ¼ cup of the vinegar mixture into a medium bowl; add the mushrooms and toss to coat until the liquid is absorbed. Reserve the remaining liquid in the skillet.

3. Arrange the mushrooms in a single layer on a large perforated grill pan. Reserve the bowl without washing it.

4. Brush the cooking grates clean. Grill the mushrooms over **indirect medium-high heat**, with the lid closed, until tender (test with a skewer) and lightly charred, 15 to 20 minutes, turning once or twice.

5. Return the mushrooms to the medium bowl. Pour the reserved liquid over the mushrooms and mix gently. Season with the remaining 1 teaspoon rosemary and with salt and pepper if needed. Serve warm.

Tandoori Cauliflower with Herb Chutney

TANDOORI CRUST

⅓ cup chopped yellow onion (½ small onion)

3 garlic cloves

2 tablespoons fresh lemon juice

¾ cup plain whole-milk or low-fat Greek yogurt

2 teaspoons ground coriander

2 teaspoons ground cumin

2 teaspoons ground ginger

2 teaspoons ground turmeric

1 teaspoon kosher salt

½ teaspoon ground black pepper

1 head cauliflower, about 1¾ pounds

Canola oil

HERB CHUTNEY

1 cup packed fresh cilantro leaves and tender stems

1 cup packed fresh mint leaves

½ small yellow onion, cut into chunks

1 tablespoon fresh lemon juice

1 small green chile pepper, such as serrano, seeded

1 tablespoon peeled, finely grated fresh ginger (½-by-2-inch piece)

2 garlic cloves, smashed

1 teaspoon kosher salt

1 cup plain whole-milk or low-fat Greek yogurt

Despite what some carnivores may think, vegetarian main courses can be showstoppers. This deceptively simple dazzler is a whole head of generously spiced cauliflower roasted over indirect heat. The crust gives the mild vegetable crazy-good color and flavor.

SERVES **4–6**

PREP: **20 MIN**

GRILL: **ABOUT 1 HOUR**

SPECIAL EQUIPMENT:
**10-INCH CAST-IRON SKILLET;
1 LARGE HANDFUL APPLE
OR CHERRY WOOD CHIPS,
SOAKED IN WATER 30 MIN**

1. Prepare the grill for indirect cooking over medium heat (350° to 400°F). In a food processor combine the onion and garlic and pulse until finely chopped. Add the lemon juice, yogurt, and all the spices and puree until fairly smooth, stopping to scrape down the bowl as needed.

2. Turn the cauliflower stem side up. Insert a small, sharp knife about ½ inch away from the stem and cut around the stem on a diagonal to remove it in one piece. Trim away any remaining leaves and discard them with the stem.

3. Lightly oil a 10-inch cast-iron skillet large enough to hold the cauliflower. Place the cauliflower, stemmed side down, in the skillet. Slather the yogurt mixture all over the cauliflower (some will run into the pan bottom, which is fine).

4. Drain the wood chips, scatter over the coals or add to the smoker box of a gas grill, and close the lid. When smoke appears, grill the cauliflower in the skillet over **indirect medium heat**, with the lid closed, until a knife slides easily into the center and the crust is nicely golden brown, 50 to 70 minutes.

5. If the cauliflower is browning too deeply, tent it with aluminum foil. Using a wide metal spatula, transfer the cauliflower to a platter, leaving behind any scorched sauce in the pan (it will taste bitter).

6. While the cauliflower is cooking, make the chutney. In a food processor combine all the ingredients except the yogurt and pulse until very finely chopped, stopping to scrape down the bowl sides as needed. Add the yogurt and puree until fairly smooth. To serve, cut the cauliflower into wedges. Serve warm with the chutney.

Grill-Baked Potatoes with Herb Butter
RECIPE ON PAGE 310

POTATOES

Did you know that our planet produces more potatoes than any other vegetable? That huge, diverse assortment of starchy tubers is split into two main types: mealy and waxy. The mealy potatoes, like the one shown on the opposite page, have a lot more starch granules that swell and break open when they are baked. They make the fluffiest baked potatoes. The waxy ones maintain a denser texture during cooking and are terrific for roasting. That slice of knowledge is just the starting point for cooking potatoes on the grill.

Top Tips for the Ultimate Baked Potatoes

1. Go with russets. For the fluffiest texture, use brown-skinned baking potatoes, such as russets or "Idaho" (which is a statement of origin, not a variety). When cooked, these starchy (mealy) potatoes have a lighter, airier interior than their waxy cousins, like the Yukon Gold.

2. Clean them up. Briefly soak the potatoes in cold water and scrub them well to remove any clinging dirt. (Be vigilant with this step.) Then dry the potatoes well with a clean kitchen towel; this helps to ensure crispy skins. Rub the skins before cooking with a little olive oil or, better yet, with bacon fat or other flavorful fat, and season with salt and pepper.

3. Let the steam go. Before grilling, pierce the potatoes in a few places with a fork or metal skewer to allow some steam to escape during cooking. They are done when most of the starch has "exploded" and lost its moisture. That dry, fluffy texture is perfect for absorbing a variety of toppings.

4. Keep them hot. To keep the potatoes piping hot, serve the toppings at room temperature, especially the refrigerated dairy products like cheeses, butter, and sour cream.

5. Skip the grate. Alternatively, cook potatoes in the embers of a charcoal grill. Let the coals burn down to medium heat, remove the cooking grate, nestle the potatoes in the coals, and cover the grill. Cook the potatoes, rotating them with long tongs every 10 minutes, until tender (open one up to check), 45 to 60 minutes. The skins will be blackened all over and the interiors will be irresistibly smoky and tasty.

6. Swap in sweet potatoes. These cooking methods work really well for sweet potatoes too. Just be aware that sweet potatoes typically cook a little faster than russets. Serve them with butter, crisp bacon, honey, brown sugar, a squeeze of lime juice, plain yogurt, chopped toasted pecans or cashews, or any combination of these ingredients.

Grill-Baked Potatoes with Herb Butter

HERB BUTTER

½ cup (1 stick) unsalted butter, softened

1 tablespoon finely chopped fresh Italian parsley leaves

2 teaspoons finely chopped fresh chives

2 teaspoons finely chopped fresh tarragon leaves

¼ teaspoon kosher salt

⅛ teaspoon ground black pepper

3 slices thick-cut bacon

4 russet potatoes, each 8 to 12 ounces

2 tablespoons rendered bacon fat, melted unsalted butter, or extra-virgin olive oil

1 teaspoon kosher salt

½ teaspoon ground black pepper

1 cup sour cream

3 tablespoons finely chopped fresh chives

It might feel a little decadent to brush bacon fat on potato skins before baking in the grill, but the properties of the fat yield a crispier outcome and a memorable flavor. Dropping some herb butter and bacon bits inside each luxurious potato makes for a mind-blowing finish.

1. In a small bowl combine all the ingredients for the herb butter and mash together with a fork to mix well. Cover and refrigerate.

2. In a medium skillet fry the bacon over medium-high heat on the stove until browned and crisp, 6 to 8 minutes, turning occasionally. Transfer the slices to a paper towel–lined plate to drain. Reserve the fat.

6. Brush the potatoes all over with the bacon fat and season the skins with the salt and pepper.

7. Brush the cooking grates clean. Grill the potatoes over **indirect medium heat**, with the lid closed, until tender, 45 minutes to 1¼ hours (use a skewer or paring knife to check doneness). Remove from the grill.

| SERVES **4** | PREP: **30 MIN** |  COOK: **6–8 MIN** (BACON) |  GRILL: **45 MIN–** 1¼ **HOURS** |

3. Pour the bacon fat (about ¼ cup) into a small heatproof bowl or liquid measuring pitcher and set aside to cool. Prepare the grill for indirect cooking over medium heat (350° to 400°F).

4. Put the potatoes in a large bowl, add cold water to cover generously, and let stand for a few minutes. Scrub the potatoes well in the water, then drain and rinse under cold running water. Dry the potatoes thoroughly.

5. Pierce the potatoes in a few places with a fork (a meat fork works best).

8. While the potatoes are cooking, coarsely chop the cooked bacon. Put the bacon, herb butter, sour cream, and chives in separate small bowls and let stand at room temperature for about 1 hour. Add a small spoon to each bowl for serving.

9. Holding each hot potato with tongs, use a small, sharp knife to cut a deep incision lengthwise into the potato and then a short incision crosswise.

10. Squeeze each potato at both ends at the same time to open up the center. Transfer the potatoes to a platter. Serve immediately with the toppings and invite guests to dress their potatoes as desired.

FLAVOR BOMB *your* GRILL-BAKED POTATO

A baked potato's greatest virtue may be its adaptability. What other vegetable is as agreeable to all of the following: an Indian curry, a riff on Mexican nachos, a French-inspired medley of mushrooms and blue cheese, and a Greek frat party of tomatoes, olives, and feta cheese with tzatziki?

TOMATO CHICKPEA CURRY POTATOES

In a medium saucepan over medium heat, sauté ½ cup chopped yellow onion in 1 tablespoon olive oil until tender, 5 to 6 minutes. Add 2 garlic cloves, minced, and 2 teaspoons minced, peeled fresh ginger and stir for 1 minute. Stir in 1 can (15 ounces) crushed tomatoes, 1 can (15 ounces) drained and rinsed chickpeas, 2 tablespoons fresh lime juice, 1 tablespoon curry powder, 1 teaspoon packed light brown sugar, and ¾ teaspoon kosher salt. Simmer over low heat for 8 minutes, stirring often. Spoon over 4 grill-baked and split potatoes (see page 310). Top each potato with 1 tablespoon sour cream and 1½ teaspoons chopped fresh cilantro.

NACHO POTATOES

In a small saucepan over low heat, combine 1 can (15 ounces) drained and rinsed black beans, 2 teaspoons fresh lime juice, 1 teaspoon ground cumin, ½ teaspoon hot sauce, and ½ teaspoon kosher salt and stir until hot, 3 to 5 minutes. Split 4 grill-baked potatoes (see page 310) and sprinkle each one with 2 tablespoons coarsely grated sharp cheddar cheese. Spoon the hot beans over the cheese. Top each potato with 1 tablespoon tomato salsa; ¼ avocado, peeled and diced; and 1 tablespoon sour cream. Garnish each potato with 1½ teaspoons chopped fresh cilantro.

CARAMELIZED ONION, MUSHROOM, AND BLUE CHEESE POTATOES

In a large skillet over medium-high heat, sauté 1 pound yellow onions, thinly sliced, in 2 tablespoons olive oil until golden, 5 to 7 minutes, stirring occasionally. Reduce the heat to medium-low and cook until lightly caramelized, about 10 minutes, stirring often. Add 8 ounces white mushrooms, sliced, and season with ¾ teaspoon kosher salt, ½ teaspoon dried thyme, and ¼ teaspoon ground black pepper. Cook until the mushrooms are tender and brown, 8 to 10 minutes, stirring often. Add 2 tablespoons balsamic vinegar and cook until evaporated, about 30 seconds. Spoon over 4 grill-baked and split potatoes (see page 310). Garnish each potato with 2 tablespoons crumbled blue cheese and 1 teaspoon chopped fresh thyme.

GREEK POTATOES

Chop 12 cherry tomatoes and 12 pitted Kalamata olives and transfer to a small bowl. Add 1 cup crumbled feta cheese (5 ounces), 1 teaspoon fresh lemon juice, and a pinch of ground black pepper and stir gently to mix. Split 4 grill-baked potatoes (see page 310) and spoon 2 to 3 tablespoons Cucumber-Mint Tzatziki (page 338) or store-bought tzatziki over each potato, allowing it to drizzle into the crevices. Spoon the salad over each potato, then garnish each potato with 1½ teaspoons chopped fresh mint leaves and a grind or two of black pepper.

Steak Fries with Chipotle Ketchup and Aioli

CHIPOTLE KETCHUP

1 cup ketchup

1 chipotle chile pepper in adobo sauce, minced, with more adobo sauce to taste

1 garlic clove, minced or pushed through a press

½ teaspoon ground cumin

¼ teaspoon ground black pepper

Kosher salt

LEMON AIOLI

¾ cup mayonnaise

1 garlic clove, minced or pushed through a press

2 tablespoons fresh lemon juice

½ teaspoon finely grated lemon zest

⅛ teaspoon ground black pepper

Kosher salt

4 large russet potatoes, each about 12 ounces, scrubbed

2 tablespoons extra-virgin olive oil

2 teaspoons kosher salt

1 teaspoon ground black pepper

For many, a steak without fries is unfinished business. This foolproof recipe for big, crispy grilled fries will ensure no steak is ever lonely again. You can keep these smoky, hearty wedges warm for at least 15 minutes in a pan set over indirect heat.

SERVES 6–8

 PREP: **15 MIN**

 GRILL: **15–25 MIN**

1. In a small bowl whisk together all the ketchup ingredients. In another small bowl, whisk together all the aioli ingredients. You should have about 1 cup of each. Set aside. Prepare the grill for direct cooking over medium heat (as close to 400°F as possible).

2. Cut the potatoes in half lengthwise, then cut each half lengthwise into about 4 wedges each ½ inch thick.

3. If you are ready to grill, place the wedges in a large bowl, add the oil, salt, and pepper, and toss to coat evenly. If you are not ready to grill, submerge the wedges in a bowl of water to prevent them from discoloring. Then drain them, pat them thoroughly dry, and coat with the oil, salt, and pepper.

4. Brush the cooking grates clean. Arrange the potato wedges perpendicular to the grate bars.

5. Grill over **direct medium heat**, with the lid closed, until golden brown and tender, 15 to 25 minutes, turning every 5 minutes (to ensure they don't break apart, use tongs and grab the center of each wedge). Serve the fries warm with the ketchup and aioli for dipping.

KEEP 'EM WARM

Some fries will probably be done a little sooner than others. That happens when some wedges are cut a little thinner than others. As each fry gets nicely browned and crispy, move it to a perforated grill pan. When all the fries are on the pan, set the pan over indirect heat. That way you can keep them warm while focusing your attention on grilling the rest of the meal, which hopefully includes some great steak.

Roasted Red Potatoes with Herbs

¼ cup extra-virgin olive oil

2 tablespoons finely chopped fresh rosemary leaves, plus more for garnish

1 tablespoon finely chopped fresh thyme leaves, plus more for garnish

2 teaspoons minced garlic

Kosher salt and ground black pepper

2 pounds red or Yukon Gold potatoes, each 1½ to 2 inches in diameter

For crispy edges worth coveting, preheat the grill pan by itself first and then spread the potatoes in a single layer. If you arrange many of them cut side down for most of the grilling time, they will brown more beautifully.

SERVES **4–6**

PREP: **20 MIN**

GRILL: **20–30 MIN**

SPECIAL EQUIPMENT:
**LARGE PERFORATED
GRILL PAN**

1. Prepare the grill for indirect cooking over medium-high heat (400° to 450°F). In a large bowl whisk together the oil, rosemary, thyme, garlic, ¾ teaspoon salt, and ¼ teaspoon pepper.

2. Cut the potatoes into chunks with sides that are 1 to 1½ inches across. Add the potatoes to the bowl with the oil mixture and toss to coat evenly. Brush the cooking grates clean. Place a large perforated grill pan over indirect heat, close the lid, and preheat for 10 minutes.

3. Use a slotted spoon to transfer the potatoes to the grill pan, arranging them in a single layer. (Do not dump them onto the pan, as the excess oil can cause flare-ups.) Reserve the bowl without washing it.

4. Grill the potatoes over **indirect medium-high heat**, with the lid closed, until nicely browned and tender when pierced with a knife, 20 to 30 minutes, shaking the pan once or twice to turn them over. Return the potatoes to the bowl, toss them with the residual oil in the bowl, and season with salt and pepper. Serve warm.

Dessert and Coffee

Summer Berry Crostata, recipe on page 326; **Whipped Cream,** recipe on page 330; **Grilled Pineapple with Blackberry Sauce,** recipe on page 320

DESSERTS

Grilled Pineapple with Blackberry Sauce

12 ounces fresh blackberries (about 2⅔ cups), plus a handful more for garnish (optional)

1 tablespoon sugar

1 tablespoon water or rum

1 teaspoon fresh lemon juice

2 tablespoons raw shelled pistachios (optional)

4 peeled, fresh pineapple slices, each 1 inch thick and cored

Canola oil

4 large fresh mint leaves, very thinly sliced (optional)

Save this recipe for summertime when blackberries are at their sweetest. Using precut fresh pineapple means this recipe comes together quickly. Place the skewered cubes over direct heat, with the exposed ends of the bamboo wrapped in aluminum foil to prevent the wood from burning.

SERVES **4**

 PREP: **15 MIN**

 GRILL: **5–10 MIN**

SPECIAL EQUIPMENT:
**4 METAL OR BAMBOO
SKEWERS (SOAK BAMBOO
IN WATER 30 MIN)**

1. In a food processor combine the berries, sugar, water, and lemon juice and puree until smooth. Do not overprocess or you'll break up the tiny seeds, which can be bitter. Using a rubber spatula, force the puree through a fine-mesh sieve set over a bowl. Discard the seeds. Cover and refrigerate until ready to serve.

2. If using the pistachios, in a small skillet over medium-high heat, stir the pistachios until they are lightly toasted, 1 to 3 minutes. Transfer to a cutting board, let cool, and then chop finely. Prepare the grill for direct cooking over medium heat (350° to 450°F).

3. Cut each pineapple slice into six equal chunks and thread them onto four skewers, dividing them evenly and making sure the flat side of each chunk faces out for optimal grill marks. Brush the pineapple chunks lightly with oil.

4. If using bamboo skewers, cut eight small pieces of heavy-duty aluminum foil. Wrap each piece around the ends of the skewers so they don't burn while grilling. Brush the cooking grates clean.

5. Place the skewers over **direct medium heat** and grill, with the lid closed, until the pineapple is well grill-marked and warm, 5 to 10 minutes, turning a couple of times to mark both sides. Remove from the grill.

6. Serve the skewers with the blackberry sauce. Top with the whole blackberries, if using, and sprinkle with the mint and pistachios, if using. Serve right away.

Banana Splits with Salted Caramel Sauce

SALTED CARAMEL SAUCE

¾ cup sugar

¼ cup water

6 tablespoons heavy whipping cream

1 tablespoon good-quality bourbon

1 teaspoon pure vanilla extract

¼ teaspoon kosher salt

4 firm but ripe bananas

2 tablespoons unsalted butter, melted

1 quart chocolate or vanilla ice cream

Whipped cream (page 330)

¼ cup chopped, toasted pecans

Maraschino cherries (optional)

Mushy, brown bananas need not apply here. The fruit needs to be firm and just ripe to stand up to the grill's heat. Leaving the skins on the split halves will help the bananas keep their shape We'll be honest: the sauce is sort of the best part.

1. Prepare the grill for direct cooking over medium heat (350° to 450°F). In a heavy saucepan stir together the sugar and water and place over high heat on the stove. Bring to a boil, swirling the pan gently, until the sugar dissolves. Brush down the sides with a wet pastry brush to prevent sugar crystals from forming.

2. Boil, without stirring, until the syrup turns a deep amber, occasionally swirling the pan and continuing to brush down the sides with the wet pastry brush, 7 to 9 minutes. Remove from the heat.

3. Stand back while carefully adding the cream, bourbon, vanilla extract, and salt (the mixture will bubble up vigorously). Stir with a heatproof rubber spatula until smooth, briefly placing the pan back over low heat if needed to dissolve any caramel bits. Set aside off the heat.

4. Cut each banana in half lengthwise, leaving the skin attached (to help the bananas hold their shape on the grill). Brush the cut sides with the butter. Brush the cooking grates clean. Grill the bananas, cut sides down, over **direct medium heat**, with the lid open, until warm and well grill-marked on the cut sides but not too soft, 2 to 3 minutes.

5. Remove from the grill. Peel the banana halves, then leave them in halves or cut each half in half again and set aside.

6. To serve, place 2 scoops of ice cream in each of four bowls. Gently set the banana pieces on opposite sides of the ice cream in each bowl. Drizzle each serving with the caramel sauce, top with the whipped cream, and garnish with the pecans and cherries, if using. Serve immediately.

Summer Berry Crostata
RECIPE ON PAGE 326

BERRY CROSTATA

When your baking skills are modest, but your dessert dreams are spectacular, this rustic, free-form tart is for you. Ripe, colorful berries become sweeter, more tender, and even more beautiful when encased in a flaky golden crust and baked right on your grill. Follow the steps on the following pages to create this easier-than-it looks dessert, and then try out other fruits, like sliced ripe peaches, nectarines, or apricots.

Summer Berry Crostata

DOUGH

1 cup plus 1 tablespoon all-purpose flour

¼ cup sugar

¼ teaspoon kosher salt

6 tablespoons (¾ stick) cold unsalted butter, cut into 16 pieces

3 tablespoons good-quality bourbon

EGG WASH

1 large egg

1 tablespoon heavy whipping cream

1 pound assorted summer berries (about 3½ cups), such as small strawberries (hulled and halved), raspberries, blackberries, and blueberries, rinsed and blotted dry on paper towels

2 tablespoons all-purpose flour

3 tablespoons sugar, divided

1 tablespoon good-quality bourbon

Whipped cream (page 330) or vanilla ice cream

Indirect heat is the key to cooking this tender, flaky crust without burning it. Also important is to use parchment paper for easy transfer on and off the pizza stone. Choose any combination of ripe summer berries for this seasonal treat.

1. In a food processor combine the flour, sugar, and salt and pulse briefly to blend. Add the butter and pulse until pea-size pieces develop. Add the bourbon and pulse just until combined.

2. Turn the shaggy dough out into a large bowl and form it into a smooth ball. Avoid overworking the dough, or the crust will be tough. Flatten the dough into a 4-inch-wide disk. Wrap in plastic wrap and refrigerate until the grill and pizza stone are preheated, at least 20 minutes.

6. Working quickly (to prevent the dough from getting too soft), toss the berries with the flour and 2 tablespoons of the sugar in a large bowl. Add the bourbon and toss to mix evenly.

7. Spoon the berry mixture onto the center of the dough circle, leaving a 2-inch border of uncovered dough around the perimeter. To create a partial top crust (with an opening in the center, exposing most of the berries), fold the edges of the dough snugly over the filling, pleating them as needed.

3. Prepare the grill for indirect cooking over medium heat (350° to 450°F). Brush the cooking grates clean. Place a pizza stone over indirect heat, close the lid, and preheat for at least 15 minutes. In a small bowl whisk together the egg and cream for the egg wash.

4. Cut a piece of parchment paper about 15 inches square. Remove the dough from the refrigerator and let sit until just soft enough to roll out. Lightly flour the parchment and the dough and set the dough on the parchment paper. Lightly flour a rolling pin and roll out the dough into a 12-inch circle ⅛- to ¼-inch thick.

5. Trim the parchment square so a 1-inch border remains around the dough circle. Slide the dough on the parchment onto a pizza peel or large rimless baking sheet (for transporting to the grill).

8. Lightly brush the top crust with the egg wash (you won't use all of it), then sprinkle the entire top evenly with the remaining 1 tablespoon sugar.

9. Using the parchment to help guide you, gently transfer the crostata to the preheated pizza stone.

10. Grill over indirect medium heat, with the lid closed, until the fruit is bubbling and the crust is browned, 30 to 35 minutes. Using the pizza peel or baking sheet, remove the crostata and parchment from the stone. Transfer to a plate or cutting board and let cool for 10 minutes. Serve with whipped cream.

Peach and Blueberry Cobbler

Nonstick cooking spray

3 ripe medium peaches, cut into bite-size pieces (about 3 cups)

1 cup blueberries

3 tablespoons packed light brown sugar

BATTER

1 cup all-purpose flour

½ cup packed light brown sugar

1 teaspoon baking powder

¼ teaspoon salt

¾ cup whole milk

½ teaspoon pure vanilla extract

Vanilla ice cream or whipped cream (page 330)

Peaches and blueberries, the high-summer staples, work well here, but 3 to 4 cups of nearly any kind of ripe stone fruit and berries would be just as delicious. If you swap out the blueberries for one of their kin, use whole raspberries or blackberries or hulled and halved strawberries.

SERVES **4**

PREP: **15 MIN**

GRILL: **30–45 MIN**

SPECIAL EQUIPMENT:
9- OR 10-INCH
CAST-IRON SKILLET
OR PIE PAN

1. Prepare the grill for indirect cooking over medium heat (350° to 400°F). Spray a well-seasoned 9- or 10-inch cast-iron pie pan or skillet with cooking spray to prevent sticking. In the pan combine the peaches and blueberries, sprinkle with the sugar, and toss to coat the fruits evenly.

2. In a liquid measuring pitcher or bowl, whisk together the flour, sugar, baking powder, and salt. Add the milk and vanilla and whisk just until the ingredients are evenly mixed; do not overmix. Spread the batter evenly over the fruit.

3. Immediately cook over **indirect medium heat**, with the lid closed, until the top is browned, the topping is set and cooked through, and the fruit juices are bubbling, 30 to 45 minutes. Remove from the grill and let cool for about 10 minutes. Serve warm with ice cream.

GRILL-BAKING

Baking on the grill is not much different from baking in an oven. It's just nicer to be outside. With your grill set up for indirect heat and the lid closed, heat will circulate evenly around the food, rather than blasting it from directly below. That means that if you can bake something in the oven, you can usually bake it on the grill.

Before getting started, pick your pan wisely. This is not the place to use a delicate glass pan or an expensive Dutch oven that might discolor on the grill. Select something sturdy and dark, like a seasoned cast-iron skillet. The thick cast iron will take a little longer to heat up than a thin metal pan, but it will keep your food warmer for longer once it's off the grill.

You may have heard that acidic ingredients such as fruit can react with metals like cast iron and develop an off flavor. If you're concerned about that, use an enamel-coated cast-iron pan like the round Weber griddle.

Chocolate Banana Bread Pudding

1 tablespoon unsalted butter, softened

3 to 4 large croissants, about 9 ounces total

2 ripe but firm bananas, peeled and cut crosswise into ½-inch-thick slices

½ cup semisweet chocolate chips or chunks

2 large eggs

¼ cup sugar

¾ teaspoon pure vanilla extract

¼ teaspoon kosher salt

1 cup heavy whipping cream

1 cup whole milk

WHIPPED CREAM

1½ cups heavy whipping cream

2 tablespoons sugar

1 tablespoon pure vanilla extract

Yesterday's breakfast is today's dessert masterpiece. The trick here is to use day-old croissants instead of the usual bread and to place the pudding over direct heat to jump-start the cooking. Then let it finish over indirect heat to achieve a decadent, rich texture.

SERVES 4–6

PREP: **15 MIN**

GRILL: **ABOUT 40 MIN**

SPECIAL EQUIPMENT:
**10-INCH CAST-IRON
SKILLET OR ROUND
GRIDDLE**

1. Prepare the grill for direct and indirect cooking over medium-low heat (about 350°F). Generously grease the griddle or skillet with the butter. Cut or tear the croissants into bite-size pieces and put into a large bowl.

2. Add the bananas and chocolate to the croissants and toss gently to mix.

3. In a medium bowl whisk together the eggs, sugar, vanilla, and salt until smooth. Add the cream and milk and whisk to combine.

4. Pour the egg mixture over the bread mixture, then fold gently with a spatula to combine. Spread the mixture evenly in the prepared pan.

5. Place over **direct medium-low heat** and bake, with the lid closed, for 10 minutes to begin the cooking. Move the pan over **indirect medium-low heat** and bake, with the lid closed, until set in the center and puffed and browned on top, 25 to 35 minutes, rotating the pan every 10 minutes. Remove from the grill.

6. In a bowl combine the cream, sugar, and vanilla and whip with a whisk or handheld beater until soft peaks form. If desired, cover and chill the whipped cream for up to 1 hour before serving. Serve the bread pudding warm, in individual bowls, with the whipped cream.

RUBS & PASTES

Beef Dry Rub

MAKES ABOUT 2 TABLESPOONS

1½ teaspoons kosher salt
1½ teaspoons prepared chili powder
1 teaspoon granulated garlic
½ teaspoon ground coriander
½ teaspoon ground cumin

In a small bowl stir together all the rub ingredients.
Use for steak and fajitas.

Chipotle-Oregano Chicken Rub

MAKES ABOUT 1 TABLESPOON

1 teaspoon kosher salt
1 teaspoon dried oregano
½ teaspoon ground cumin
½ teaspoon chipotle chile powder
¼ teaspoon ground black pepper

In a small bowl stir together all the rub ingredients.
Use for chicken pieces.

Pork Rib Rub

MAKES ABOUT ⅓ CUP

1 tablespoon kosher salt
1 tablespoon smoked paprika
1 tablespoon granulated onion
1 tablespoon prepared chili powder
2 teaspoons ground cumin
1 teaspoon celery seed
1 teaspoon ground black pepper

In a small bowl stir together all the rub ingredients.
Use for baby back ribs or spareribs.

Pork Shoulder Rub

MAKES ABOUT ¼ CUP

1 tablespoon packed dark brown sugar
1 tablespoon sweet paprika
1 tablespoon kosher salt
1½ teaspoons garlic powder
1 teaspoon onion powder
1 teaspoon ground black pepper
½ teaspoon dry mustard

In a small bowl stir together all the rub ingredients.
Use for pork shoulder roast (pulled pork).

Seafood Rub

MAKES ABOUT 2 TABLESPOONS

2 teaspoons kosher salt
1 teaspoon prepared chili powder
1 teaspoon granulated garlic
½ teaspoon ground coriander
½ teaspoon celery seed
½ teaspoon ground black pepper

In a small bowl stir together all the rub ingredients.
Use for fish fillets or shellfish.

Red Chili Rub

MAKES ABOUT 2 TABLESPOONS

2 teaspoons prepared chili powder
1½ teaspoons kosher salt
1 teaspoon packed dark brown sugar
1 teaspoon granulated garlic
½ teaspoon ground black pepper

In a small bowl stir together all the rub ingredients.
Use for pork tenderloin, pork chops, or chicken pieces.

Five-Spice Poultry Rub

MAKES ABOUT 2 TABLESPOONS

2 teaspoons granulated garlic
1½ teaspoons Chinese five spice
1 teaspoon ground coriander
1 teaspoon kosher salt
½ teaspoon ground black pepper

In a small bowl stir together all the rub ingredients.
Use for chicken, turkey, or duck.

Caribbean Rub

MAKES ABOUT ¼ CUP

1 tablespoon packed light brown sugar
1 tablespoon granulated garlic
1 tablespoon dried thyme
2¼ teaspoons kosher salt
¼ teaspoon ground black pepper
¼ teaspoon ground allspice

In a small bowl stir together all the rub ingredients.
Use for chicken, turkey, or duck.

Steak Spice Paste

MAKES ABOUT ¼ CUP

3 tablespoons extra-virgin olive oil
1 teaspoon sweet paprika
1 teaspoon kosher salt
½ teaspoon dried oregano
½ teaspoon ground coriander
½ teaspoon granulated garlic
¼ teaspoon ground black pepper

In a small bowl mix together all the paste ingredients. Brush the paste evenly over both sides of the meat before grilling. Use for steaks.

Toasted Fennel Paste

MAKES ABOUT ½ CUP

1½ tablespoons fennel seeds
4 tablespoons extra-virgin olive oil, divided
2 garlic cloves, minced or pushed through a press
2 teaspoons dried oregano
1½ teaspoons kosher salt
1 teaspoon sweet paprika
¾ teaspoon crushed red pepper flakes
¾ teaspoon ground black pepper

Toast the fennel seeds in a skillet over medium heat on the stove until fragrant, about 1 minute, stirring often. Transfer the fennel seeds to a cutting board. Drizzle 1½ teaspoons oil on the fennel seeds and finely chop them. Transfer the fennel seeds to a small bowl, add all the remaining rub ingredients including the remaining 3½ tablespoons oil, and mix to form a paste. Use for pork chops, pork tenderloin, or lamb chops.

Tuscan Herb Paste

MAKES ABOUT ½ CUP

3 garlic cloves
2 tablespoons chopped fresh rosemary
2 tablespoons chopped fresh sage
1 tablespoon fresh lemon juice
½ teaspoon finely grated lemon zest
½ teaspoon kosher salt
¼ teaspoon ground black pepper
3 tablespoons extra-virgin olive oil

Using a mortar and pestle (or a small food processor), grind together the garlic, rosemary, sage, lemon juice and zest, salt, and pepper until a relatively smooth paste forms. Blend in the oil. Rub the herb paste all over the meat. Cover and refrigerate for at least 3 hours and up to 8 hours. Remove from the refrigerator just prior to preparing the grill. Use for pork or chicken pieces.

Dijon-Herb Paste

MAKES ABOUT 3 TABLESPOONS

1 tablespoon Dijon mustard
2 teaspoons Worcestershire sauce
2 teaspoons dried thyme or dried Italian seasoning blend
2 large garlic cloves
¾ teaspoon kosher salt
½ teaspoon ground black pepper

In a small bowl whisk together the mustard, Worcestershire sauce, and thyme. On a cutting board smash the garlic cloves with the side of a knife and then mince. Sprinkle with the salt and then use the side of the knife to mash the garlic and salt together to make a paste. Stir into the mustard mixture along with the pepper. Use for whole chicken or chicken pieces.

Garlic-Rosemary Paste

MAKES ABOUT 1 CUP

6 garlic cloves, smashed and peeled
1 cup packed fresh Italian parsley leaves and tender stems
2 tablespoons fresh rosemary leaves
1 tablespoon fresh thyme leaves
¼ cup Dijon mustard
2 tablespoons extra-virgin olive oil

In a food processor, process the garlic until chopped and it sticks to the sides of the bowl. Scrape down the sides of the bowl; add the parsley, rosemary, and thyme and pulse until finely chopped, occasionally scraping down the sides of the bowl as needed. Add the mustard and oil and process just until blended. Use for prime rib, beef tenderloin, or leg of lamb.

North African Spice Paste

MAKES ABOUT 1 CUP

⅓ cup extra-virgin olive oil
⅓ cup packed fresh cilantro leaves, very finely chopped
⅓ cup packed fresh basil leaves, very finely chopped
2 tablespoons sherry vinegar
2 to 3 garlic cloves, minced or pushed through a press
1½ teaspoons sweet paprika
¾ teaspoon kosher salt
¾ teaspoon ground cumin
⅛ to ¼ teaspoon cayenne pepper or ground black pepper

In a large bowl whisk together all the ingredients for the paste until smooth and emulsified. Alternatively, add the ingredients to a food processor and process until smooth. Use for chicken pieces, pork tenderloin, or lamb chops.

MARINADES & BRINES

Cuban Citrus Marinade

MAKES ABOUT 1½ CUPS

Finely grated zest and juice of 1 large lemon
Finely grated zest and juice of 1 large lime
½ cup fresh orange juice
⅓ cup extra-virgin olive oil
1½ teaspoons kosher salt
1 teaspoon ground cumin
1 teaspoon dried oregano
1 teaspoon granulated garlic
½ teaspoon ground black pepper

In a large bowl whisk together the lemon zest and juice, lime zest and juice, orange juice, oil, salt, cumin, oregano, garlic, and pepper to make a marinade. Transfer ⅓ cup of the marinade to a separate small bowl and set aside to serve later as a sauce. Put the chicken in a large resealable plastic bag and pour in the marinade. Press the air out of the bag and seal closed. Turn the bag to distribute the marinade. Put the bag in the large bowl and refrigerate for at least 4 hours and up to overnight. Use for whole chicken or chicken pieces.

Lemon-Herb Marinade

MAKES ABOUT ¾ CUP

½ cup packed fresh Italian parsley leaves and tender stems
¼ cup extra-virgin olive oil
5 or 6 garlic cloves
Finely grated zest of 1 lemon
1 tablespoon fresh lemon juice
1 tablespoon dried oregano leaves
1 teaspoon kosher salt
½ teaspoon ground black pepper

Combine all the marinade ingredients in a food processor and process until a coarse paste forms. Place the poultry or seafood in a bowl and add the marinade. Mix well to coat evenly. Cover and refrigerate for 1 to 4 hours, turning occasionally in the marinade. Use for boneless chicken thighs and breasts, shrimp, or fish fillets.

Mediterranean Marinade

MAKES ABOUT ½ CUP

¼ cup finely chopped fresh mint
3 tablespoons extra-virgin olive oil
2 tablespoons fresh lemon juice (from 1 lemon)
1 tablespoon dried oregano
3 garlic cloves, minced

1 teaspoon kosher salt
½ teaspoon ground black pepper

In a medium bowl whisk together all the marinade ingredients. Put the meat or poultry in the bowl and stir to coat evenly. Cover and refrigerate for 2 to 4 hours. Use for pork loin, rack of lamb, or chicken pieces.

Beer Marinade

MAKES ABOUT 1¼ CUPS

1 cup dark Mexican beer
2 tablespoons dark sesame oil
1 tablespoon finely chopped garlic
1 teaspoon dried oregano
1 teaspoon kosher salt
½ teaspoon ground black pepper
¼ teaspoon cayenne pepper

In a medium bowl whisk together all the marinade ingredients. Add the meat or poultry to the bowl and mix well. Cover and refrigerate for at least 1 hour and up to 24 hours. Use for pork or chicken.

Tequila Marinade

MAKES ABOUT 1¾ CUPS

1 cup fresh orange juice
½ cup tequila
2 tablespoons fresh lime juice
2 tablespoons packed light brown sugar
2 teaspoons ground cumin
1 jalapeño chile pepper, thinly sliced

In a medium bowl whisk together all the marinade ingredients until the sugar dissolves. Add the meat or poultry to the bowl and mix well. Cover and refrigerate for at least 1 hour and up to 24 hours. Use for beef, pork, or chicken.

Smoked Paprika and Lemon Marinade

MAKES ABOUT ½ CUP

¼ cup extra-virgin olive oil
Finely grated zest of 1 lemon
2 tablespoons fresh lemon juice
1½ teaspoons smoked paprika
1 teaspoon kosher salt
1 teaspoon granulated garlic
¼ teaspoon ground black pepper

Combine all ingredients in the food processor and process until well combined. Use for chicken pieces.

Catalan Marinade

MAKES ABOUT 1½ CUPS

4 large garlic cloves
1 cup packed fresh Italian parsley leaves and tender stems
1 cup packed fresh cilantro leaves and tender stems
1 teaspoon finely grated lemon zest
1 teaspoon smoked paprika
½ teaspoon ground cumin
½ teaspoon kosher salt
⅓ cup extra-virgin olive oil

Combine the marinade ingredients in a food processor and process until finely chopped. Spread the marinade evenly over the meat. Cover with plastic wrap and refrigerate for 6 to 8 hours. Let stand at room temperature 1 hour before grilling. Use for lamb chops or leg of lamb.

Thai Marinade

MAKES ABOUT ½ CUP

¼ cup vegetable oil
2 tablespoons fresh lime juice
2 teaspoons Thai red curry paste
2 garlic cloves, minced
1 teaspoon kosher salt
¼ teaspoon ground black pepper

In a medium bowl whisk together all the marinade ingredients. Add the meat or poultry to the bowl and mix well. Cover and refrigerate for at least 1 hour and up to 24 hours. Use for pork or chicken.

Asian Soy Marinade

MAKES ABOUT ⅔ CUP

¼ cup soy sauce
¼ cup mirin or dry sherry
1 tablespoon toasted sesame oil
2 teaspoons peeled, finely grated fresh ginger
2 teaspoons minced or grated garlic
2 teaspoons packed light brown sugar
1 teaspoon Sriracha or other hot chili-garlic sauce

Whisk together all the marinade ingredients in a glass baking dish large enough to accommodate the main ingredients in a single layer. Turn to coat all sides with the marinade. Cover and refrigerate for at least 1 hour and up to 24 hours. Use for fish fillets, chicken pieces, or pork.

Adobo Marinade

MAKES ABOUT 2 CUPS

6 large garlic cloves, smashed and peeled
2-by-1-inch piece fresh ginger, peeled and coarsely chopped
2 teaspoons black peppercorns

1 cup distilled white vinegar
½ cup soy sauce
2 tablespoons vegetable oil

In a food processor combine the garlic, ginger, and peppercorns and pulse until finely ground, about 3 minutes, scraping down the sides of the bowl occasionally. Add the vinegar, soy sauce, and oil and process until pureed, about 30 seconds. Add the meat or poultry to the bowl and mix well. Cover and refrigerate for 2 to 4 hours. Use for pork or chicken.

Basic Brine

MAKES ABOUT 2 QUARTS

8 cups water
⅓ cup kosher salt
⅓ cup sugar
4 garlic cloves, smashed
1 tablespoon dried thyme
1 tablespoon ground black pepper

Combine all the brine ingredients in a large bowl or baking dish, whisking until the salt and sugar are dissolved. Submerge the meat or poultry in the brine. Cover and refrigerate for at least 3 hours and up to 24 hours. When ready to grill, remove the meat or poultry from the brine, discard the brine, and pat dry with paper towels. Brush lightly with olive oil. Use for whole chicken or other poultry, chicken pieces, or pork.

Herb-Wine Brine

MAKES ABOUT 5½ CUPS

1 cup dry white wine
½ cup cold water, plus 4 cups ice-cold water
½ cup kosher salt
¼ cup packed light brown sugar
2 fresh rosemary sprigs
2 fresh sage sprigs

In a saucepan combine the wine, ½ cup cold water, salt, sugar, rosemary, and sage. Bring to a simmer over medium-high heat and simmer until the salt and sugar dissolve, stirring often. Remove from the heat and add the 4 cups ice-cold water. Let the brine cool to room temperature.

Put the meat, fat side up if applicable, into a container just deep and wide enough to contain it with room for the brine to cover it completely. Pour the brine over the meat. If the meat is not fully submerged, add just enough cold water to cover. Refrigerate, covered, for at least 6 hours and up to overnight. Use for whole chicken or other poultry, chicken pieces, or pork.

SAUCES, DRESSINGS & MORE

Maple-Bourbon BBQ Sauce

MAKES ABOUT 1 CUP

¾ cup ketchup
¼ cup maple syrup
¼ cup bourbon
2 tablespoons cider vinegar
¼ teaspoon chipotle chile powder

In a saucepan over high heat, bring all the sauce ingredients to a boil, then reduce the heat to a simmer and cook for 12 to 15 minutes, stirring occasionally. Remove from the heat. Use for chicken pieces.

Cola Barbecue Sauce

MAKES ABOUT 1½ CUPS

1 cup ketchup
1 cup cola
3 tablespoons cider vinegar
2 tablespoons molasses
2 tablespoons yellow mustard
1 tablespoon Worcestershire sauce
1 teaspoon prepared chili powder

In a saucepan over medium-high heat, bring all the sauce ingredients to a gentle boil, stirring often. Reduce the heat to low and simmer until the mixture thickens, 15 to 20 minutes, stirring occasionally. Use for pork ribs, brisket, or chicken.

Smoked Onion BBQ Sauce

MAKES ABOUT 2 CUPS

1 Vidalia or other sweet onion, unpeeled, halved lengthwise
2 tablespoons extra-virgin olive oil
2 large garlic cloves, minced
1¼ cups ketchup
¼ cup cider vinegar
¼ cup packed dark brown sugar
1 tablespoon Worcestershire sauce
2½ teaspoons prepared chili powder
2 teaspoons smoked paprika

Smoke the onion halves over indirect low heat, with the lid closed, for 1½ hours. Transfer the onion to a cutting board. Peel and mince the onion (about 1 cup). In a saucepan over medium heat, warm the oil. Add the onion and cook, stirring, until soft and golden brown, 5 to 10 minutes. Add the garlic and cook for 30 seconds, stirring. Stir in the remaining ingredients. Reduce the heat to low, and simmer, stirring frequently, until thickened and reduced to 2 cups, about 5 minutes. Use for pork ribs, brisket, or chicken.

Carolina Vinegar Sauce

MAKES ABOUT 1 CUP

¾ cup cider vinegar
¼ cup water
4 teaspoons packed dark brown sugar
1½ teaspoons sweet paprika
1½ teaspoons hot sauce, such as Tabasco®
1 teaspoon crushed red pepper flakes
¾ teaspoon dry mustard
¾ teaspoon garlic powder
¾ teaspoon kosher salt

In a medium bowl whisk together all the sauce ingredients until the sugar and salt dissolve. Use for pulled pork.

Tangy Barbecue Sauce

MAKES ABOUT 3 CUPS

1½ cups ketchup
¾ cup unsweetened apple juice
¾ cup cider vinegar
3 tablespoons packed light brown sugar
3 tablespoons tomato paste
1½ tablespoons unsulfured molasses (not blackstrap)
1 tablespoon Worcestershire sauce
1½ teaspoons mustard powder
¾ teaspoon hot sauce, such as Tabasco®
¾ teaspoon kosher salt
½ teaspoon ground black pepper

In a heavy saucepan whisk together all the sauce ingredients. Bring to a simmer over medium heat on the stove. Cook until fragrant, about 5 minutes, stirring occasionally. Use for pork ribs, pulled pork, or chicken pieces.

Hoisin Barbecue Glaze

MAKES ABOUT ½ CUP

1 tablespoon toasted sesame oil
1 teaspoon grated garlic
1 teaspoon peeled, finely grated fresh ginger
¼ cup hoisin sauce
2 tablespoons soy sauce
2 tablespoons packed light brown sugar
2 tablespoons honey
1 tablespoon rice vinegar

In a saucepan over medium heat warm the sesame oil. Add the garlic and ginger and cook for 30 to 60 seconds, stirring constantly. Add the remaining glaze ingredients, mix well, and cook until simmering, 1 to 2 minutes. Use for chicken pieces or pork tenderloin.

Honey-Teriyaki Glaze

MAKES ABOUT 1 CUP

1 tablespoon toasted sesame oil

3 tablespoons peeled, finely chopped fresh ginger

3 garlic cloves, minced

1 tablespoon sesame seeds

⅔ cup honey

⅓ cup reduced-sodium soy sauce

2 tablespoons seasoned rice vinegar

1 tablespoon chili-garlic sauce, such as Sriracha

1 tablespoon cornstarch, dissolved in 3 tablespoons cold water

In a saucepan over medium heat, warm the oil. Add the ginger, garlic, and sesame seeds and cook, stirring, until fragrant, 2 to 3 minutes. Add the honey, soy sauce, vinegar, and chili-garlic sauce, bring to a simmer, and cook for 2 minutes, stirring occasionally. Increase the heat to medium-high and bring the mixture to a boil. Stir the cornstarch mixture briefly to recombine, then gradually add it to the pan while whisking constantly and boil until thickened, about 1 minute. Use for pork ribs.

Buffalo Wing Sauce

MAKES ABOUT ⅔ CUP

⅓ cup hot sauce, like Frank's RedHot® or Crystal

¼ cup unsalted butter

2 teaspoons distilled white vinegar

½ teaspoon garlic powder

½ teaspoon Worcestershire sauce

Kosher salt

In a small saucepan over medium heat, stir together the sauce ingredients until the butter is melted. Remove from the heat and let cool slightly. Season with salt. Use for chicken pieces.

Creamy Horseradish Sauce

MAKES ABOUT 1¼ CUPS

1 cup sour cream

2 tablespoons prepared horseradish

1 tablespoon Dijon mustard

2 teaspoons Worcestershire sauce

½ teaspoon kosher salt

¼ teaspoon ground black pepper

In a medium bowl whisk together all the sauce ingredients. Use for beef or lamb.

Thai Peanut Sauce

MAKES ABOUT ¾ CUP

½ cup unsweetened coconut milk, stirred

¼ cup smooth peanut butter

1 tablespoon fresh lime juice

1 tablespoon soy sauce

2 to 3 teaspoons Thai red curry paste

In a small saucepan over medium heat, whisk together the sauce ingredients until smooth. Remove from the heat and let cool slightly. Use for chicken, pork, beef, or seafood.

Honey-Mustard Sauce

MAKES ABOUT ¾ CUP

¼ cup honey

¼ cup Dijon mustard

2 tablespoons mayonnaise

2 teaspoons fresh lemon juice

In a small bowl mix together all the sauce ingredients. Use for chicken pieces.

Arugula Pesto

MAKES ABOUT 1½ CUPS

3 tablespoons pine nuts, toasted

1 garlic clove

2 cups packed baby arugula leaves

1 cup packed fresh basil leaves

¼ cup freshly grated Parmigiano-Reggiano® cheese

¼ teaspoon kosher salt

⅛ teaspoon ground black pepper

⅓ to ½ cup extra-virgin olive oil

In a food processor, pulse the pine nuts and garlic until minced. Scrape down the sides of the bowl. Add the arugula, basil, cheese, salt, and pepper and pulse until finely chopped. Scrape down the bowl again and, with the motor running, add enough oil to create a smooth, emulsified sauce. Use for beef, chicken, or pork.

Chimichurri Sauce

MAKES ABOUT 2 CUPS

3 garlic cloves

2 cups loose-packed fresh Italian parsley leaves

½ cup loose-packed fresh cilantro leaves

¼ cup loose-packed fresh oregano leaves

¾ cup extra-virgin olive oil

2 tablespoons red wine vinegar

1 teaspoon kosher salt

¼ teaspoon crushed red pepper flakes

¼ teaspoon ground black pepper

Put the garlic in a food processor and process until it sticks to the sides of the bowl. Scrape down the bowl, then add the parsley, cilantro, and oregano and pulse until coarsely chopped. Add the oil, vinegar, salt, red pepper flakes, and black pepper. Process just until the sauce is blended; you want to see big flecks of herbs. Use for beef, chicken, or fish. >

Green Goddess Dressing

MAKES ABOUT 1½ CUPS

⅔ cup mayonnaise
½ cup buttermilk
½ cup chopped fresh Italian parsley leaves
⅓ cup chopped fresh chives
2½ tablespoons chopped fresh tarragon leaves
1 garlic clove, chopped
1 teaspoon white wine vinegar
¼ teaspoon kosher salt
¼ teaspoon ground black pepper

In a food processor combine all the dressing ingredients and process until the herbs are minced and the dressing is a uniform light green, 2 to 3 minutes. Use for seafood or chicken pieces.

Green Herb Salsa

MAKES ABOUT 1½ CUPS

1 cup packed fresh Italian parsley leaves and tender stems
½ cup packed fresh cilantro sprigs
½ cup packed fresh mint leaves
2 large garlic cloves
1 small jalapeño or serrano chile pepper, stemmed and quartered
1 tablespoon red wine vinegar
1 tablespoon fresh lemon juice
1 teaspoon finely grated lemon zest
¾ teaspoon kosher salt
½ cup extra-virgin olive oil

In a food processor combine all the salsa ingredients except the oil. Pulse to chop coarsely. With the motor running, add the oil through the feed tube in a steady stream, processing until a pesto-like consistency forms. Use for chicken, pork, seafood, or vegetables.

Cilantro-Mint Chutney

MAKES ABOUT 2 CUPS

1 cup packed fresh cilantro leaves and tender stems
1 cup packed fresh mint leaves
½ small yellow onion, cut into chunks
1 tablespoon fresh lemon juice
1 small green chile pepper, such as serrano, seeded
1 tablespoon peeled, finely grated fresh ginger
2 garlic cloves, crushed
1 teaspoon kosher salt
1 cup plain whole-milk or low-fat Greek yogurt

In a food processor combine all the ingredients except the yogurt and pulse until very finely chopped, scraping down the bowl as needed. Add the yogurt and puree until fairly smooth. Use for chicken, pork, seafood, or vegetables.

Gremolata Sauce

MAKES ABOUT ¾ CUP

¼ cup extra-virgin olive oil
Finely grated zest of 1 orange (about 1 tablespoon)
2 tablespoons fresh orange juice
¼ cup chopped fresh cilantro
1 tablespoon capers, rinsed and drained
½ teaspoon kosher salt
¼ teaspoon ground black pepper

Whisk together the oil, orange zest, and orange juice in a small bowl. Stir in the cilantro, capers, salt, and pepper. Use for seafood, chicken, or vegetables.

Cucumber-Mint Tzatziki

MAKES ABOUT 2 CUPS

¾ cup coarsely grated English cucumber
Kosher salt
1 cup plain whole-milk Greek yogurt
2 tablespoons finely chopped fresh mint leaves
1 tablespoon extra-virgin olive oil
1 tablespoon fresh lemon juice
1 garlic clove, minced or pushed through a press
¼ teaspoon coarsely ground black pepper

In a fine-mesh strainer, toss the cucumber with ½ teaspoon salt, then press against the cucumber with the back of a spoon to force out excess moisture. In a bowl, combine the cucumber and remaining ingredients, stir to mix, and season with salt. Cover and refrigerate until serving. Use for lamb, pork, chicken, seafood, or vegetables.

Lemon-Dill Sauce

MAKES ABOUT 1 CUP

⅔ cup mayonnaise
2 tablespoons finely chopped fresh dill leaves
Finely grated zest of 1 lemon
1 tablespoon fresh lemon juice
1 garlic clove, minced or pushed through a press
½ teaspoon Worcestershire sauce
4 to 8 drops hot sauce, such as Tabasco® (to taste)

In a small bowl combine all the ingredients for the sauce and whisk until smooth. Cover and refrigerate until ready to serve. (The sauce can be made up to 4 hours ahead.) Use for seafood and chicken.

Lemon Aioli

MAKES ABOUT 1 CUP

¾ cup mayonnaise
2 tablespoons fresh lemon juice
1 garlic clove, minced or pushed through a press

½ teaspoon finely grated lemon zest
⅛ teaspoon ground black pepper
Kosher salt

In a small bowl whisk together all the aioli ingredients. Use for chicken, pork, beef, seafood, or vegetables.

Chipotle Ketchup

MAKES ABOUT 1 CUP

1 cup ketchup
1 chipotle chile pepper in adobo sauce, minced, with adobo sauce to taste
1 garlic clove, minced or pushed through a press
½ teaspoon ground cumin
¼ teaspoon ground black pepper
Kosher salt

In a small bowl whisk together all the ketchup ingredients. Use for burgers or steak fries.

Sweet-and-Sour Sauce

MAKES ABOUT ⅓ CUP

½ cup balsamic vinegar
½ cup fresh orange juice
2 tablespoons sugar
2 tablespoons cold, unsalted butter

In a saucepan over high heat, bring the vinegar, orange juice, and sugar to a boil. Reduce the heat to medium-low and simmer, stirring to dissolve the sugar, until syrupy, about 20 minutes. Remove from the heat and swirl in the butter. Use for pork, poultry, or seafood.

Spicy Ginger Sauce

MAKES ABOUT ½ CUP

¼ cup soy sauce
2 tablespoons seasoned rice vinegar
1 tablespoon packed dark brown sugar
2 teaspoons chili-garlic sauce, such as Sriracha
½ teaspoon toasted sesame oil
⅓-inch piece fresh ginger, peeled

Stir together all the sauce ingredients except the ginger in a small bowl. Use a fine-rasp grater to grate about ½ teaspoon ginger directly into the bowl. Use for beef, pork, poultry, seafood, or vegetables.

Spanish Romesco Sauce

MAKES ABOUT 1 CUP

2 large red bell peppers
¼ cup whole natural almonds, toasted
1 garlic clove

½ cup loosely packed fresh Italian parsley leaves
1 tablespoon sherry vinegar or red wine vinegar
½ teaspoon kosher salt
¼ teaspoon ground black pepper
¼ teaspoon dried thyme
¼ cup extra-virgin olive oil

Prepare the grill for direct cooking over high heat (450° to 550°F). Brush the cooking grates clean. Grill the bell peppers over direct high heat, with the lid closed as much as possible, until black and blistered all over, about 20 minutes, turning occasionally. Place the peppers in a bowl and cover with plastic wrap; let steam 10 to 15 minutes. Cut away the stem and core from each pepper, then slit each pepper lengthwise, spread it open, and remove the seeds and membranes. Peel away and discard the charred skin. Roughly chop the peppers. In a food processor combine the almonds and garlic and pulse to chop finely. Add the bell peppers, parsley, vinegar, salt, black pepper, and thyme and process to create a coarse paste. With the motor running, slowly add the oil and process to create a fairly smooth sauce. Taste and adjust the seasoning if needed. Use for pork, poultry, seafood, or vegetables.

Red Wine Sauce

MAKES ABOUT ¾ CUP

6 tablespoons (¾ stick) cold unsalted butter, divided
1 large shallot, minced (about ⅓ cup)
3 cups full-bodied red wine, such as Cabernet Sauvignon
1 cup unsalted or low-sodium beef broth
3 fresh thyme sprigs
1 bay leaf
1 teaspoon balsamic vinegar
1 teaspoon packed light brown sugar
Scant ½ teaspoon kosher salt
½ teaspoon ground black pepper

In a wide saucepan over medium heat, melt 1 tablespoon butter. Add the shallot and sauté until soft and translucent, 3 to 4 minutes. Add the wine, broth, thyme, and bay leaf, bring to a boil, and boil until the mixture is reduced to about 1 cup, 20 to 25 minutes. Strain the sauce through a fine-mesh sieve into a small saucepan, pushing down on the solids to extract as much liquid as possible. You should have about ¾ cup. Bring to a simmer over medium heat, stir in the vinegar and sugar, and boil until slightly syrupy and reduced to a scant ½ cup, 3 to 5 minutes. Set aside. When ready to serve, reheat the sauce gently over medium-low heat on the stove. Whisk in the remaining 5 tablespoons butter, 1 tablespoon at a time, until emulsified (do not boil or the sauce will "break"). Remove from the heat, stir in any juices from the cutting board, and season with the salt and pepper. Use for beef or lamb. >

Pico de Gallo

MAKES ABOUT 1½ CUPS

3 plum tomatoes, cored, seeded, and cut into ¼-inch dice
¼ cup roughly chopped fresh cilantro leaves
3 tablespoons finely diced red onion
1 tablespoon seeded and minced jalapeño chile peppers
1½ tablespoons fresh lime juice
½ teaspoon kosher salt
¼ teaspoon ground black pepper

In a bowl, combine all the salsa ingredients and mix well. Use for beef, chicken, pork, seafood, or vegetables.

Tomatillo Salsa

MAKES ABOUT 1½ CUPS

1 pound tomatillos, husked
1 large jalapeño chile pepper
½ cup chopped yellow onion
½ cup packed fresh cilantro leaves
2 tablespoons fresh lime juice
1 large garlic clove, chopped
½ teaspoon kosher salt

Grill the tomatillos and jalapeño over direct medium heat until charred all over, about 10 minutes. Stem and seed the jalapeño. In a food processor combine the tomatillos, jalapeño, and remaining ingredients. Pulse to a chunky salsa consistency. Use for beef, pork, chicken, or seafood.

Tropical Salsa

MAKES ABOUT 4 CUPS

½ pineapple, peeled and cut crosswise into ½-inch slices
½ cup diced red bell pepper, in ¼-inch dice
2 tablespoons chopped fresh cilantro
1 tablespoon finely chopped jalapeño chile pepper
1 tablespoon fresh lime juice
¼ teaspoon kosher salt

Grill the pineapple slices over direct medium heat until charred and tender, 10 to 12 minutes, turning every 2 minutes. Transfer the pineapple to a cutting board to cool, then cut away the core and cut into ½-inch dice. Transfer to a bowl and add the remaining ingredients. Toss to combine. Use for poultry, pork, or seafood.

Avocado Crema

MAKES ABOUT 1½ CUPS

1 large ripe avocado, halved, pitted, and peeled
½ cup sour cream
2 tablespoons fresh lime juice
1 garlic clove, minced
½ teaspoon kosher salt

¼ teaspoon chipotle chile powder
¼ teaspoon Mexican hot sauce, such as Cholula®

In a food processor process the ingredients until smooth, scraping down the bowl once or twice. Transfer to a bowl, cover, and refrigerate for up to 6 hours. Use for chicken, pork, seafood, or vegetables.

Guacamole

MAKES ABOUT 1 CUP

2 ripe Hass avocados
1 tablespoon fresh lime juice
2 small garlic cloves
¼ teaspoon kosher salt
1 tablespoon finely chopped fresh cilantro leaves
⅛ teaspoon ground black pepper

In a bowl mash the avocados with the back of a fork, then mix in the lime juice. Roughly chop the garlic with a chef's knife. Sprinkle the salt over the garlic, mince the garlic with the salt, and then use the side of the knife to crush the garlic into a smooth paste. Add the garlic mixture, cilantro, and pepper to the avocado and mix well. Serve at once or refrigerate, covered with plastic wrap, until ready to serve. Use for beef, chicken, pork, seafood, or vegetables.

Mediterranean Relish

MAKES ABOUT 3 CUPS

1 cup finely diced roasted red bell peppers (2 to 3 peppers)
1 cup grape tomatoes, halved (or quartered if large), or 1 cup diced fresh tomatoes
½ cup pitted black or green olives, halved or quartered lengthwise
⅓ cup roughly chopped fresh Italian parsley leaves
3 tablespoons extra-virgin olive oil
1 tablespoon balsamic or red wine vinegar
½ teaspoon kosher salt
½ teaspoon dried thyme or oregano
¼ teaspoon crushed red pepper flakes (optional)
⅛ teaspoon ground black pepper

In a bowl, stir together all the relish ingredients. Use for chicken, pork, seafood, or vegetables.

Balsamic Vinaigrette

MAKES ABOUT 1 CUP

¼ cup balsamic vinegar
1 tablespoon Dijon mustard
¾ cup extra-virgin olive oil
Kosher salt and ground black pepper

In a bowl whisk together the vinegar and mustard, then add the oil in a slow, steady stream while whisking constantly to emulsify. Season with salt and pepper. Use for beef, poultry, or vegetables.

Italian Vinaigrette

MAKES ABOUT 1¼ CUPS

¼ cup red wine vinegar
1½ tablespoons minced shallot
2 teaspoons fresh lemon juice
1 tablespoon Dijon mustard
1 teaspoon mixed Italian herb seasoning
¾ cup extra-virgin olive oil
Kosher salt and ground black pepper

In a bowl whisk together the vinegar, shallot, lemon juice, mustard, and dried herbs. Add the oil in a slow, steady stream while whisking constantly to emulsify. Season with salt and pepper. Use for poultry or vegetables.

Lemon Vinaigrette

MAKES ABOUT ⅓ CUP

¼ cup extra-virgin olive oil
1 teaspoon finely grated lemon zest
2 tablespoons fresh lemon juice
1 garlic clove, minced or pushed through a press
¾ teaspoon kosher salt
½ teaspoon Dijon mustard
½ teaspoon sugar
¼ teaspoon ground black pepper

In a bowl whisk together all the vinaigrette ingredients. Set aside until ready to serve. Use for seafood or vegetables.

Blue Cheese Dressing

MAKES ABOUT 1¼ CUPS

¼ cup buttermilk
¼ cup plain whole-milk Greek yogurt
2 tablespoons cider vinegar
2 tablespoons mayonnaise
¼ teaspoon kosher salt
⅛ teaspoon ground black pepper
⅓ cup crumbled blue cheese (about 1½ ounces)

In a bowl whisk together all the ingredients except the cheese. Stir in the cheese. Cover and refrigerate until ready to serve. Use for beef, chicken, pork, seafood, or vegetables.

Honey-Mustard Dressing

MAKES ABOUT 1¾ CUPS

1 cup mayonnaise
¼ cup plus 2 tablespoons Dijon mustard
¼ cup honey
2 tablespoons fresh lemon juice
Kosher salt and ground black pepper

In a bowl stir together all the ingredients. Season with salt and pepper to taste. Use for chicken, pork, or seafood.

Vietnamese Dressing

MAKES ABOUT 1½ CUPS

3 scallions, white and light green parts only, chopped
⅔ cup soy sauce
Finely grated zest of 2 limes
¼ cup fresh lime juice (from 2 to 3 limes)
2-inch piece fresh ginger, peeled and cut into chunks
4 garlic cloves, smashed
2 tablespoons fish sauce
2 tablespoons toasted sesame oil

In a food processor combine all the dressing ingredients and process until smooth, about 30 seconds. To use as a marinade, add ½ cup of the dressing to a bowl and whisk in ¼ cup canola oil and 2 tablespoons packed light brown sugar. Use for beef, chicken, pork, seafood, or vegetables.

Thai-Style Dressing

MAKES ABOUT 1 CUP

¼ cup fish sauce
3 tablespoons packed dark brown sugar
3 tablespoons fresh lime juice
3 tablespoons thinly sliced shallot
2 tablespoons toasted sesame oil
2 tablespoons finely chopped fresh cilantro leaves
2 tablespoons finely chopped fresh mint leaves
1 to 2 teaspoons crushed red pepper flakes

In a bowl whisk together all the ingredients, using 2 teaspoons red pepper flakes if you prefer a spicy dressing. Set aside to allow the flavors to develop. Use for beef, chicken, pork, seafood, or vegetables.

Creamy Coleslaw

MAKES ABOUT 8 CUPS

¾ cup mayonnaise
3 tablespoons white wine vinegar
2 tablespoons sugar
1 teaspoon celery seed
¾ teaspoon kosher salt, plus more to taste
½ teaspoon ground black pepper, plus more to taste
4 cups cored and very thinly sliced green cabbage (½ head)
2 medium carrots, peeled and coarsely shredded, about 2 cups
1 large red bell pepper, cored and finely diced, about 1 cup
½ cup roughly chopped fresh Italian parsley

In a large bowl whisk together the mayonnaise, vinegar, sugar, celery seed, salt, and pepper to dissolve the sugar and salt. Add the cabbage, carrots, bell pepper, and parsley. Mix well. Taste and add more salt and/or pepper, if desired. Cover and refrigerate until chilled, at least 2 hours and up to 1 day. Drain in a colander and transfer to a serving bowl. Serve chilled.

INDEX

AUTHOR AND EXECUTIVE PRODUCER

Jamie Purviance

CREATIVE TEAM

Producer and Lead Editor: Kim Laidlaw

Art Director and Lead Designer: Ali Zeigler

Senior Production Designer: Diana Heom

Photographer: Ray Kachatorian

Illustrators: Felicita Sala and Joel Holland

Food Stylist: Kim Kissling

Prop Stylists: Jennifer Barguiarena and Glenn Jenkins

Photo Assistants: Toven Stith, Jeff Johnson, and Mario Kroes

Food Stylist Assistants: Becca Martin, Karen Santos, Huxley McCorkle, Stormie Ingram, JM Hunter, and Cassandre Ursu

CONSULTING GLOBAL PUBLISHING DIRECTOR

Susan J. Maruyama, Round Mountain Media

WEBER-STEPHEN PRODUCTS LLC

Brand Godfather: Mike Kempster

VP Global Marketing: Brooke Jones

HOUGHTON MIFFLIN HARCOURT

Editor-in-Chief: Deb Brody

Editor: Stephanie Fletcher

Managing Editor: Marina Padakis Lowry

Art Director: Tai Blanche

Production Director: Thomas Hyland

CONTRIBUTORS

Lynda Balslev, Brigit Binns, Lena Birnbaum, David Bonom, Linda Carucci, Danielle Centoni, Michael P. Clive, Sheri Codiana, Dan Cooper, Sarah Epstein, Suzy Farnworth, Tobi Francz, Mike Gerrish, Anders Jensen, Allison Kociuruba, Kevin Kolman, Mike Lang, William Lendway, Kemp Minifie, Diane Morgan, Bart Mus, Cynthia Nims, Rick Rodgers, Cheryl Sternman Rule, Tracey Seaman, Sarah Tenaglia, Kerry Trotter

For information about permission to reproduce selections from this book, write to **trade.permissions@hmhco.com**

or to

Permissions
Houghton Mifflin Harcourt Publishing Company
3 Park Avenue, 19th Floor
New York, NY 10016

Weber, the kettle configuration, and the kettle silhouette are registered trademarks of Weber-Stephen Products LLC, 1415 S. Roselle Road, Palatine, IL 60067 USA.

www.hmhbooks.com
www.weber.com®

Library of Congress Cataloging-in-Publication Data is available.

ISBN 978-1-328-58993-4 (paper over board)
ISBN 978-0-358-15716-8 (Weber edition)
ISBN 978-0-358-16148-6 (Barnes & Noble special edition)
ISBN 978-0-358-19759-1 (Target special edition)
ISBN 978-1-328-59276-7 (ebook)

Printed in the United States of America

DOW 10 9 8 7 6 5 4 3 2 1

Parmigiano-Reggiano is a registered certification trademark owned by Consorzio Del Formaggio Parmigiano-Reggiano, Republic of Italy; Pecorino Romano is a U.S. trademark registration owned by Consorzio Per La Tutela Del Formaggio Pecorino Romano, 226, Corso Umberto I, 08015 Macomer-Nuoro, Italy

AUTHORIZED BY WEBER-STEPHEN PRODUCTS LLC